"Herman Selderhuis gives a well-organized, source-based short account of Luther's life, putting him into his context. Written by one of the most respected international scholars in Reformation history, this book may be fruitfully used as an introduction to Luther's life."

Volker Leppin, theologian and professor of church history, Eberhard Karls University of Tübingen; president, Interdisciplinary Medieval Association

"With a keen eye for the details that make Luther come alive for twenty-first-century readers, and with an ear for those often-false rumors spread by other scholars about the man, Selderhuis guides us through the life of the Wittenberg professor, depicting his genius and his temperament within the context of his time and its challenges. This well-balanced journey at the reformer's side provides readers with insights into the development of his thought and his path toward prominence and influence that shaped the last quarter century of his life. The often-slighted later years, in which his writings and personality created a sphere of influence equaled by few in any age, are here given due attention, with helpful explanations of the setting in which Luther's reform movement matured."

Robert Kolb, international research emeritus professor, Institute for Mission Studies, Concordia Seminary; author, *Martin Luther: Confessor of the Faith*; coauthor, *The Genius of Luther's Theology*

"The complexity of Luther is staggering, but Herman Selderhuis has given us a detailed portrait of the reformer that captures both his blemishes and the beauty of his faith in Christ. This book is a fascinating read about one of the most significant figures of history. Both students of Christian history and admirers of Reformation theology will find it helpful."

Joel Beeke, president, Puritan Reformed Theological Seminary

"There have been more books written about Martin Luther than any other figure in the last millennium of church history. With such a Luther-glutted market, what more could possibly be said about him? Well, this latest volume from the hand of the gifted Reformation scholar Herman Selderhuis does indeed give us a fresh perspective on the German reformer. With his own translations of Luther's writings and his comprehensive knowledge of Luther's world, both theological and social, this new biography is both deeply instructive about the things that mattered most to Luther and a delight to read. This is how biography should be written!"

Michael A. G. Haykin, professor of church history and biblical spirituality, The Southern Baptist Theological Seminary

"Among the many new biographies of Martin Luther, this one stands out for its fresh engagement with Luther's own assessment of his life and work. Well researched and engagingly presented."

Timothy George, founding dean, Beeson Divinity School; general editor, Reformation Commentary on Scripture

"What makes this Luther biography distinct is its explicit attention to Martin Luther's spiritual journey as a sixteenth-century person haunted by his demons and driven by his passions, and the way it presents Luther's own voice and reflection throughout, paired with a restrained but poignant analysis that invites the reader to dig deeper. Luther is introduced as a 'problem' in his church context with evolving roles in which he is shaped by his relationships. He is assessed as a 'unique phenomenon' on the one hand, while as a flesh-and-blood human being with a temperament, strong emotions, and tragic ailments on the other. Selderhuis's clearly written and immediately engaging narrative, with wit, offers an abundance of detail and apparatus for the reader to understand one of the most fascinating personalities in Christian history and the complexities of his Reformation hermeneutics."

Kirsi Stjerna, First Lutheran, Los Angeles / Southwest California Synod Professor of Lutheran History and Theology, Pacific Lutheran Theological Seminary; author, *Women and the Reformation*

"This richly illustrated and succinctly written book, based on anything but superficial knowledge, is very much a life of Luther for everyone. While announcing itself as a 'spiritual biography,' it actually presents Luther in body and soul in his day-to-day contexts. Selderhuis catches very well Luther as a reformer stumbling daily from one unconcealed existential crisis to another, often beset with spiritual, mental, religious, family, political, physical, and personality problems. Here we have the real Luther—potent prophet of God, astonishing theologian, prolific writer, and phenomenal communicator indeed, but also a flawed genius whose attributes included buffoonery, vulgarity, vindictiveness, and downright rudeness. While many have viewed the reformer as a Hercules of the faith and the thirteenth apostle, this book reminds us that Luther was also no saint and that he had no pretensions to be one."

W. Ian P. Hazlett, honorary professorial research fellow, University of Glasgow; editor in chief, *Reformation and Renaissance Review*; author, *The Reformation in Britain and Ireland*; coauthor, *A Useable Past*

"At this half-millennium anniversary of the birth of the Protestant faith, there is scarcely a better place to (re)discover Martin Luther than in this fresh biography by internationally recognized Reformation scholar Herman Selderhuis. Here is where to start your investigation of an amazing man whose remarkable courage, controversial ministry, and persuasive writings changed the world—for good and for ill. Don't miss reading this fascinating, fun, and poignant foray into the spiritual life and tumultuous times of the one who, as Calvin described, 'gave the Gospel back to us.'"

Peter Lillback, president and professor of historical theology and church history, Westminster Theological Seminary

"*Martin Luther: A Spiritual Biography* offers a new and fascinating approach to Luther's life. In this book, political and theological contexts are paid attention to, but priority is given to the story of Luther's religious life, from childhood to old age. The account is based on an extensive use of primary sources—not least Luther's letters and *Table Talk*—and the reformer's own words are frequently quoted. At the same time, the interpretation of Luther's texts is closely related to specific places and concrete situations in his life. In this way, the reader is brought closer to Luther's person than what is often the case in other biographies."

Tarald Rasmussen, professor of general church history and research director, University of Oslo; editor, *Teologisk Tidsskrift*

"Herman Selderhuis is a fine scholar but also a churchman and a teacher. Thus, he writes with an enviable, conversational ease, which makes his teaching accessible to the nonspecialist audience. In this brief biography of Martin Luther, he brings the reformer alive, from his birth in humble circumstances to his death as the most (in)famous man in Europe. Those who have never encountered the narrative of Luther's life before will find this an accessible and satisfying introduction that wears its learning lightly and points to the deep truths to which Luther's life and thought testified."

Carl R. Trueman, Paul Woolley Chair of Church History and professor of church history, Westminster Theological Seminary; author, *The Creedal Imperative* and *Luther on the Christian Life*

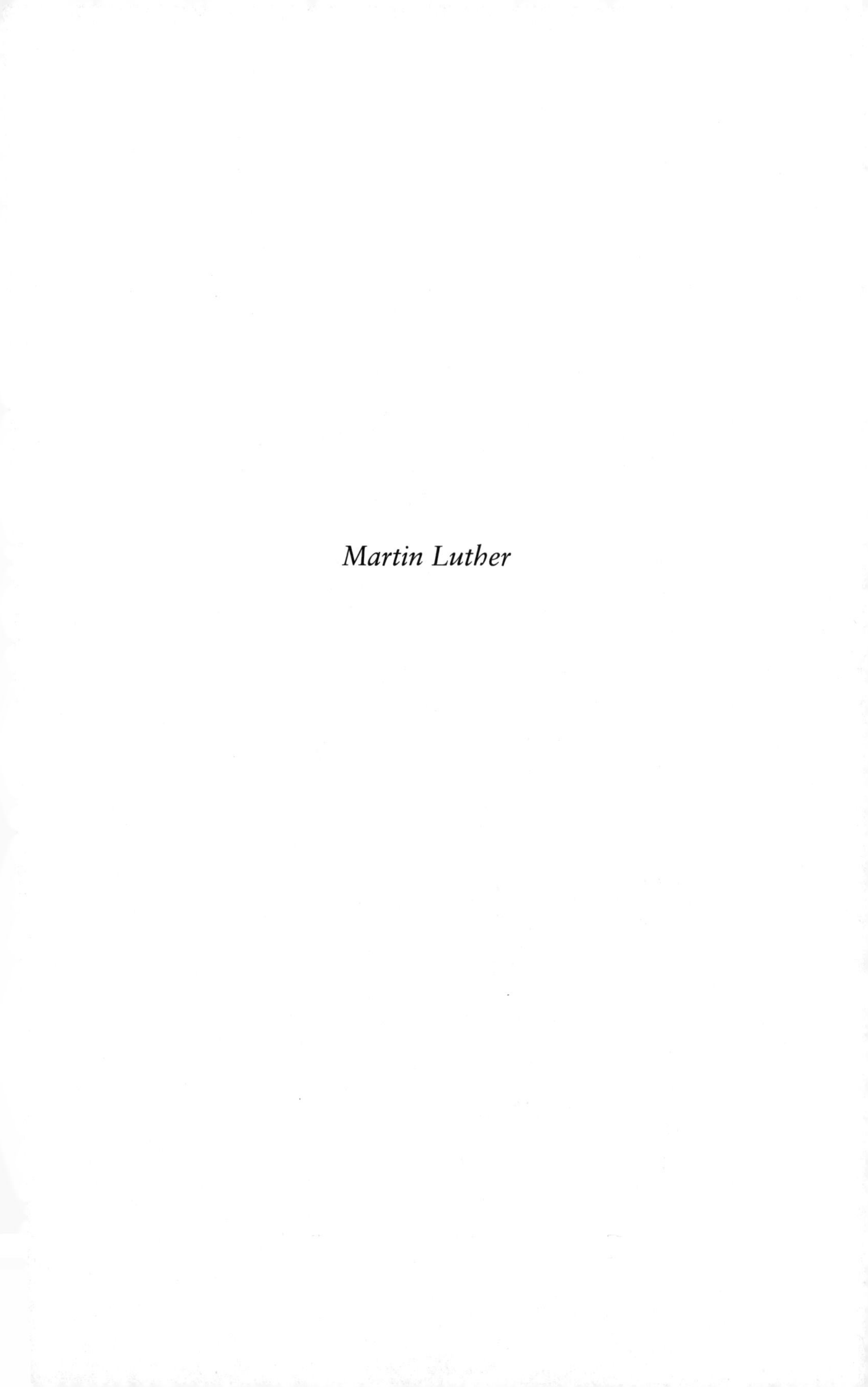

Martin Luther

Martin Luther

A Spiritual Biography

Herman Selderhuis

WHEATON, ILLINOIS

Martin Luther: A Spiritual Biography

Published by Crossway
1300 Crescent Street
Wheaton, Illinois 60187

This book is translated from the original Dutch version, *Luther: Een mens zoekt God*, by Herman Selderhuis, © 2016 by Uitgeverij De Banier in Apeldoorn, the Netherlands.

Cover design: Josh Dennis

Cover image: Germanisches Nationalmuseum, Nuremberg, Germany / Galleria degli Uffizi, Florence, Italy / Bridgeman Images

First printing 2017

Printed in the United States of America.

Hardcover ISBN: 978-1-4335-5694-4
ePub ISBN: 978-1-4335-5697-5
PDF ISBN: 978-1-4335-5695-1
Mobipocket ISBN: 978-1-4335-5696-8

Library of Congress Cataloging-in-Publication Data

Names: Selderhuis, H. J., 1961– author.
Title: Martin Luther : a spiritual biography / Herman Selderhuis.
Other titles: Luther. English
Description: Wheaton : Crossway, 2017. | Includes bibliographical references and index.
Identifiers: LCCN 2016058580 (print) | LCCN 2017032809 (ebook) | ISBN 9781433556951 (pdf) | ISBN 9781433556968 (mobi) | ISBN 9781433556975 (epub) | ISBN 9781433556944 (hc)
Subjects: LCSH: Luther, Martin, 1483–1546.
Classification: LCC BR325 (ebook) | LCC BR325 .S45413 2017 (print) | DDC 284.1092 [B] —dc23
LC record available at https://lccn.loc.gov/2016058580

Crossway is a publishing ministry of Good News Publishers.

SH 27 26 25 24 23 22 21 20 19 18 17
16 15 14 13 12 11 10 9 8 7 6 5 4 3 2 1

Contents

Timeline of Luther's Life

1483	November 10: Born in Eisleben, Saxony
	November 11 (The Feast of St. Martin): Baptized in the St. Peter and Paul Church of Eisleben
1484	Moves with family to Mansfeld
1490	Starts at the Latin school of Mansfeld
1497	Sent by his parents to a school in Magdeburg
1498	Allowed to move to Eisenach, where he attends the priests' school associated with St. Georgenkirche
1501	Begins his legal study in Erfurt
1505	Early 1505: Completes his master's degree and begins his actual study of law in Erfurt
	July 2: Caught in a terrible thunderstorm and promises to become a monk
	July 17: Enters the Augustinian monastery in Erfurt
1507	Consecrated as priest; reads his first mass
1508	Starts his theological studies at the University of Wittenberg
1509	Obtains two doctorates in theology and starts teaching but is recalled to the monastery in Erfurt soon after
1510–1511	Journeys to Rome because of a conflict within the Augustinian order and returns to continue studying at the University of Wittenberg
1512	Obtains a doctorate in theology and becomes professor of (biblical) theology
1513–1515	Starts teaching, beginning with his *Lectures on the Psalms*
1515–1516	Delivers his *Lectures on Paul's Epistle to the Romans*
1516–1517	Delivers his *Lectures on Paul's Epistle to the Galatians*
1517	October 31: Posts his "Ninety-Five Theses"

1517–1518	Delivers his *Lectures on the Epistle to the Hebrews*
1518	Early 1518: Publishes *Sermon on Indulgence and Grace*
	April: Attends Heidelberg Disputation
	October 12–14: Appears before Cajetan at Augsburg
1519	Continues his *Lectures on the Psalms*; attends conference in Leipzig with Eck and Carlstadt
1520	August 12: Publishes *To the Christian Nobility of the German Nation*
	October 6: Publishes *On the Babylonian Captivity of the Church*
	Mid-November: Publishes *On the Freedom of a Christian*
	December 10: Burns the papal bull threatening excommunication
1521	January 3: Excommunicated
	April 17–18: Attends hearing at the imperial Diet of Worms after a long journey through Germany but does not retract his books
	May 4: Kidnapped and taken to the Wartburg, where he starts translating Erasmus's edition of the Greek New Testament into German
	May 8: Banished from the empire and declared an outlaw
	Summer: Hears about the escalating situation in Wittenberg
1522	March 1: Returns to Wittenberg and starts to set matters straight
	March 9: Begins his "Invocavit Sermons"
1523	April 4: Helps twelve nuns escape from the monastery in Nimbschen
1525	June 13: Marries Katharina von Bora
1526	June 7: First son is born
1529	Early 1529: Publishes Large and Small Catechisms
	Spring: Lutheran members of the imperial Diet of Speyer protest its confirmation of the Edict of Worms, giving birth to the term *Protestant*
	September 30: Arrives for the Colloquy of Marburg
1530	April–October: Stays in the Coburg during the Diet of Augsburg
1534	September: Completes translation of Old and New Testament and Apocrypha
1535	Begins his *Lectures on Genesis*
	Appointed dean of the theological faculty at the University of Wittenberg
1536	May 29: Signs Wittenberg Concord

1536–1537	December 1536–February 1537: Meets in Schmalkalden, which, after two months of discussion, leads to the formation of the Schmalkaldic League
	February 1537: Leaves Schmalkalden dangerously ill
1539–1541	Revises his translation of the Bible
1541	Conducts the ordination of Nicholas von Amsdorf to become bishop of Nuremburg
1542	Publishes *Concerning the Jews and Their Lies*
1544	December: Publishes *Contra the 32 Articles of the Theological Sharpshooters in Leuven*
1545	December: Publishes *Contra the Papacy in Rome Established by the Devil*
1546	February 14: Gives last sermon (in the St. Andreas Church in Eisleben)
	February 18: Dies in Eisleben
	February 22: Buried in Wittenberg

Illustrations

Figure 0.1 Map of Germany

Introduction

Luther was a problem. Certainly for the pope and the emperor, but often he was also a problem for his fellow reformers. Prone to outbursts of rage and coarse language, Luther was frequently stubborn and undiplomatic, even with allies. As one fellow reformer put it,

> He's a person who often loses his path and who is reluctant to consider a return: he's a human who fears God uprightly and earnestly seeks his honor but becomes irritated the moment he is reprimanded. This is how God gave him to us, and this is how we will have to use him.[1]

The man who had to learn humility as a monk had an ego that combined with his quick temperament to swiftly make enemies and exasperate even his most intimate circle of friends. "We must, and we will take him the way he is," John Calvin remarked, "because it was Luther who gave the Gospel back to us."[2]

Of course, Luther could only "give back" the gospel to the church after he had found it himself. And he had long been searching for it. He was a man searching for God. Luther was a phenomenon—a fascinating human being. His opponents thought so too. Luther consistently displayed a brilliant richness of thought, a command of language, and an irascible humor. He was honest about his struggles of faith, often using them to comfort and encourage others. The same ego that could sometimes alienate people also buffered his sense of calling and resolve, enabling him to achieve an astonishing number of accomplishments in his life.

The temptation for any biographer of Luther is to merely let the reformer speak for himself. In this biography I have attempted both to reveal Luther in his own words and to give the reader an objective portrait. My hope is that I have at least achieved a balance.

It should be said at the outset that this is a biography of Martin Luther and not a history of the Reformation, though of course we cannot understand Luther without at least a basic understanding of the historical context that formed him. The translations from Luther's works, letters, and *Table Talk* are nearly all mine. The endnotes indicate where I used existing translations. Translating Luther is nearly impossible since his German and Latin are as dynamic as the man himself. I hope some of that dynamism comes through in this book.

1

Child (1483–1500)

Devils Everywhere

God, the Devil, and death were everyday topics in the world into which Martin Luther was born. As a child, Luther learned that God was a Judge more righteous than merciful. The Devil was out to snatch your soul and turn women into witches. Death was not the end of life, Luther was taught, but instead it was the moment you appear before God and enter purgatory. With these dour lessons firmly in his head, is it any surprise that years later Luther would say that every mention of God was "as a clap of thunder in [his] heart"? The god that Martin Luther was told to believe in as a child was a god who signaled his righteousness chiefly through punishment.[1]

The presence of devils and witches certainly did not make life more pleasant. Luther grew up regularly hearing and thinking about Satan. In Luther's time, stories from the Bible and folklore had been blended together to create many terrifying representations of the Devil and his cohorts. Miners, who worked in darkness deep underground, were terrified at the thought of meeting an evil spiritual being.[2]

Among other things, Luther was taught that the pealing of the church bells would drive out demons, that the Devil influenced the weather, and that he could command the cattle. Luther also believed that a witch had poisoned his brother, almost certainly following the beliefs of his mother, who was convinced that a neighbor was secretly a witch, preying on the Luther children. The neighbor appeared again in a 1533 comment recorded in Luther's *Table Talk*:

> Doctor Martinus told us a lot about sorcery, about anxiety, and about elves, and that his mother had had so many problems with a neighbor who was a sorceress. Therefore, his mother had to do her utmost to remain on good terms with the neighbor by being friendly and forgiving. Whenever the neighbor took one of her children onto her lap, she screamed bloody murder. This woman punished a preacher without even mentioning his name and cast a spell on him so that he had to die. He couldn't be helped with any medicine. She had taken dirt from the ground where he had walked, threw it in water, and bewitched him, because without that earth he could not become better again.[3]

The accusation of witchcraft devastated many women in Luther's day, and some paid for the rumors with their lives. In the culture in which Martin Luther was raised, the Devil was everywhere and behind everything. Luther relates,

> When I was still a boy, a story was told that there was no way that the Devil could cause a quarrel between a man and his wife who really loved each other. Nevertheless, he managed to make it happen using an old woman who put a razor under both their pillows and then told them that they were there. The man found it and murdered his wife. Then the Devil came and, using a long stick, gave the old woman a pair of shoes. When she asked why he wouldn't come near her, he answered her, "Because you are worse than I am, because you accomplished something with that man and woman that I couldn't." In this way we see once again that the Devil is always the enemy of everything that the Lord God brought about.[4]

Luther had difficulty throwing off such superstition, but over time he eventually gained a more theologically responsible view of spiritual warfare. Luther would write that he viewed his frequent stomach ailments as direct attacks from the Devil. According to Luther, that struggle happened especially when he was sitting on the latrine, where he spent quite some time due to his intestinal issues, alternating between constipation and diarrhea. Luther experienced many physical struggles in that place, and he saw those struggles as attacks of Satan on his work. Moreover, the Devil likes nothing more than to envelop people in a noxious stench, and he manages that especially on the latrine. A person tries his utmost quietly and privately to have his bowel movement, but subsequently, Satan begins to stir in it so that everyone, especially God, will notice that there is a bad smell hanging around him.[5] The imagery of the latrine as a place where Satan does his filthy work and where a person experiences his lowly position was not new and was already present in a medieval song. What was new was Luther's discovery that this was also the place where the Holy Spirit taught him to combat Satan by trusting in Christ.[6] Before he would come that far, however, much would still have to take place in Luther's life.

Few Details

Little can be said about Luther's earliest years, simply because we know little about them. Here is what Luther wrote in a letter about his first years:

> I was born in Eisleben and also baptized there, namely, in St. Peter's Church. Of course, I cannot remember anything about this, but I believe my parents and the other people from my native town. My parents moved to the neighborhood of Eisenach because most of my family live in Eisenach, and they all knew me and still know me because I went to school there for four years, and no other city knows me as well as this one. . . . The time after this I spent at the University of Erfurt and in the monastery there, until I came to Wittenberg. I also went to Magdeburg for a year, but I was fourteen then. Here you have my life story and where I came from.[7]

Fortunately, we know more about the young Luther than these few sentences indicate. He recounted a lot in his letters but also in his so-called *Table Talk*, which is as famous as it is notorious. Luther did leave us some memory of his earliest years, though it is debatable how much of what he says about himself is accurate.

Name and Face

In Luther's time, surnames varied more in spelling and pronunciation than they do today. Luther's father, Hans, wrote his surname as Lüder, Loder, Ludher, Lotter, Lutter, or Lauther, reflecting the cultural habit of spelling names as they sound. When Martin Luther himself began publishing, it was more important to have a consistently spelled name; thus, from 1517 onward, he used *Luther* exclusively, save for a brief time in which he indulged a mildly elitist habit of using a pen name, *Eleutherios*, a wordplay on the Greek for "free man."

In time, Luther would feel the need to distance himself yet again from his name. He was bothered that he had become synonymous with the Reformation. Luther wrote that everyone who realized that he was bound to the rediscovered Christian truth

> must be silent concerning my name and should not call himself Lutheran but Christian. What is Luther? Does the doctrine belong to me? I have not been crucified for anyone. . . . How would I as a poor, sinful bag of maggots [this is the way Luther viewed his body] allow people, the children of Christ, to bear my unwholesome name? I am no master and don't want to be one either. Together with the congregation I share in the universal doctrine of Christ, and he alone is our master.[8]

Regardless of Luther's sentiment, those who followed in his theological legacy would continue to bear his name: Lutherans.

What did Luther look like? In a time in which we are awash with photographs, it's almost unimaginable that someone would reach thirty-seven years of age before appearing in his first portrait. In Luther's time, however, most people were never painted. The images we have of Martin Luther were all made by Lucas Cranach the Elder (1472–1553), the famous court painter of the elector. The first shows us a scrawny monk with tonsure and serious-looking eyes (see fig. 1.1). This is an image with a message: here stands a serious man and not a heretic with wild plans. Then as now, portraits and images were part of the public relations division. Gradually, Luther becomes fatter. It seems as if the insight that a person cannot earn his way into heaven by means of fasting had convincingly tempted Luther into a calorie-rich lifestyle. It would

Figure 1.1 *Martin Luther, Bust in Three-Quarter View*. Engraving by Lucas Cranach the Elder, 1520. The Museum of Fine Arts, Houston.

also become evident that his innards would have difficulty adapting to these foods. He continues to look serious in the portraits, both the ones portraying him as professor and those in which he appears as a married man—clearly, a man you could trust. At least that is the message conveyed in the portraits. They also picture a man whose look makes you restless. In the spring of 1523, a representative from the Polish king visiting Luther wrote, "His face is like his books; his eyes are penetrating and glitter almost fearfully, as you sometimes see with lunatics."[9]

Origins

> I am the son of a farmer; my great grandfather, my grandfather, and my father were real farmers. Actually, I should have become a village head, a sheriff or whatever they would have in a village, a

> function that would have placed me just a bit higher than others. But my father moved to Mansfeld, and he became a miner. That's where I come from.[10]

Now and again, Luther would recount something about his origins and his childhood, but as those descriptions were almost totally dependent on his memory, the images he created did not always fit with reality. Luther said, for example, that his parents were not well off: "In his youth, my father was a poor miner. On her back my mother carried all the firewood home. That's the way we were brought up. They endured a lot of difficulty, difficulty that the world today does not want to endure anymore."[11]

In reality, it appears that the poverty suffered by his parents was not as bad as he claimed. Hans Luther (1459–1530) was not a simple miner as portrayed by his son but rather was the enterprising son who had come out of a fairly prosperous farmer's family. He lived in Möhra in Thüringia, and at twenty years old he married Margarethe Lindemann (1460–1531), also twenty (see fig. 1.2). She came from a middle-class family in Eisenach; her brothers were jurists. She was neither the child of bitter poverty mentioned by some of Luther's more romantic biographers nor the whore of the bathhouse invoked by some of Luther's theological enemies.

Luther's father had a younger brother, and in accordance with local inheritance customs, the farm went to the youngest brother, not the eldest. Subsequently, Hans sought employment in copper mining, a growing industry in the county of Mansfeld, which was rich with copper and would thus see a major economic resurgence. Like many other families, the Luthers moved to Mansfeld and purchased a mine. On November 10, the Luthers' second son was born. He was baptized the next day, November 11, on the Feast of St. Martin—Hans and Margarethe named their newborn son after the saint. The baptism took place close by, in the St. Peter and Paul Church. In that time a child's birthday was associated with a saint's day and was deemed to be more important than the actual birth year. Hence it is not definite that Luther was born in 1483, as virtually every biography has claimed. According to newer research, there are good reasons to believe that Luther was actually born a year later, in 1484.

Figure 1.2 *Portrait of Hans Luther, Luther's Father / Portrait of Margarethe Luther, Luther's Mother*. Paintings by Lucas Cranach the Elder, 1527. Wartburg-Stiftung, Wartburg.

Whatever year he was born, a year after his birth the family moved a couple of miles farther, to Mansfeld, a small city with approximately two thousand inhabitants. There Hans received a leadership position in the copper mines, thanks to one of Margarethe's uncles. Seven years later he owned three copper smelters, two hundred acres of land, a large farm, a number of buildings, and enough capital to become a prodigious lender. It's not clear exactly how large the family became, but we do know that Martin had four brothers and four sisters. The family's relative prosperity has been confirmed by archeological analyses of the family refuse pit, in which was found seven thousand food remains that clearly testify to the diverse and luxurious meals they would have often enjoyed.

Nevertheless, the times were not always plentiful. Hans was weighted by significant debt, which accrued in the down seasons of the mining business. It would be a mistake to assume that the Luthers lived like royalty. While they enjoyed some variety of food, they also faced economically challenging times. Without any question, Luther experienced periods of poverty at home. That his parents had to work hard, even when they were financially better off, is obvious from the look on their faces in their portraits. As mentioned above, Luther would recollect years later that his mother gathered firewood and carried it home every day. This shouldn't be interpreted as a sign of destitution but as a typical life for this era's middle-class family.

Impression

Why did Luther give the impression that he had lived his early life in extreme poverty? The best answer is that this description of his life fit his image of himself. Luther wanted to be known as a man who, though the son of a poor, ignoble father, was nevertheless able to successfully oppose a powerful pope and emperor. Luther enjoyed drawing this kind of contrast about himself: "I admit that I am the son of a farmer from Möhra near Eisenach, and yet I am a doctor in the Holy Scriptures and an enemy of the pope."[12] Luther knew that this "David and Goliath" narrative was appealing. At the same time, it would be a mistake, as we will see later, to simply dismiss Luther's account as untrustworthy.

Tourists today can visit the town of Eisleben, where Luther was born and where he died (see fig. 1.3). Shortly before his birth, Luther's family came to Eisleben, and only a few months later they had already left. The house that is now shown as his birthplace is the correct location but is not actually the house in which he was born (which burned down in 1689). Moreover, Luther did not die in the house that they now show as his place of death (he died a few houses down the street, and immediately after his death, they brought him to the house that is now claimed to be the place of his death). Not everything fits, but it is close enough to make a good story. All in all, Eisleben did not actually play a primary role in Luther's life like Mansfeld did. It was there that he grew up until he was fourteen. When he went to Erfurt to study, approximately fifty-five miles from home, he was registered as "Martin Ludher from Mansfelt" (*Martinus ludher ex mansfelt*).

Strict

While Luther's claims of family poverty were exaggerated, his claims of strictness and discipline in his upbringing almost certainly were not.

Figure 1.3 Luther's birth house in Eisleben.
Photo courtesy of Touristoffice Eisleben.

A common form of corporal punishment in Luther's day was a rap on the knuckles. Whether this was an effective method of discipline is questionable, but it certainly made an impression on the young Luther:

> My parents brought me up so strictly that it sometimes scared me. My mother once hit me until I bled simply because I had secretly taken a nut. Because of this hard-nosed discipline, they finally drove me into the monastery. Even though they meant well, it made me scared. They did not know the appropriate relationship between someone's character and the manner in which one should be disciplined. You should punish in such a way that you place the apple beside the rod.[13]

Luther would later record that his father had once berated him in frustration for over an hour.[14] The reformer was not bitter about such parenting, and he even admitted that his father had the right to do that, because this little hour was insignificant over against the ten years of work that his father had to devote to him. Besides, this outburst of rage had not harmed him. This should call into question the very common claim that Luther's strict upbringing had imparted to him a psychological problem that had shaped his idea of God. Aside from the fact that four remarks about a person's upbringing are rather meager data on which to build a psychological profile, there is little evidence of neuroses or other complexes when Luther talks with and about his parents later on. The comforting letter he wrote to his father when he was afraid to die says enough.[15] Luther was relieved to hear that his father, shortly after the reading of this letter, died peacefully and in faith.[16] Luther's opinion of his father is made clear in a letter dated June 5, 1530, to his colleague Philipp Melanchthon, when he heard that his father had passed away:

> Today Hans Reinicke wrote me that my dear father, Hans Luther, the old man, has left this life, on Sunday, *Exaudi* (May 29), exactly at one o'clock. His death has made me extremely sad, not only because of my father's nature but also because of his unique affectionate love and because through him, my Creator has given me everything that I am and have. And even though it comforts me that he writes that he died in Christ in the strength of his faith, the grief and the memories of that extremely loving relationship with him, has affected me intimately so much that I have hardly ever despised death as now. But "*the righteous perish* . . . ," Isaiah 57:1, because before we really die, we die so frequently. I am now the one who will function as the heir of the Luther name, and I am almost the oldest Luther in the family. Not only coincidentally but also in a legal perspective I have the right to follow him through death into Christ's kingdom. He graciously grants us that right, though we are the most miserable among humanity and a shame of the whole world.[17]

These are not the words of someone who needs psychological or emotional recovery from his parents.

Luther expressed the same sentiments to his mother in a later letter.[18] It has been suggested that the lack of correspondence between Luther and his mother indicates a strained relationship, but this is an unnecessary interpretation. More likely, Luther's mother, like many others in her time, could not read. The depression and irritability that Luther would become known for are better attributed to extreme physical and mental stress, something to which many people today can surely relate. Luther's parents were not perfect, of course, but we are told that his father prayed with his children when they went to bed and that his mother was known as a pious woman.[19] In the context of all the strictness, it is piety, not cruelty, that characterized the Luther home.

School

When Martin was seven years old, his father sent him to the Latin school in Mansfeld. At this time, a Latin school represented the best chance for an elite education; it would prepare young students for a lifetime of scholarship. Though certainly Hans would have seen Latin school as a way to give his son a stable and strong future, Luther would later severely criticize his school years, calling them a time of tortures, a time in which a child learned nothing more than a lot of nonsense.[20] These schools were often harsh; Latin was hammered into students' heads and occasionally beaten into them with the rod. Luther recounted that one time he received fifteen stripes because he did not know how to decline a number of Latin words, though he had never been taught how to do this.[21]

Yet the lessons in classics were not lost on him. Years later, Luther would relish the fables of the Greek poet Aesop so much that he published them himself. The music of the school also made an impression on the reformer, especially the Latin prayer that began and ended each day, "Come, O Creator, Spirit Blessed," which Luther eventually reworked and republished.

Luther's World

Luther's childhood context was one of relative prosperity. Luther's family always had plenty of food, plenty of room, and plenty of funding for schools. Most of Luther's childhood friends were expected to work and earn income, as were a majority of children; thus, literacy was often a privilege reserved for those who could afford it. It is difficult for most of us to imagine having few friends who can read or write, but that is the reality in which Luther lived. Luther's world was a world largely without written words.

In the main, it was also a world without images. Images were typically seen only in church, and then likely only a woodcutting. A watery reflection or the mirroring of glass was the most that many people ever beheld. It was a world silent in the countryside but ceaselessly noisy in the city. Luther's world was also a world of odors, a world in which brushing one's teeth was unknown, where people seldom washed or put on clean clothes, a world without underwear, where streets were open sewers, where fleas, flies, and lice were everywhere.

The world at large did not offer Luther much, but it would become determinative for him. It was the world of the Holy Roman Emperor of the German Nation, a name highlighting that it concerned the German portion of the old Roman Empire. That German part consisted of a great number of large and small political principalities, such as city-states, kingdoms, and duchies. This German Empire also included areas such as modern-day Hungary, the Czech Republic, Croatia, Slovakia, Slovenia, Spain, parts of Italy, Luxemburg, and the Netherlands. Though the emperor was the highest sovereign, each nation sought to act as independently as possible. Such independence was possible because the emperor was far removed; Emperor Charles V, for example, was a Spaniard who treated the German portion of his empire as a secondary concern (that is, until Luther launched his reforms).

During a diet (a formal deliberative assembly), more than a hundred sovereigns, princes, counts, and city representatives would gather under the chairmanship of the emperor to discuss imperial matters. For many years these governors had received orders from their spiritual head seated in Rome, the pope. In their opinion, the Roman rulers had too much political power, demanded too much German tax money, did not concern themselves sufficiently with spiritual matters, and were occupied instead with too many secular issues. Princes who didn't want to follow the pope's demands only exacerbated internal strife. In the preceding century, there had been a number of attempts to institute political and ecclesiastical reform, but other than a few local revivals of piety, they had left no lasting impact. Under the surface of German social and religious life lay many explosive issues; Luther would be the one to ignite them.

Luther's world was evolving in more ways. The Middle Ages were being transformed into a new era. It should be noted that the so-called Dark Ages were often not as dark as its commentators have suggested. Likewise, monasteries were not as corrupt or lethargic as many anti-Catholic critics maintained, both then and later. That the situation was problematic, however, was generally accepted, and many felt that monasteries needed to be changed at least to some degree.

What this means is that the Reformation was not something that originated with Luther. Luther's arrival was not the beginning of demands for reform; indeed, some reforms had actually begun before Luther's work. Accounts about church visitations, for example, reported improvements in the monasteries.[22] Luther's work was, however, radically different from these other reforms. Luther was not content to merely fix abuses. He wanted to articulate an entirely different vision of man's relationship to God.

Frightening

When Martin was thirteen, his parents sent him to Magdeburg, a city at that time of approximately twenty-five to thirty thousand inhabitants. He went there together with his friend from Mansfeld, Hans Reinicke. The city was growing stronger in Luther's time, often fortifying its walls. According to Luther, they entered a school of the "Brothers and Sisters of the Common Life,"[23] but there was never such a school in Magdeburg. He did, however, live with people who were followers of the Modern Devotion. It was through this association that Luther became acquainted with the dysfunctions and corruptions of the church. He received Latin instruction at the local cathedral school. Otherwise, very little is known about Luther's stay in Magdeburg. One event in particular, though, left a deep impression on him:

> When I went to school in Magdeburg in my fourteenth year, I myself saw one of the princes of Anhalt. It was the brother of the dean and the later bishop Adolf of Merseburg. He was walking on the Breite Strasse in a monk's tunic begging for bread and carrying a cloth bag much like a donkey carrying his load so that he was constantly forced to bend over. His brother monks walked beside him and didn't carry anything, so that the pious prince alone was the best example that clearly showed the world what the meaning

> is of the raw reality of a holy life. In the monastery they had given him such a lowly position that he had to perform the same chores as all the other brothers. Additionally, he had fasted so rigorously, kept vigils, and chastised himself so that he looked like death itself. He was not more than skin over bone, and died shortly afterward. . . . Whoever looked at him was stricken with silence and could only feel ashamed of his own situation.[24]

Luther's stay in Magdeburg was short; a year later his parents allowed him to move to Eisenach, probably under the watch of relatives there. Eisenach was small but had many churches and monasteries. Luther described Eisenach as a "priests' nest and a massive gathering of clerics."[25] Luther attended the priests' school associated with St. Georgenkirche (see fig. 1.4). That did not mean, however, that he was enrolled in the training for the priesthood, only that he would receive instruction to prepare him for a higher study. As a student, he would also be engaged in the celebrations of mass. Thus, Luther became involved in the veneration of St. Anna, a popular saint at that time. Her veneration took place especially in the church that Luther attended. Most likely, Luther received accommodation in the house of Heinrich Schalbe, a leading citizen of Eisenach and burgomaster of the city between 1495 and 1499. It is also possible that he was simply a frequent guest, because Schalbe often allowed students to join his family for free meals.[26]

One of the residents in that house was Ursula Cotta, Heinrich's daughter, and her husband, Kunz Cotta. Whether Luther was received in that house because Ursula had noticed him singing or begging, as was said, is not completely clear. Luther himself recounted that he had to earn money for his studies as *partekenhengst*, a word that is derived from the Latin word *particula*, which means "part," whereas *hengst* means "horse." So Luther had to earn money by going door-to-door and singing, just as a horse neighs for a piece of bread. Though this kind of behavior was looked down on, Luther does not appear to have been ashamed of it.[27]

In the Schalbe household Luther was exposed to the Franciscan monastery. The most important aspect of Luther's spiritual devotion, though, was his belief that Christ is, more than anything, a Judge:

Figure 1.4 St. Georgenkirche of Eisenach. Photo by CEphoto, Uwe Aranas (CC BY-SA-3.0).

"Ever since my childhood I had gotten used to blanching and becoming frightened whenever I simply heard the name of Christ mentioned. For I had not been taught anything else other than that I had to see him as a strict and wrathful Judge."[28] This attitude also appears from one of the stories Luther told to make the message of the gospel clear:

> Christ offers himself to us with the forgiveness of sins, and nevertheless, we still flee from his face. That's the way it was when, as a boy still living at home, we went out to sing songs to collect sausages. Once someone called out to us with a joke: "What are you

> doing there, you rascals? Just you wait a moment!" And at the same time, he approached us with two sausages. But my friends and I fled and ran away from him who came to us with a gift. In exactly the same manner it is with us before God. He grants us Christ with all his gifts, and yet we flee away from him and see him as our Judge.[29]

The question that haunted so many people in Luther's day, young and old alike, was whether they could do enough good to outweigh their sins and thus be acceptable to God:

> Therefore, it is scandalous that men under the papacy taught people to flee from Christ. I preferred that his name would not be mentioned within my hearing because they had instructed me in such a manner that I had to provide satisfaction for my sins and that on the last day Christ would say, "How well did you keep the Ten Commandments? What's your condition?" Whenever someone described him to me, I was terrified of him, just like I was of the Devil, because I could not bear his judgment.[30]

This terror made the sale of indulgences successful. To help people deal with temptations, special booklets were developed, meant primarily for clerics, to provide dying people with as much surety as possible. In Latin these booklets were called *ars moriendi*, literally, "the art of dying well." Since most people could not read, these books contained pictures, which illustrated what Satan would try to do to make one's deathbed a horror. The spirituality of Luther's culture was almost completely about awareness of sin and guilt, and ghastly images like these functioned to instill fear in spiritually dull people. In this context, Luther recounted that even as a child he knew that playing cards and dancing were sins and that one would have to confess these sins if he or she had hope of life after death.[31]

The Middle Ages may not have been as dark as they have often been portrayed, but from a spiritual perspective, the world in which young Martin Luther grew up was more like a haunted house than a playground.

2

Student (1501–1505)

Erfurt

Luther was a bright student. His parents, apparently having both ambition and financial means, sent Luther in 1501 to begin his legal training in Erfurt. The plan was for Luther's younger brother to continue the family mining business and for Martin to become a lawyer.

Erfurt was a large city, with about twenty-five thousand citizens, thirty-five churches, at least eleven monasteries, and a major university that was established in 1392. This city was known for its flourishing religious life with its more than eight hundred clerics, numerous processions, and a rich treasure of popular relics spread over its several churches. While Erfurt boasted an admirable heritage of great preachers, many of its clerics had casually abandoned their vows of celibacy.

Erfurt's university was respected throughout Europe. At Erfurt, like most universities at the time, many different philosophical and theological traditions flourished alongside one another. For Luther's development, however, the philosophical school of nominalism was most significant. This philosophical current supported a new way of reasoning in which the authority of the Bible received more emphasis than the authority of church tradition and scholarly luminaries such as Thomas Aquinas and the Greek philosopher Aristotle. The movement's most important thinkers included John Duns Scotus (ca. 1266–1308), William of Ockham (ca. 1288–1347), and Gabriel Biel (ca. 1420–1495).

The nominalists concentrated not so much on universals (e.g., mankind in general) but rather on particulars (e.g., this specific man). Experience was considered more important than reason, though the nominalists retained the importance of logic as a system of reasoning. Above all, the nominalists emphasized the search for truth, especially truth about the nature of God and the relationship between God and mankind. In general, the nominalists were younger scholars, a newer generation that interacted and often conflicted with older traditions—a common phenomenon throughout church history. Nominalism's impact on Luther would be apparent very quickly.

Luther registered as a student at Erfurt at the beginning of the summer 1501 semester, either late April or early May. The Matriculation Register, which records the names of every student, reads, "Martin Ludher from Mansfelt" (*Martinus ludher ex mansfelt*). Like other students, Luther experienced the customary initiation into student life: he put on an animal mask with donkey ears, horns, and boar tusks before being "baptized" with a mixture of water and wine. This ritual was meant to convey the message that he had left his animal existence behind and had been incorporated into the world of real people, the world of the university.

Luther lived among his peers in one of the houses that was part of the student community in Erfurt, apparently belonging to a group of student houses called "the gate of heaven." The house established fixed times for studying, prayer, and Bible reading. Strict rules regulated the use of alcohol and closing time; women were forbidden entry. Everyone in these communities had to obey the rector. These student houses had copied the structure of the monasteries, and in many ways they resembled them in daily life.

One of Luther's peers described him as "a well-educated philosopher and musician."[1] The term *philosophy* at this point referred not to one specific discipline but rather to the initial period of one's schooling, which included the more general subjects. The reference to Luther's being a "musician" indicates involvement in humanism, which encouraged collaborative musical activities.

Luther himself did not recount much about this period except that around Easter in either 1503 or 1504, he had an accident that almost caused his death:

> Tuesday after Easter I had a serious accident. I was on my way home, somewhere in a field quite a distance from Erfurt, I accidentally stabbed my dagger into my thigh, and into the artery. I bled profusely. Regardless of what I did, the bleeding would not stop. Fortunately, I was accompanied by someone who quickly got a doctor from Erfurt. He bound up the wound, but I was close to death and appealed to Mary. That night, the wound broke open again so that I still almost bled to death. But I prayed again to Mary.[2]

More than twenty-five years later, in 1531, Luther related this story, vividly recalling that he had appealed to Mary twice. Two things stand out in this account. First, as a student, Luther's pious and spiritual behavior in his personal life was typical of his peers. Furthermore, after Luther became known as a great reformer, he had no difficulty talking about his former devotion to St. Mary. It is especially important to note that in mentioning the mother of God, he wanted to show that when he almost died, he had come close to putting his trust in Mary rather than in Christ. The choice between placing faith in either Mary or Christ serves as an apt symbol of the quest Luther was on to flee from his sense of guilt.

Bible

Luther's first direct contact with the Bible appears to have been just as striking. At one point in his *Table Talk*, Luther said that it was in the university library that he saw a Bible for the first time in his life. He read a portion from the book of Samuel and was smitten: "But the bell pealed and I had to return to lectures. I wanted to read the whole book, but there was no time."[3]

Luther did not mean, of course, that he had absolutely no previous contact with the Bible. Throughout his youth he had heard Bible texts in church. Even though the passages had been read in Latin, he would have understood much of that language at an early age. Luther tended to exaggerate the degree to which the Bible was ignored (or despised) in his surrounding culture. Perhaps he related this to his own experience; indeed, at the university in Erfurt, relatively little Bible explanation was given.

That was certainly not the case at every university. Many Bible commentaries of the church fathers and medieval theologians were available and were used for Bible study. The content of the Bible was familiar and studied. But when Luther said, "When I was twenty years old I had never seen a Bible,"[4] that was very likely true. He continued to read the Bible and recounted that in 1505, he studied Scripture to fight his temptations.[5]

For university students, the Bible only began to play a part when they studied theology. But before they could start this, they first had to complete a foundational program. After that, they could choose from the disciplines of medicine, law, or theology. That first foundational study was in the faculty of philosophy, also called the study of the arts—subjects that included grammar, dialectics, rhetoric, mathematics, geometry, music, and astronomy. These foundational courses taught skills that would enable students to continue their studies in other areas. The works of the Greek philosopher Aristotle were given an important place because he was a master in logical thinking and formulation. His thinking was structured in cause-and-effect relationships, enabling him to reason in a transparent but objective way. Years later, Luther would critique Aristotle's thought, but the Greek's influence on Luther's intellectual formation would remain.

At the end of September 1502, Luther concluded the first part of his studies and obtained his bachelor's degree, the first and lowest academic degree. At this point he would also have been expected to teach a number of lessons himself. He completed his master's degree in early 1505. In accordance with the general practices of the day, this milestone was celebrated with a parade for the class and an elaborate party with an abundance to eat and drink. Luther's enjoyment appears to run together with his worries about sin and guilt, and he attempted to assuage his anxieties by diving into Bible study: "As I was a young master in Erfurt, I would grieve about temptation and then on account of my grieving I would become even sadder. Therefore, I spent a lot of time reading the Bible."[6] These two sides of Luther would remain with him throughout his life.

Law

On May 19, 1505, the day of St. Ivo, the patron saint of lawyers and of the law faculty, the semester was opened, and Luther began the actual study of law. For Luther this day was both solemn and exciting. His father could be proud of him. Luther himself, however, wondered whether this direction of study was the right choice for him. Was this really what God wanted him to do?[7] He did not complete much of this program. For several weeks he was involved in studying civil law, aided by his father's gift of a number of law books and his own copy of the old Roman law book *Corpus Iuris Civilis*, a hefty tome that spelled out civil rights.[8]

Soon the young student discovered that lectures were rather boring. Learning about the rules of Roman law was one thing, but having to listen to what innumerable scholars had said about these laws throughout the centuries practically put him to sleep. Additionally, Luther was frustrated by the contradictory arguments that his various professors would make. This ideological conflict flew in the face of the clarity he craved.

Luther found refuge in student life. After the boring lectures, he would often go to the popular student cafe and enjoy fresh beer, food, and recreation. Nevertheless, Luther did not find what he really wanted there. He recounted that one time after he had left the pub, he entered a church. He was shocked by the images of death he observed in paintings of the dance of death. Death, guilt, God, and judgment: the words bounced back and forth in his head. He imagined what would happen if he were suddenly to die. Occasionally these worries disappeared, but then they would suddenly return—the fear of dying and having to appear before God.

This preoccupation with his death intensified as Luther witnessed the tragic deaths of those close to him. Luther wrote that in 1505, his brothers Heintz and Veit died from the plague. The bubonic plague, a gruesome disease, resulted in black-colored boils on a person's skin and was therefore often called the "Black Death." In Europe in the late Middle Ages, the bubonic plague killed more victims than any war, economic crisis, or other disease. This epidemic, spread by fleas on rats, claimed an incredible number of victims due to generally poor hygiene. The outbreak of the plague that swept across Europe between 1347 and 1353 alone claimed twenty-five million lives, more than a third of the population of Europe. In some places more than half the population died.

This terrible plague returned frequently. Luther was stunned by the news that three professors at the university in Erfurt had died in quick succession. The overwhelming number of victims meant that the city stank of death and decay. Everyone was scared, and that included Luther. On June 13, all the students were expected to attend a mass for the dead and the funeral for the three professors. He was particularly struck by what two of the professors had said on their deathbeds: "Ah, would that I had been a monk."[9] For these professors, a monastic life would have been wiser because they believed that they would have died with greater assurance of salvation as a cleric than as a lawyer. This event confused Luther even more, and with increasing desire he craved clarity and certainty.

Stotternheim

By the end of June, he had made up his mind. This study was not for him; it was pointless and had not provided what he was looking for. It was around this same time—June 30—that Luther went to visit his parents in Mansfeld. The timing of this visit is notable because the summer semester would have still been in session. It's unclear why he suddenly decided to go home. But in consideration of subsequent events, there is a strong possibility that he had his doubts about the direction of his study and wanted to talk to his parents about it.

Some of Luther's biographers believe that he was summoned home because his father had found a suitable marriage partner for him. In 1521, Luther wrote his father that it was almost sixteen years since he had decided to become a monk and since his father tried to thwart his plans by means of a marriage: "It was even your intention to pledge me to an honorable and rich marriage."[10] A marriage alone, however, cannot explain his trip home, because a marriage could easily have been put off for several weeks. Also, Luther's father would never have interrupted his studies for such a reason. Quite possibly it concerned a decision Luther had made, and the matter was so pressing that it could not wait until the holidays. Or had Hans Luther sensed that his son was considering holy orders and called him home to convince him that marriage would be a better route?

In any case, on July 2, Martin returned to Erfurt. Near Stotternheim, about four miles from Erfurt, he was caught in a terrible thunderstorm. The thunder and lightning were so violent that he feared for his life. This was a "fear of sudden death,"[11] a fear for an unexpected and insufficiently prepared appearance before the Judge of heaven and earth. After lightning struck close by again, he invoked the aid of St. Anna—who was seen as the mother of Mary—and promised her that he would become a monk if she rescued him from this horrible weather.

At least, this is the way the story is usually presented. Does it fit with the facts? It is more likely that Luther had gone home to tell his parents that he wanted to become a monk and that in the thunderstorm he made his definitive vow. According to Luther's own words thirty years later, he had begged, "Help me, holy Anna; I want to become a monk."[12] As it was, Luther had wanted to become a monk anyway. Therefore, it is incorrect to assume that a soaking wet and deadly afraid Luther made a rash vow in Stotternheim. At an earlier date he had also invoked the aid of St. Anna to help him while he considered holy orders to clear his guilt before God, because his death would have come at a very inopportune time. Apparently, Anna must have agreed with him because Luther's life was spared, which confirmed for him that he should enter the monastery (see fig. 2.1).

Why did he appeal to Anna and not to Mary? Anna was the patron saint of miners, and therefore, we may presume that Luther had learned at home to call on her in emergencies. A year earlier, though, he had appealed to Mary when he accidentally stabbed himself with his dagger. Had his trip home once again brought Anna closer to him? It is also quite possible that Luther had not called out to Anna at all. The first time he mentioned her in the above circumstances was thirty years after the fact. Before that, he had never mentioned Anna.[13]

Whatever the case, Luther survived the storm and entered the monastery as he had pledged. Luther's thunderstorm promise was not binding, however, because according to canon law, a person was not obliged to keep vows made in crises such as he experienced near Stotternheim. But Luther was committed. A stronger motivation than the vow in the storm was the deep fear he felt about dying unprepared to encounter God. Friends at that time compared this change to Paul's conversion on

Figure 2.1 Monument in Stotternheim. In 1917, this monument was raised in Stotternheim with the inscription "Holy Anna, I will become a monk." Photo courtesy of Touristoffice Erfurt.

his way to Damascus.[14] Luther was very clear that this was a heavenly call that resounded deep in his soul.[15]

In reality, this change in his life was not that radical; he had been preoccupied with seeking God for some time already. He was seeking the God who could provide him with peace in his heart and rest in his conscience. From a very young age, Luther had learned to search his heart and earnestly confess his sins daily. This demand became such a burden for his conscience that at times he almost collapsed from it.[16] Luther sought God and sought him everywhere. The fact that he thought he could find him in the monastery was simply the next step in his quest. While it was his next step, though, it was also a life-changing step.

Father Luther

Luther was now also confronted with the question of how he should inform his parents. He understood quite well that they would not rejoice at his decision, but he could not avoid this. In fact, they reacted as he expected. When he told his father about his decision, a different kind of thunderstorm burst loose. Though Luther perceived the lightning near Stotternheim as the voice of God, his father saw it as something entirely different: "You've heard nothing less than the voice of the Devil!"[17] As far as Hans Luther was concerned, his son's decision to enter the monastery would have yet another devilish consequence: Hans would have very little chance of ever receiving a grandson. For his part, Luther would always remember this moment:

> My father almost went crazy when I told him I wanted to become a monk. He was totally displeased and would not give me his consent. Nevertheless, I wanted to do this with his knowledge and permission. When I wrote that to him, he responded in writing and addressed me again with *du* [the familiar address of *you*]. Before that he addressed me with *sie* [the polite address] because I had obtained my master's degree. But now he denied me every sign of his favor and paternal benevolence. Subsequently, the plague broke out, and two of his sons died. With this news, he had also received the news that I had died. But as long as God wills, I still live. After this, some people urged my father to relinquish part of his pride and sacrifice something holy so that I would join a holy order and become a monk. My father, however, had all kinds of objections and refused until he was convinced and finally consented, though it was with a grudging and grieving will. He said, "May God permit that something good will come out of this," but he did not accept this joyfully or enthusiastically. "With all my heart" was missing.[18]

Luther's entry into the monastery was a surprise for his parents and friends. But on the whole it was not unusual that students would choose to become a monk. Luther's choice was not unique in his day. Though some people today may think that Luther was the only one who made such a choice, we do well to remember that monks and nuns were not born in a monastery. What was unique was not Luther's decision but the circumstances surrounding it.

For centuries men and women chose to embrace a monastic lifestyle. No one could be sure of his or her salvation, but those who had lived as monks or nuns could be a bit more assured. Monasteries were everywhere, both inside and outside the cities. Monks and nuns were an integral part of city and country life. Of course, Luther's entrance into the monastery was notable, since he would eventually be responsible for the exodus of thousands of monks and nuns. It is interesting to observe what Luther said about his motivation. He was convinced that forsaking the world and embracing the strict monastic lifestyle were clear signs of obedience to God.[19] His purpose, however, was neither obedience to God nor the desire to serve God but concern for his own salvation: "For the sake of my salvation, I made my vow."[20] He had been taught that via the monastery one could again become a friend of God, and that was what Luther wanted: "That was, after all, our doctrine. . . . Would you like to become holy and pious through penance? Then you should become a monk to torture yourself with fasting and prayer until God wants you to be his friend again. With that purpose in mind, I entered the monastery."[21]

Luther's primary focus was not God but himself: "I thought: O, if I were to enter the monastery and serve God with cowl and habit, then he will reward me and welcome me."[22] He had it all figured out: "With my works I wanted to live so piously and strictly so that I could appear before God and say: 'Please, here you have my holiness.'"[23] Later, Luther would also admit that he used this transition to escape other responsibilities: "Serving God meant fleeing into solitude and forsaking authority, politics, and business."[24] He could run away from the study of law and whatever else he found empty.

Entry

On July 16, 1505, Luther was received into the monastery. Because Erfurt, like many other cities, had a number of monasteries, Luther could pick which one he desired. Luther chose the Augustinian monastery, where the monks lived in accordance with the rules set out by Augustine. Some people have assumed that he chose this monastery because they kept a more rigorous rule, but if that had been the reason, he would have been better off entering the Carthusian order. It is possible that his choice was driven more by the fact that in this monastery he could continue his studies.

The Augustinian monastery in Erfurt at this time had fifty residents and was known as an organization devoted to Bible study. But the monks also spent considerable time begging because the monastery survived on gifts. Therefore, Luther frequently had to go into the streets to gather in money. Luther ended up exchanging the rowdy table in the student pub for the silence and solitude of the monastic cell. This change also confronted him with the question whether this would really provide him with the purpose of his quest. The evening before his entrance into the monastery he celebrated his departure from student life with a party. Just once more he wanted to eat, drink, and make music with his friends. He wrote that during that evening he played his lute the last time. Luther sold his law books, which claimed a good price.[25] Getting rid of his books did not cause him any grief. He claimed that he experienced joy only in the study of the Holy Scriptures. The next day, however, Luther had to hand in all the money from the sale of his books and property to the monastery. That didn't appear to be a problem for Luther because he was not attached to these things. Would he be able, though, to give himself completely? At dawn, his friends accompanied him to the entrance of the monastery, where they said goodbye. According to Luther, this was forever: "You see me now, but afterward never again."[26] It would not, in fact, turn out that way.

The day that he entered the monastery remained with Luther for the rest of his life. From the words that he spoke in 1539, it is clear that he always remembered the date:

> On July 16, the day of [St.] Alexius, he said, "Today it is the anniversary of my entry into the monastery in Erfurt." And he began to recount the story how he had made a vow almost fourteen days earlier when underway he was upset by a lightning bolt near Stotternheim, not far from Erfurt. In his fear he had called out, "'Help me holy Anna, I want to become a monk.' At the time, however, God regarded my vow in Hebrew: Anna, that is to say, in grace, and not under the law.[27] I regretted my vow, and many told me that I shouldn't keep it. I persisted, however, and on the day before [St.] Alexius, I invited my best friends to say goodbye so that they could accompany me to the monastery the next day. When they wanted to hold me back, I said, 'Today you will see me for the last time.' Under tears they brought me away. Also, my father was very angry about the vow, but I stuck to my decision. I never considered leaving the monastery. I was completely dead to the world."[28]

In later life, Luther said that he knew that God had wanted to use his entry into the monastery so that he could learn about the many sins committed there[29] and could discover the gospel of grace again. While the latter would certainly have been most relevant for him, it's doubtful that Luther learned much about the former. The Augustinian monastery was widely recognized as strict and pious. It's more likely that his negative judgment of monasteries was influenced by his attitude toward his pre-reformed period, a phenomenon that was prevalent among Protestant converts.

Actually, Luther was plagued more by his own sins than by those of others. Nor did he have to enter the monastery in a quest of self-discovery—which was not the purpose of monasteries. Instead, he needed to seek and find God's grace. In the normal introduction process, a potential monk would be asked, "What do you seek here?" The monastic candidate would answer, "God's grace and your grace." Luther's search was exclusively the former. "In the monastery I never thought about women, money, or possessions, but my heart trembled and pondered about the question of how I could gain God's grace."[30]

Luther's search was to find the grace of God, and therefore, the monastery was not so much a flight from the world as a dedication to God. Seen in retrospect, it was a decision that he forced himself to take, a decision taken against the coercive pressures of everything and everyone else: "I became a monk under duress, and did so against the will of my father, my mother, God, and the Devil."[31] Against the latter he especially chose this course because Luther made a discovery in the monastery that would cause the Devil to strike his banner, as he would write later in "A Mighty Fortress Is Our God."

Reception

Luther entered and was immediately received into the monastic community, where his path forward was clearly and carefully set out. During the first several weeks, Martin lived separately from the other monks so that he would become used to being alone and would have an opportunity to reflect on his choice. Also during these weeks, people in the monastery could observe who this novice was. During this time, he had to submit to a thorough confession of his sins, which involved a review of his whole life. Subsequently, he started his probation, officially called his novitiate, which lasted for a period of one year and a day.

The novitiate began in the presence of the whole monastic community. In a gathering in the chapter house, the prior of the monastery told the novice how heavy life as a monk would be. He mentioned all aspects of obedience, dedication, and poverty, and then posed the question whether the novice really wished this life. After Luther said yes, they sang, removed his regular clothes, and gave him the habit of a novice. In the meantime, he was shorn almost completely bald. Whenever he was not wearing his hood, the hairstyle typical of a monk would be visible. All his hair had been removed except a circlet around his head, called a tonsure. After prayer and a hymn, all the monks went to the church together, and there the novice would lie down in front of the altar, facedown and his arms spread out in the form of a cross, expressing his dedication and willingness to sacrifice himself for Christ and his congregation. Then a mentor would be assigned to him who would guide him very carefully throughout his novitiate and teach him all aspects of monastic life. This was not only to include the outward learning of rules and attitudes but also especially to affect an inward change. Personal development was not the purpose. Rather, it was about the reshaping of the person into someone who, with heart and soul, would obediently engage himself in a life dedicated to God. During the novitiate, a novice still had the opportunity to leave, but Luther never considered that thought.

Luther's mentor was Johann von Greffenstein. He taught Luther that in the confessional they would occasionally be confronted with situations of sin and guilt that were almost impossible to resolve. In those situations they should especially focus on developing understanding and seeking grace. Von Greffenstein was Luther's confessor, and it was to him that he confessed his inner struggle. He directed the novice to Christ. If the mentor gave a positive report, the novice could definitely be taken up into the order. That was also what happened with Luther. In a solemn gathering of prayer and song led by the prior, the novice's clothing was exchanged for the black Augustinian cassock with a hood. The change of clothing signified that he had put off the old self and put on Christ. The clothing was coarse, simple, cold, and black. Barely visible under the black cassock was a white undergarment.

At that point, Luther had to make his vow and to promise absolute obedience to God, Mary, and the prior—a life of poverty and eternal chastity. Luther was then given a burning candle, and the whole procession went to the church, where, as was customary, he kneeled in front of the altar and prayed three times: "Lord, take me up in accordance with your promise, and I shall live." As a sign that he was now a member of the community, the prior and the other monks gave him the kiss of peace. This was an auspicious beginning, but especially here he hoped to find peace with God. Before he came to that point, much had to happen; part of that story would include his work as a monk.

For Luther it had to have taken a while to get used to life in a monastery. His cell measured only about eight by ten feet (see fig. 2.2). He also soon discovered that monks do much more than simply pray and meditate. He had entered a mendicant order, and they rubbed that in as well. That he had to beg in the streets, he could live with that. But the fact that when he returned to the monastery, he still had to empty the latrines was a bit much for him. How could they think that begging and scrubbing served monastic life better than studying the Bible?[32]

No Peace

In the monastery he did not find the peace that he sought. He kept the rules to obtain salvation. To find this peace and salvation he had—with some hesitancy and despite his parents—entered the monastery:

> Though I became a monk under pressure, and against the will of my father, my mother, of God and the Devil, in the time that I was a monk I reverentially respected the pope in such a way that I could challenge everyone who was papist and who still are because I didn't make my vow for the sake of my stomach but for the sake of my salvation. I kept all the rules rigorously.[33]

Unfortunately, that salvation appeared far away. In fact, in the monastery this inward struggle only worsened. For example, Luther recounted nights during which he didn't sleep a wink because his fear of Christ was so great that he could not believe that Christ would save him: "Constantly I see him before me, enthroned on the rainbow as a strict, terrible Judge who will punish me for my sins. I cannot believe

Figure 2.2 Luther's cell in the Augustinian priory in Erfurt. Photo courtesy of Touristoffice Erfurt.

in him. The moment the day begins, I go to confession. Confess some more, and then again."[34]

In the course of history, the biblical injunction to confess one's sins and to fight against them developed gradually into the practice of formal confession. This confession was connected to the call to repent and do penance and to the promise of forgiveness and renewal. The church had tried to take data from God's Word and formally organize this, eventually arriving at the three "acts" of the confession. The penitent (i.e., the confessing sinner) began with the confession of sins to the priest (Latin: *confessio*). He in turn would ask if the penitent was sorry (Latin: *contritio*). If that were the case, the priest would declare, "I absolve you of your sins" (Latin: *absolvo te*). But this was not the end of the matter because the forgiveness would not be completed until the sinner had made satisfaction (Latin: *satisfactio*). In essence, the process drawn from the Bible ended up being more tightly defined than what the Bible actually prescribed. Consequently, the belief arose that only sins that were confessed could be forgiven. That led to people really digging deeply in their conscience and memory so they would not forget any sins, because sins that were forgotten had to be paid for in purgatory. Additionally, the penitent had to do his or her utmost to complete *satisfactio*; otherwise, forgiveness was invalid.

This process presented an enormous difficulty for Luther because he wanted to do everything possible to clear up his guilt before God. He sought God and outside of that nothing: "I myself was a monk for twenty years. I tortured myself with prayer, fasting, vigils, and freezing cold. The cold alone could have killed me. It caused me pain such as I will never inflict on myself again, even if I could. What else did I seek by doing this but God?"[35]

Once again it's this seeking of God. This search led him to be a zealous penitent frequently at the confessional. As could be expected, he worked hard to accomplish every possible form of satisfaction. According to his own opinion, though, he made little progress. He entertained the notion that the people in the monastery did not take him seriously. After he told Winand von Diedenhofen, the prior during Luther's first years at the monastery, what he did to live a righteous life before God, Diedenhofen said to him, "You're trying to knock down twelve bowling pins when in actual fact there are only nine."[36] That was friendly pastoral advice, but according to Luther it was the other way around. There were twelve, and he could never achieve more than nine, three short that would have eternal and fatal consequences for him.

Luther also discussed these problems with Johann von Staupitz (ca. 1468–1524), who served as his pastor, teacher, friend, and superior (see fig. 2.3). He provided leadership at the Augustinian monasteries and sought to revive the strict rule of the monastery. Additionally, he served as adviser to Elector Frederick III of Saxony (1463–1525)—known as Frederick the Wise—and he was the first dean of the new university in Wittenberg. In his theology he emphasized the electing grace of God. Based on this divine grace, von Staupitz consistently advised Luther to stop looking at himself and instead direct his attention to Christ. Eventually, this advice would have a great impact on Luther, though initially his focus revolved exclusively around his own small circle of spiritual problems, much to the annoyance of von Staupitz. At one point when

Figure 2.3 Johann von Staupitz (ca. 1468–1524). Unknown artist, ca. 1600. Bildarchiv, Austria.

Luther was again wallowing in the confession of his sins, von Staupitz suddenly interrupted him: "I really do not know what you are talking about." When he added, "That temptation of yours, no one else really has that," Luther felt like he had become as a "dead corpse."[37] The fact that he referred to himself in this fashion shows that he was in a very sorry state of mind. According to him, it felt like he was lying in the sick bay and that, as Luther put it, "there was no one who could comfort me, including von Staupitz. When I asked him about this, he said, 'Master Martin, I don't understand you.'"[38]

Bible

His brother monks could not understand Luther, nor could he understand them. He didn't understand what they were doing and felt that since he had been ordained as priest, they had tried to hold the Bible at arm's length from him. Instead, they wanted to redirect his attention to books written by medieval theologians. In contrast, Luther believed that they all needed to return to the source. Did not God's Word teach much more than whatever people had written? He recalled that one night he "secretly snuck into the library to read a Bible."[39]

It's an open question whether Luther's experience matched the facts. Monasteries were not anti-Bible institutions. It is more likely that Luther wanted to study the Bible at a time in his program when the monastery had prescribed the study of other books. Luther had ended his legal studies, but that did not mean that he quit studying altogether. When he entered the monastery, just like all other monks, he was given a personal copy of the Bible. He began to study this Bible thoroughly, as he had done before. The fear of being lost forever, the fear of God, and his consciousness of sin and guilt led to a zealous study of Scripture in the hope that there he would find inner peace and rest.

Luther's quest for answers matched the spirit of the time, in which many subjects in church and theology were vigorously discussed. During the first centuries, the church had made all kinds of declarations—especially about the Trinity and the natures of Christ. In the twelfth century, they had established the doctrine of transubstantiation. Concerning the meaning of baptism or the doctrine of predestination, however, theologians were a long way from agreement, and consequently, the church had not established any dogmas on these and other questions. Besides all this, there were all kinds of theological schools of thought that debated God's essence, God's grace, and the value of human volition. Luther would have been confronted with many of these currents of thought, though it's not really clear which current had the strongest influence.

The fact that the Bible was quite relevant to these discussions is also clear from the influence that humanism exercised on Luther. In essence, humanism was also a reform movement, in the sense that it strove to achieve purity and the renewal of scientific study, literature, and lifestyle. Humanists also wanted to return to the Bible sources, the church fathers, and the classical writers. Unlike later forms of humanism, sixteenth-century humanism had nothing to do with the belief that man should be central instead of God. Rather, it emphasized that faith and piety should be freed from unnecessary and unbiblical ballast. It was therefore no wonder that a number of humanists joined the Reformation, following the lead of Luther the humanist student.

3

Monk (1505–1511)

Prayer

Life in a monastery was tightly regulated, and residents paid close attention to make sure that the order of the prayers and the celebration of the masses were properly upheld (see fig. 3.1). It's fairly easy to reconstruct what Luther's daily experience would have been like, including what activities he pursued. We should note here that when Luther looked back on this period of his life, in which he experienced so much difficulty, he often expressed himself quite negatively. No doubt, what Luther actually experienced was more nuanced than he indicated. When he said, for example, that prayers were rattled off as nothing more than lip service, he neglected to admit that he could speak only for himself. Conversely, he mentioned repeatedly that he himself took prayer very seriously.

The twenty-four-hour day was divided into eight three-hour blocks, day and night, each of which began with communal prayer. Prayers were seen as a means to seek reconciliation with God, and therefore, they were focused on personal salvation. That was a problem for Luther: how could he know if his prayer was good enough for and acceptable to God? Failure to keep the hours of prayer or to forget them was also seen as sin. Luther was very conscious of this. When he had to conduct lectures in the monastery in addition to his regular work, he could not meet all the prayer requirements during the week, and thus he would make up for these on weekends: "I locked myself up for three days in my cell, and I did not eat or drink anything until I finished all my prayers. Because of this, I became so frantic that afterward I didn't sleep for five nights."[1] That still did not appear to be enough: "The prayers piled up until I was sick to death of them." When at a certain time he was three months behind, he recalled, "It was simply too much for me, and I had to give it up."[2] An event in Wittenberg in 1515 characterizes Luther's attitude: he had been so busy with promotions during the day that he had not been able to keep his prayers. When thunderstorms broke out that night, he was so scared that God was going to punish him for his neglect that in the middle of the night he arose to pray the prayers he had missed the previous day.[3]

In the meantime, prayer ended up giving him more stress and fear than merit and grace. It was not until at least 1520 that he realized that this manner of prayer was legalistic and had nothing to do with the freedom provided by Christ. After this awakening, he discontinued the liturgical hours of prayer,[4] three years after the fateful year of 1517. Other old habits were harder to break; Luther would continue, for example, to wear the monk's habit until 1524.[5]

Confessions and Fasting

Every Friday after the communal Bible reading, the monks participated in the public confession of sins. Each friar was expected to confess the sins that he had committed against the monastic order. At such a public confession, it was also possible to remind brother monks of their sins. Sins corresponded with four categories of guilt: light, grave, more grave, and very grave. Light sins included, among others, being late for Bible reading, laughing or making others laugh, singing poorly, or putting a book back in the wrong place. Penance for these sins involved reading one or more psalms. Grave guilt was incurred by grievous sins such as lying, speaking with a woman, or breaking a fast. Penance for these was three days of fasting. The long list of rules and prohibitions demonstrates how much Luther's life was controlled from minute to minute, every hour of every day, by the consciousness of guilt and the pressure to do good works. It was impossible not to sin against these rules that overtaxed the conscience. Was it a wonder that later on Luther would speak about a "tyranny over the

Figure 3.1 The Augustinian priory in Erfurt. Photo courtesy of Alupus, Thüringer Landtag, and in collaboration with Skillshare e.V. (CC BY-SA-3.0).

consciences?"[6] He was completely stuck. Regardless of how hard and how often he tried to do good, something would go awry. Nor did he accept the concept that different sins carried different degrees of guilt, because in his view, every sin, regardless of how trivial, would bring enmity with God.

The regulations on fasting were also very strict. The monks held a fast every Friday—the day of the Lord's death—and on every liturgical feast day. True, after every fast, ample good food was served, but Luther took no part in that. Sometimes he would fast for three consecutive days, neither eating nor drinking anything, to perform penance and to gain God's goodwill. Luther did not want to be the perfect monk but just aimed at doing—and forgoing—everything he could to find peace with God: "We wanted to be the most devout of all and thought that we could earn heaven with the horrible idolatry of the mass, with the veneration of saints, and with our own monastic holiness."[7] Luther attempted to do all these things to the very best of his ability and said concerning himself, "I was holy. I did not murder anyone but myself. I went to an extreme, and with my body and soul I wanted to sacrifice myself to our Lord God."[8]

The conclusion was clear: "If there was ever a monk who reached his goal, then that should have been me. All my brothers in the monastery who knew me can testify to that. If it had lasted longer, I would have tortured myself to death with vigils, prayers, reading, and other works."[9] Luther was the ideal monk. Later, for example, he recounted that he had never had any sinful thoughts about women: "I didn't even look at the women when they came to confession because I did not want to recognize the faces of those to whom I had listened. In Erfurt I did not take confession from any women at all, and in Wittenberg, from only three."[10]

The confessional was the place where sins were confessed and forgiveness could be attained. Sins caused alienation from God, and confessing sins and receiving forgiveness restored this relationship. Formal confession was established based on an interpretation of Scripture concerning penance and confession of guilt. In an atmosphere of trust, sinners could confess their sins to a priest, who would prescribe some form of penance, which would secure the penitents' forgiveness.

Luther took confession very seriously: "At one time, I confessed my sins nonstop for six hours."[11] This admission fits well with someone who was constantly preoccupied with self-evaluation and wanted to confess every single sin and who was likewise scared that he would accidentally miss one. The clerics who listened to his confessions sometimes felt that he was too extreme. One of them interrupted Luther when he was in full swing in a long session of confessions, reminding him that God had commanded his people to place their hope in his grace.[12] Von Staupitz, to whom he had confessed his sins in a letter, reacted in a different tone and informed him that Luther actually did not have any real sins at all. Despising God, murder, adultery—those were the truly evil works. Of such sins Luther was advised to make a list so that Christ could forgive him those. He should not preoccupy himself with trivialities and imaginary sins and with turning every little mistake into a sin.[13]

His Personal Bible

Luther writes that when he had become a member of the monastic community, "the monks gave him a red leather-bound Bible. He familiarized himself so thoroughly with the contents that he knew exactly what was on each page and could identify the reference immediately if someone started reading."[14] Luther "began to read the Bible and read it again and again."[15] He read his Bible from front to back and then would start anew. He would make summaries of each chapter so he could better remember them. He gained such a tremendous growth in his Bible knowledge while he lived in the monastery that Carlstadt would later praise him for this.[16] While in the monastery, Luther learned that Bible reading is actually "listening to the Bible": a text had to be read but also heard, again and again, as frequently as necessary until one gained an understanding of what the text said. This manner of Bible reading was called *lectio divina*, literally, "godly reading." The goal of *lectio divina* was to read and listen until one heard God's voice in the Word:

> If you want to become a Christian, you must take the word of Christ, realizing that you will never be finished learning, and then with me, you will recognize that you still do not even know the ABCs. If one was to boast, then I could certainly do that about myself, because day and night I was busy studying the Bible, and yet I have remained a student. Everyday I begin like someone in the primary school.[17]

Because Luther relied so much on the Bible in his search for God, he was quite disappointed when, first in Erfurt and later again in Wittenberg, he had to give lectures in philosophy and delve into books about scholasticism. With passion he said that he would have loved to exchange philosophy for theology, but he meant real theology, the theology that "searches out the pit in the nut, the germ in the wheat, and the marrow of the bone."[18] Luther was searching for the heart, for the real essence of theology. That essence is searching out God as he really is, in addition to searching out who man really is and how God and man are related to each other. Luther searched in the Bible, he "knocked" on the texts, he shook them like the branch of a fruit tree, and then he listened to find words of comfort and reassurance to drive away his fears.

But initially, the Bible reading shocked him, especially the psalms that he had to pray many times a day. He prayed using the Psalms but did not understand them, chiefly because his prayers were not meant to help him understand the Psalms but to merit good works. In Psalm 71:2, Luther read, "In your righteousness deliver me and rescue me." Luther could only see righteousness as judgment, condemnation, and a punishing justice. Luther even said that he hated Psalm 2:11 because God's people are told to serve the Lord with fear and trembling.[19] As if Luther wasn't gripped by enough fear as it was! In praying these psalms, the Bible itself made life even more burdensome for Luther: "What I wouldn't have given if someone had delivered me from the mass and the fear in my conscience and had shown me the true meaning of a psalm or one of the chapters in the Gospels. I would have crawled on my knees to St. James [of Santiago de Compostella]."[20] From this he would take a lifelong interest in the Psalms, especially when Luther was convinced that God was different from what he had always thought. He realized then that the book of Psalms does speak about temptations but also about comfort for those who are tempted.

Priest

Similar to most Augustinian monks, Luther, on decision of the prior, had to become a priest. The monastery needed priests to celebrate the many masses. The mass was seen as a repetition of Christ's sacrifice on the cross, which, on behalf of one or more church members, the priest would bring to God. With the pronouncement of the words that Jesus had spoken at the institution of the Last Supper, the bread and wine were believed to change into the body and blood of Christ. After this sacrificial ritual, the body of Christ was given to the celebrants in the form of the host. As a prerequisite to celebrate mass, it was expected that the believers had previously examined themselves, confessed their sins, and were free of sin. They had to be worthy; otherwise, they could not receive Christ, since the mass, as a sacrifice to God, was seen as a meritorious work. It was also believed that it would benefit those who had died and were still in purgatory. Consequently, many people requested the celebration of mass not only for their own salvation but also for that of others.

To prepare for this office, Luther was thoroughly instructed in the meaning of the mass and the manner in which it should be celebrated.

The priest by means of his words and actions effected Christ's presence, and as priest he was directly involved with Christ. Therefore, he had to be extremely careful about every word spoken, each vestment worn, and every gesture made. A verbal stumble or even a stain on the priest's vestment was seen as a serious sin. Purity in speech, gestures, and heart was far more important for a priest than for the ordinary believer. All the expectations associated with the celebration of the mass led to a tremendous spiritual struggle for Luther, especially when he celebrated the sacrament for the very first time.

On April 3, 1507, Luther was formally consecrated as priest in a chapel of the cathedral church in Erfurt. His first celebration of the mass took place on May 2. For every priest this first mass was celebrated with a large ceremony attended by friends and family. It was also the only occasion when women, such as the mother and sisters of the priest, were allowed in the monastery. It is not known whether Luther's mother was in attendance. His father had apparently reconciled himself with his son's decision because he "had even sent twenty florins to the monastery kitchen. He had come with twenty people for whom he assumed the costs."[21] Other members of his family plus a number of friends also attended the ceremony.

Before they could have a festive meal together, however, a very important and serious event had to take place. Luther was not only nervous and stressed, as one could expect at such an event, but he also realized that a mistake in the pronouncement of the ritual of the mass would be seen as a sin.[22] Luther was terribly frightened and overcome with dread to think that through his sinful hands bread and wine would be changed into the body and blood of Christ, and he would be directly involved with God. "I, ash, dust, and full of sins, was speaking with the living God, the eternal and true God. At such a time someone should shake with fear such as when I read my first mass."[23] And he did mess up:

> When I was still a monk, and read the words in the liturgy of the mass for the first time, "Therefore, O merciful Father" etc., "We present to You, the Living, True and Eternal One," I was utterly stupefied, and terror-stricken by these words. Because I thought: how can I as a mere man address the divine Majesty as if I was in the presence of or in discussion with a sovereign or king?[24]

In the middle of the celebration, he told the priest assisting him that he wanted to stop. But the priest became angry and said, "You will continue, and quickly too!"[25] That fear stayed with Luther as long as he presided over and received mass. Whenever his celebration of the mass went well, he was happy that he had presented the sacrifice of Christ to God. But more often he was afraid, and this fear stifled the celebration. He was tormented by thoughts whether he was worthy enough, whether he had confessed all his sins, or whether he had truly received forgiveness of his sins. He often avoided participating at all. It would take years before Luther would come to the conviction that it was not the worthiness of the person but the command of Christ that determined whether someone should or should not celebrate the Lord's Supper. After this first service, Luther was relieved and thankful, but his inward problems were far from over.

Study

Around the same time, in the spring of 1507, Luther was consecrated as priest, and he began his theological studies. The monastery leadership motivated many monks to study theology at the university because the church needed theologians. Luther so excelled that as a twenty-four-year-old, he was the top student in his monastery. This distinction brought admiration from some but envy from others, so much so that some of his colleagues attempted to thwart his theological career.[26] In Erfurt he received instruction in the *Four Books of Sentences* by Peter Lombard (ca. 1095–1160), a standard textbook used by every university in Europe. Through this book and others, Luther became acquainted with the church fathers. He learned how complex some theological questions could be and how those questions could lead to even greater spiritual problems.

Like many, Luther's life was shaped by books, but it was also shaped by other people, especially Johann von Staupitz, mentioned earlier. Von Staupitz had assisted in the founding of the University of Wittenberg in 1502, and he served there as professor for ten years. Additionally, he served as vicar general of the Augustinian monasteries that wanted to maintain the old rules rigorously. He also supported a new relationship between the university and the monastery and led by example since he worked in both organizations. Von Staupitz was recognized for his erudition as well as for his orthodoxy, and it was he who served as Luther's confessor. As a consequence, he was acquainted with all of Luther's doubts, temptations, and questions, and he helped him to find deliverance, even though he did not completely follow Luther on that road himself. He remained faithful to the pope and simultaneously a friend of Luther. His importance for Luther's development was such that in 1545 Luther said, "If I do not want to be an accursed and ungrateful popish donkey, I must praise doctor von Staupitz because he was my first father in this teaching, and it was he who facilitated my birth in Christ."[27]

Before von Staupitz fulfilled this role, he was Luther's superior. Quite suddenly, in October 1508, von Staupitz sent Luther to the young University of Wittenberg. He had heard that this monk was inordinately focused on Bible study. He asked Luther to continue his studies in Wittenberg and give lectures on the ethics of Aristotle. For Luther this change came about quite unexpectedly as he wrote in a letter to Johann Braun on March 17, 1509:

> Do not be alarmed that I left without telling you. My departure went so quickly that hardly any of my friends even noticed. I had wanted to write you, but because of a lack of time and rest I did not get around to it. I am deeply sorry—that is the least I can say—that I was forced to leave you so suddenly without even saying goodbye. I am now in Wittenberg, by God's command, or at least not without his permission! Do you want to know about my situation here? Well, thanks be to God, I am well, though the studies are arduous, especially philosophy, which right from the outset I would have preferred to trade for that of theology, and then, that theology which penetrates to the heart of the matter, into the germ of the grain, into the marrow of the bone. But God is God, and the judgment of people is often wrong, yes, actually it always is. And he is our God; he will always lead us in gentleness.[28]

Luther was bound to the educational system of instruction that was found in all European universities, namely, lecturing in philosophy and studying in one of the higher faculties of medicine, law, or theology. If Luther, in his driven search to understand the relationship between God and mankind, had had his way, he would have preferred to study theology and nothing else. But he could not avoid having to teach. That teaching involved giving lectures—every afternoon from two o'clock to three—on the ethics of Aristotle. These ethics were also what caused him the greatest grief, something von Staupitz must have gotten wind of.

So, Luther recounted, in a discussion under the pear tree in the cloister garden, von Staupitz encouraged him to seek promotion to doctor in theology. Luther immediately replied that his health was too poor for all the teaching responsibilities that were associated with a doctorate. Over against von Staupitz he complained that the combination of teaching and studying would be too much: "I will not survive that for long." Von Staupitz's response was clear: "Our Lord God has planned great things. Also, above he needs good and wise people who can assist him. If you should die, you will have to be his adviser there."[29] Not even Luther's threat to die would help him escape this responsibility; God would have a solution for that. The moment he entered heaven, he would still have to become a doctor to assist God, "because at this time, God has a lot to do in heaven."[30] Luther simply had to comply; if he did not survive, then he wouldn't even receive an opportunity to study theology and serve as God's adviser. He continued to consider himself unqualified and unworthy for this position but could not withdraw from von Staupitz's request. According to von Staupitz's plan, once Luther had received his doctorate, he would take over his chair in theology. Luther's description of this discussion confirms the image he often preferred to communicate, that is, that he had not wanted this at all, but God, through others, had forced him to take this road.

In any case, this choice was made quickly, and Luther did what was requested of him. He continued his theological studies in Wittenberg, and in March 1509, he obtained his first doctorate, *baccalaureus biblicus*. This degree meant that he had sufficient knowledge to offer first lectures, in which he simply had to explain chapters from the Bible. Only half a year later, he obtained his second degree, *baccalaureus sententiarus*, which entitled him to teach lectures on the *Four Books of Sentences* by Peter Lombard. He had just begun this task when in the fall of 1509 he was recalled to the monastery in Erfurt. Why this happened is not completely clear. Did they need him more in Erfurt because one of the teachers had died, creating a vacant chair? Or did they not want him to become the top theologian too quickly in Wittenberg? Regardless, within two years, he was back in Wittenberg.

Seeking and Studying

Not much is known about Luther's study years. There are indications that already in these years he criticized the popular mode of thinking about the relationship between God and mankind. We do know that in the course of his personal search, in 1508, he obtained a little book of sermons written by the Dominican friar Johann Tauler (ca. 1300–1361). This had been written in German and therefore written for the common people, since Latin was the language of the academy. Here Luther found a theology that affected his mind and his heart. He learned that only an attitude of humility and resting in God would make one pleasing to God. God works where we let him work. A person should have an attitude of passivity and submit completely to whatever God wants with the sinner. God wants to put the old Adam in us to death, and in this we should let God do his work.

This appealed to Luther. He was likewise drawn to the sermons of Bernard of Clairvaux (1090–1153), which stressed personal humiliation, self-denial, and the development of a devout inner being. These sermons would have a lasting effect on him. He also read mystical theologians who often spoke about fellowship between God and the soul, which was exactly what Luther desired. But these did not bring him any further in his own quest. He felt that the mystics placed too much emphasis on a manner of believing that expected people to ascend to God through their faith experience. Luther simply could not achieve this. This difficulty was typical of the spiritual and theological world as portrayed in the books of that time, which Luther found confusing and pointless, especially theology and preaching in which people were summoned to prepare themselves for the grace of God but were unclear when they had done enough or whether they were sufficiently prepared inwardly to be worthy of such grace. It was a form of religion that drove people to self-examination, to a consciousness of their guilt, and to the confession of sin. They were motivated and driven to live a Christian lifestyle, in which people were told at the same time that they could never be sure whether God loved them or hated them, whether he had rejected or chosen them. The only surety was that Christ would be Judge and that they would have to appear before him. In other words, there was nothing certain other than judgment.

Rome

In terms of public opinion, the church, which included the pope and the rest of the clergy, had a rather poor score. The pope needed large amounts of money to wage war in defense of the Papal States and to maintain the pomp and luxuries of the papal court. Most people believed that these expenses stood in shrill contrast to the teachings of Scripture concerning church leaders. Many bishops saw themselves primarily as political leaders and acted accordingly. Neither did many of the clergy remain faithful to their vows of chastity and celibacy, often failing to suppress their sexual desires. Though these sins taxed their consciences, ridding themselves of this guilt was simple: paying penance. In this fashion, guilty consciences, first burdened by the church, provided the church with significant financial support! Increases in the number of indulgences and frequency of masses caused questions and suspicions.

In addition to the latter problems, other sources of conflict emerged. In Erfurt, for example, in 1509 and 1510, fierce social conflicts erupted that led to violence between the citizens and the government. The death and bloodshed that Luther saw led him to ask God, "Who can serve God when he uses such force?"[31] It was Luther's constantly recurring question: How was it possible to serve God in a satisfactory way?

Nor did he receive an answer to his question in 1510 when he made the journey of a lifetime to Rome. This journey had been prompted by a conflict within the Augustinian order. A group of monasteries wanted to keep the monastic rule rigorously, but another group believed that less strenuous maintaining of the rules was acceptable. They felt that personal possessions such as clothing and books should be permissible. Attempts to resolve this dispute internally had failed. A prospect for resolution appeared when Luther's old friend Johann von Staupitz, a supporter of reform, became the superior over both groups. When he attempted to use this opportunity to implement his plans for reform, though, it was met with opposition. A number of monasteries feared that this reform plan would mean that monasteries would become embroiled in all kinds of church issues. As a result, monks would be taxed with new duties that would interfere with their normal monastic tasks. Objections against the influential position that von Staupitz would receive could only be submitted to the pope. Therefore, the priories of Erfurt and Nuremberg each sent a monk to Rome to argue their case before the pope. Erfurt sent Luther, burdening him with the task of opposing the policies of his friend von Staupitz. Despite his personal objections, his earlier promise of eternal obedience when he had taken the monastic vow compelled him to go. Luther was only twenty-seven, indicating the important position of trust he had achieved even at such a relatively young age.

This journey would remain vivid in his memory for a long time, and not because of the issues that had prompted his trip to Rome in the first place. In later remembrances the questions concerning von Staupitz were not even mentioned. The vivid impressions were made due to the sharp contrast between his expectations of Rome and what he actually experienced there: "Whoever goes to Rome with lots of money will receive forgiveness of sins. I also was so foolish to go to Rome with onions and return with garlic."[32] In other words, you bring an odor to Rome, and you return with an even bigger stench. The problems Luther brought to Rome were not solved, merely exacerbated.

In early November, the two friars began their journey. Each day they could average about twenty-five miles. Augustinian monastic rules forbade travel by horse for monks. Instead, the journey would consist of walking together with a fellow friar—never alone, to prevent sin and accidents, yet always one behind the other, to inhibit them from chatting together. Clearly, this style of travel did not make the journey any shorter or more amicable. Nights were spent in monasteries along the way. Though the two had a choice of pilgrim routes, they chose the worst one, via Switzerland, Milan, and Florence. That route meant mountains and, because they left at the end of October, treading through snow, not to mention the danger of robbers. They had already traveled from Wittenberg to Nuremberg, a walking journey of ten days, when they had a meeting to discuss the contentious issues. Little is known about the actual journey. Luther mentioned only a few details: that Switzerland was unproductive because they had only pastures and that the mountains made farming impossible. He also noted that Italian tailors made nicer trousers than the Germans. Though the travels led them through Florence and Siena, he said nothing about the beauty of those cities. After forty-eight days of walking, they finally reached Rome, on Christmas Eve in 1510.

Distressing Impressions

The long journey was finally rewarded with a terrible shock. Luther had often been told about Rome but could not believe possible much of what he had heard. At first, he was appropriately impressed: "In the year 1510 when I first saw the city, I fell on the ground and cried: 'Greetings, holy Rome! Indeed, truly holy because of the blood of the holy martyrs that drips from this city.'"[33] That sentiment changed rapidly. In most churches, masses were rattled off in a hurried pace, so that they could take in as much money as possible. In the St. Sebastian Basilica, he observed two priests reciting mass at the same altar, each to a side, separated by a painting. In this way, they could present seven masses in one hour. Exceptions to this practice were rare, and according to Luther, it was only in the church of Santa Maria dell'Anima on the Piazza Navona that he observed a mass done with reverence and respect. He later recalled,

> I was not in Rome for a very long time, but I presided at many masses and observed many masses. I still shudder with horror when I think of them. In addition to the things that I saw there among the clergy at the table, I also heard them laugh mockingly about how others spoke when they offered up the bread and wine—"Bread thou art, and bread thou shalt remain"—and then held it up on high. At that time I was a very young and a very devout monk, and such words hurt me. What was I to think? What else could I think other than the thought that people at the table here in Rome apparently conducted themselves very freely and frankly? Imagine if

> all of them—the pope, the cardinals, and the whole curia—would administer mass in such a fashion. Then I would have been deceived by all of them whose masses I attended! And above all, I developed such an aversion to the "quick, quick" administration of the mass. It appeared like it was a game to them.[34]

For someone who presided at mass with such fear and trembling because he believed that he, as a sinful person, came into such close contact with the holy God, this cavalier fashion of offering up mass must have come as an enormous shock. The realization was painful for Luther. Five years earlier, Erasmus of Rotterdam (ca. 1466–1536) had been in Rome and had also expressed disgust at the blasphemous practices he had observed there. Other visitors expressed their amazement and shock as well. For Luther, it was more than disgust. It brought him great grief. Complaining to the pope was not an option because he was not available; he was commanding his armies to suppress rebellions in several Italian cities.

St. Peter's

Since 1506, construction on the new St. Peter's Basilica had begun in earnest. At the time that Luther was in Rome, Michelangelo was busy working on the Sistine Chapel, and Raphael was working on decorations for the papal residence. Bridges had been built across the Tiber to facilitate pilgrim travel to the Vatican. In fact, one of those bridges had been built with revenue from a prostitution tax. For every pilgrim coming to Rome, visits to the seven main churches were compulsory (see fig. 3.2). In one day, without eating or drinking, people were expected first to visit St. Paul's Church outside the city gate and then afterward to visit the tomb of St. Paul. Subsequently, they would visit the St. Sebastian Church, the Cathedral of St. John Lateran, the Basilica of the Holy Cross, the St. Lawrence Church, the papal Church of St. Maria Maggiore, and finally St. Peter's.

All pilgrims were expected to climb the Scala Sancta, a long stairway that was reputed to have come out of the palace of Pontius Pilate. It was also claimed that the bloodied Jesus had climbed these stairs on Good Friday. In the fourth century, Helena, the mother of Emperor

Figure 3.2 *Pilgrims Visiting the Seven Churches of Rome during the Holy Year of 1575*. Engraving by Antonio Lafreri, ca. 1575. Metropolitan Museum of Art, New York.

Constantine the Great, had these stairs brought to Rome. Everyone who would climb these stairs on their knees reciting the Lord's Prayer on every tread would supposedly deliver a soul from purgatory. Luther went through this exercise to rescue his grandfather. He recalled,

> In Rome I wanted to rescue my grandfather from purgatory. Therefore, I climbed the stairs of Pilate and prayed the Lord's Prayer on every tread. There was a conviction that whoever prayed in this way could save a soul. But when I arrived at the top, I thought, who knows whether this is really true?[35]

Also here in Rome, he tried his utmost to acquire as much grace as possible. In a way he felt sorry that his father and mother were still living because he would dearly have loved to rescue them from purgatory.[36]

There was more that Luther did not achieve, however. On Friday he had been in the Cathedral of St. John Lateran, the official church of the bishop of Rome, but decided to return to that church the following day. He had wanted to preside at mass there because of a rule that stipulated that if a priest led mass on Saturday in the St. John Lateran, he would bestow a special blessing on his mother. It turned out that there were many more priests on pilgrimage who wanted to do this for their mothers. It was so busy with competing priests on pilgrimage that there was no way he could get a turn. Disappointed, he finally left and treated himself to a smoked herring.[37]

From a practical perspective, the trip was also a disappointment, because Luther and his colleague were not admitted to the leading clergy. They had walked to Rome for nothing and then walked all the way back via the Brenner Pass, Innsbruck, and Augsburg. At the end of March 1511, they had finally returned to Nuremburg, probably much lighter but weighed down with many experiences. Luther was stunned to realize that in Rome he had not been able to find any answers, and worse, his questions had only grown more troublesome. Did God really extend his grace to Luther because he had presided at mass in so many churches or climbed that old stairway? Was what he had seen and experienced in Rome really what Jesus Christ had meant the church to be? Luther was familiar with the expression that wherever the Lord builds a church, the Devil builds a chapel next door.[38] He would have liked to believe that that was the case in Rome. But his experience proved that it was much worse than he had supposed, a feeling corroborated by what others said: "When I was in Rome, I heard people openly saying on the street: 'If there is a hell, Rome was built upon it.'"[39]

Luther had gone to Rome to address the von Staupitz issue, but his reports about his activities and experiences clearly indicate that his personal salvation and that of his family preoccupied him most of all. If people were to obtain righteousness before God, then Rome—of all places—should have been the place where people could have achieved this. But for Luther, a devout monk, all he obtained was disappointment and doubt.

4

Exegete (1511–1517)

Transfer

In many places throughout Europe, rulers tried to increase their influence and prestige by establishing universities, hoping to provide their subjects with competent doctors, jurists, and theologians. The University of Wittenberg was founded in 1502. To give it extra luster, the name was changed to *Leucorea*, a combination of the Greek words meaning "white" and "mountain" (see fig. 4.1). The luster, however, was visible not just in the fancy name but also in the program taught, specifically, the humanist program. In those days humanism meant nothing more than taking a fresh new look at the old subjects, with an emphasis on the knowledge of the original Greek and Hebrew languages. The oft-repeated refrain was "Back to the original sources!"

In 1508–1509, Luther had temporarily lectured in Wittenberg on the ethics of the Greek philosopher Aristotle. He therefore knew where he was going when von Staupitz transferred him there in 1511. One reason for the transfer was some internal problems in Erfurt, where a large group of monks wanted renewal and a smaller group wanted to rigorously keep the monastic rules. Because Luther belonged to the latter group, it was deemed that he should leave. His friend Johann Lang (1487–1548), who had come to the monastery in Erfurt shortly after him, accompanied him. After five years, Lang returned to Erfurt but then left the monastery altogether in 1522 to help with the work

Figure 4.1 Wittenberg University Alma Mater Leucorea, established 1502. Photo courtesy of Touristoffice Wittenberg.

of the Reformation. Luther, on the other hand, remained in Wittenberg permanently.

In 1511, Wittenberg, in contrast to Erfurt, with its many churches and monasteries, was a small town of about four hundred houses—most of them built from wood and straw—and thus not a world-renowned center. Going to this glorified village could hardly be seen as a promotion. Wittenberg was home to about two thousand citizens. Luther sensed that he had come to the edge of civilization.[1] If they had traveled just a little farther, "they would have ended up in a complete wilderness."[2] Wittenberg—named after the white sands on the shores of the Elbe River—was simply a long street with the castle on one side and the so-called Black Cloister on the other. Somewhere in the middle was a market square and the town hall. There was no church of local significance unless one counted the Castle Chapel, which was under construction when Luther arrived. This was the case with many of the buildings, since the elector was preoccupied with the university. The City Church had two beautiful towers but was relatively modest in size and adornment. The university was only ten years old, and though it was making a name for itself, it was still in an entirely different class than the University of Erfurt. Housed in a former hospital, a monastery had been established at the same time as the university but was constantly under construction. Attached to the cloister was a decrepit chapel about thirty feet by twenty feet. The monastery housed about thirty monks, a considerable number for such a small cloister. Additionally, the city boasted three book printers and expected more to come if the university continued to grow.

This small city experienced interesting political times because the elector, Frederick the Wise, lived there in his castle. He strove for the political independence of the church. But at the same time, he wanted a healthy church, free from wrongs and faithful to the Catholic tradition. Clearly, this was a policy that appeared to fit exactly with the views of Luther. Neither the elector nor Luther realized this when he arrived. According to Luther, he had no contact with the elector and never met him during his first fifteen years in Wittenberg. One of his students asked him, "My lord doctor, they say that you have never spoken with Duke Frederick." He answered, "That is true."[3] The two communicated through the humanist priest and teacher Georg Spalatin (1484–1545), who also served as tutor of the young princes, librarian of the university, curator of the collection of relics, and adviser and secretary to the elector (see fig. 4.2). Spalatin maintained a very close relationship with Luther, as the more than four hundred preserved letters he wrote to Luther attest.

Doctor

Luther had followed the earnest advice given earlier by von Staupitz and finished his studies to obtain his doctorate in theology. Following the presentation of the required documentation, discussions, and the payment of academic fees, the promotion took place on October 18–19, 1512. In the afternoon of the 18th, Luther participated in a three-hour disputation. Senior students and university instructors engaged the prospective doctor in a theological debate, in which he had to demonstrate his expertise and knowledge. Andreas Bodenstein (1486–1541), usually called Carlstadt after the name of his birthplace, served as Luther's promoter. (Years later Luther would experience a sharp difference of opinion with him.) Carlstadt ended the first day with a humorous address.

Figure 4.2 *Portrait of Georg Spalatin* (1484–1545). Painting by Lucas Cranach the Elder, 1509. Museum der bildenden Künste, Leipzig.

The following morning an official promotion ceremony began in the Castle Church. The promoter, Carlstadt, delivered a speech, which was followed by Luther's swearing of the doctor's oath. In this oath Luther formally pledged that he would not proclaim anything that disagreed with the doctrine of the church. Afterward, he was presented with the symbols of his doctor's position: an open and a closed Bible, a beret, and a doctor's golden signet ring engraved with three intertwined circles, signifying the divine Trinity, the greatest theological mystery known to the church. The new doctor then gave an address about the tremendous value of theology. Subsequently, there was another disputation and finally a festive meal with the faculty to close off the events of the day.

Luther was twenty-eight when he became doctor, quite young for that time. Though he claimed that he had not wanted the title, it would become essential to his later deeds. After Luther had acquired his doctorate, he was given the chair called *Lectura in biblia*, or professor of theology. Though the teaching assignment was broader than the Bible subjects, he would be mostly involved with exegesis. A professor in those days had essentially three tasks: lecturing (*lectio*), organizing academic disputations (*disputatio*), and preaching (*praedicatio*). Teaching consisted primarily of presenting lectures in which the lecturer would explain the Bible content or, using standard theological works, lecture on dogmatics. Luther concentrated on explaining the content of Scripture. Beginning in the summer of 1513, he spent almost two years on the Psalms, then continued with Paul's letters to the Romans (1515–1516) and the Galatians (1516–1517), and in the 1517–1518 school year explained the letter to the Hebrews. The letter to the Romans would become, and remain, the most important book in the New Testament for him:

> This letter is the most important chapter in the New Testament and is the purist gospel. It would be worth a Christian's effort not only to memorize this letter word for word but also to work with it on a daily basis like daily bread for the soul. One can never read or reflect on it too often or too thoroughly. The more frequently you engage yourself with this letter, the more valuable and appetizing it becomes.[4]

Beginning in 1519, he again lectured on the Psalms. Luther enjoyed teaching, especially because he could then lecture in the beautiful hall given the nickname "heavenly lecture hall" (*auditorium coelium*). This hall was part of the church and situated above the crossing. In the summer he taught from six to eight o'clock in the morning, and in the winter from seven to nine. Sentence by sentence, word by word, he explained the text, using only the Bible rather than books about the Bible, as he would have done formerly. He had the printers produce special Bibles with lines that were spaced to leave ample room for students to take notes both between the lines and in the margins. What made Luther's teaching style unique was his combination of scholarship and devotion: he explained the Bible texts carefully using the most recent scholarly insights and then applied these to faith life.[5] During the Middle Ages, people had felt that academic theology was sterile and of little practical use. Monastic theology countered this sterility with an emphasis on the practice of a godly lifestyle. Luther's exegesis merged these two traditions of university and monastery; this was novel but eagerly accepted by the students. It was also attributed to Luther's success as professor that from 1515 to 1520 the number of students in Wittenberg doubled.

Besides the lectures, there was the phenomenon of disputations. A *disputatio* was essentially a discussion about a number of theses drafted by the professor. Usually it concerned discussions between students, who used these opportunities to gain more knowledge and to learn to articulate and defend their point of view. The exchange of perspectives became a vehicle to learn collaboratively. Because the professor established the theses, he could direct the substance of the debate. In the context of this function, the professor's regular preaching in the Black Cloister, as well as his preaching for the laity in the City Church, were integral to the process.

Commentaries

None of the materials from Luther's first years of teaching in Wittenberg were saved. His development as a professor can only be followed, albeit in a limited fashion, from 1513 to 1514. It is easier to see the actual result of that development rather than designating the exact periods of that process. We know that in the spring of 1513, Luther began his commentaries on the Psalms. This is the book of the Bible that looks into the hearts of believers, he said. Many exegetes before him had also spent considerable time on the Psalms, so his choice was not unique. Nevertheless, his own heart and inner conflicts would have played an important role in Luther choosing the Psalms. By carefully and painstakingly taking his students through these texts, the professor provided instruction for his students but also for himself. Subsequently and not surprisingly, he followed with the letter to the Romans.

In 1516, Erasmus's Greek New Testament was published. For the first time in many centuries, it was again possible to go directly to the original text of the Bible. Luther immediately began using this new publication and soon discovered that key words in Greek sometimes had entirely different meanings than those given in the Latin Vulgate, the official translation used by the church. However, Luther was obligated to use this translation as the starting point in his lectures.

In his lectures from 1513 to 1517, one can see how Luther searched for an understanding of the relationship between God and man. His thinking about sin and grace was changing, and in that process the interaction of his personal experiences, the voices of the church fathers, and the teachings of the medieval theologians played a major role. But he strove to let the Word of God drown out the inner and outer voices. Progressively, the Bible became his only norm. In a 1515 sermon he clearly said that while the Bible was not Christ, through the Bible we come to Christ.

Whoever reads the Bible must be very careful not to wander, Luther insisted. One can expound the Scriptures, but this should never be directed by feeling. Instead, one must allow the Bible to lead back to the source, that is, to the cross of Christ. Then the student of Scripture will reach his goal and will not go amiss.[6]

The influence of Erasmus's methodology of exegesis was quite evident when Luther spoke about the Old Testament. Erasmus had warned that exegetes should note carefully who is speaking in the Bible text and who is addressed in the Bible text. Luther taught similarly:

> God spoke with Adam, but I am not Adam. He commanded Abraham to strangle his son, but I am not Abraham, and therefore, I should not strangle my son. In this way God also spoke to David. It's all God's Word; that is certainly true. But God's Word here or there, I must know and pay close attention to whom God addresses his Word.[7]

By means of these lectures, Luther learned things that he in turn could also pass on to others: one becomes a theologian through *oratio*, *meditatio*, and *tentatio*—prayer, meditation, and trial. For Luther, reflection was not a vague or woolly feeling about a text. Rather, it meant weighing the Word while listening in prayer, thinking deeply about the meaning of a Hebrew concept or a Greek term. According to Luther, it concerned the "rechewing" of the text[8] until it opened up, as it were, and revealed the content.[9] As a result of engaging with the Word of God in this way, Luther became increasingly convinced that people have no inherent means by which they can access God. Man does not only sin; he is a sinner. Before God he stands only as a sinner, and if he denies that, then he makes God into a liar.[10] Every attempt to make oneself right before God—whether in consciousness of guilt, knowledge of sin, distress of the conscience, or remorse—is senseless. God's grace only gets its due and honor when a person acknowledges that he or she is a sinner.[11]

During these years, Luther's consciousness of sin and perception of Christ were like the dawning light that gradually drove away the darkness. At this stage we can perceive a humble theology in Luther, a realization that he was guilty and lost. But Luther was careful not to make his humility into a new condition for grace. Luther's perception of God's righteousness as a punishing justice was still a problem, though that would soon change.

Preaching

When he obtained his doctorate and became professor, he also received the charge to preach. It is not clear whether this charge came from von Staupitz or from the city council of Wittenberg. Initially, Luther did not want to preach,[12] but once he began, he couldn't be stopped. His preaching assignment was normally at the City Church, though occasionally he also preached in the Castle Church, when members of the regal family wanted to attend a service there. In this way, through Luther's sermons, the pulpit and the lectern were linked, and the professor was able to reap the fruits of his exegesis as teacher and pass these on to the people as preacher. Some of his sermons from 1514 have been saved. Here we can read things that students had already heard in the lectures. Luther indicated that he had great difficulty forcing people to achieve a Christian life and sanctification that was impossible to attain. Such a theology and preaching denied not only the power of sin but also the power of God's grace. According to Luther, this was unmerciful and blasphemous. It was unmerciful to say that people should do all kinds of things when they really couldn't, and it was blasphemous to misrepresent what God required. It is better to acknowledge that we are and remain sinners and that God first gives and only then asks.

In his sermons Luther strongly criticized the veneration of saints. At this time he did not object to appealing to saints but instead objected to using them only to address earthly matters, such as healing a cow or finding a missing ring. If we used saints for only such matters, then, according to Luther, we would be preoccupied with matters of this life when we should be focused on eternal life. Luther was questioned about this by Spalatin, who asked on behalf of the elector why he criticized the veneration of saints. Luther answered him in a lengthy letter, writing,

> I was never of the opinion that the veneration of saints would be superstitious in itself, not even when they were invoked for the sake of corporal matters. . . . For it is better to desire all kinds of things from God's saints (because everything is a gift from God) than that people would seek these things from the Devil by means of magic or witchcraft, like many people do. I only wanted to say that it would be superstitious, indeed, ungodly and wrong, to desire only corporal things from God and the saints, and completely fail to concern ourselves with what is needed for our souls and our salvation, indeed, what God wants us to do, as if we would forget his word and would not believe what he says (Matt. 6:33): "Seek first his kingdom and all these things will be given you as well." Indeed, Jesus teaches everywhere to have little concern for the body and everything that comes with it. And if it is permitted to pray for other things, then that only counts for those who are imperfect in their faith and live under Moses more than under Christ. Therefore, such a veneration of saints should only be tolerated on account of those who are weak, but it is definitely not to be recommended as something that fits with a Christian lifestyle. Look at the common people and see if they venerate a saint to receive chastity, patience, humility, faith, hope, love, and other spiritual gifts. The saints that the people find attractive, for whom people build churches and chapels, are all saints who help protect against fire, sickness, poverty, and other corporal things. When you only invoke saints for earthly needs, that is superstition.[13]

Ripple in the Pond

Luther's search for God gradually became more apparent. His sermons increasingly attracted attention, not only because of his emotional and enthusiastic style but also because of the content. He sounded similar to the well-known preachers of repentance, but his message was still different, as his students noticed. A growing number of his colleagues noticed it too when they gathered for a disputation prompted by theses drafted by other professors. Luther's theses spoke of a different approach to the themes of guilt and grace, God and man. Both in the city and beyond, people spoke about it, saying that in Wittenberg there was a professor who heavily criticized scholasticism (the medieval theology that focused on questions about the essence of God and angels, which tended to be highly theoretical and impractical for normal churchgoers). Luther criticized the humanists who obsessed over form, language, and style but who showed apathy toward the theological content. He argued that the church needed reform but that this reform must come from God:

> The church needs reform [*reformatio*], and that is not the work of a pope, nor the work of a lot of cardinals, such as the most recent councils proved. But it is a matter of the whole world—indeed, a matter of God himself. When the time for this reform has come only he who created time will know. But in the meantime we cannot ignore all wrongs. The keys of the kingdom are being misused and have been subjected to greed and zealous ambition.[14]

The Protestant Reformation, which we now see as Luther's reformation, was not the reformation he meant here. Here by *reformatio* Luther meant the restoration of all things with Christ's return on the last day. But there were too many things that had gone wrong to put off reform and wait for the end of time. Luther preached that something had to happen now, that this reform had to go deeper than changing external wrongs. He became known as the preacher who railed against the notion that sins were only mistakes. The Bible teaches not only that we *make* mistakes but also that we *are* mistaken and wrong, indeed sinful. With his remarks, Luther sharply criticized the theological authorities who set the direction of the universities. These universities in turn had determined the character of the ministry and the preaching.

Erfurt was upset and annoyed by Luther's insights.[15] Luther clarified that he did not reject everything taught by the great theologians. They had said many good things, but the moment they spoke about faith and mercy, virtue and hope, they were wrong.

During the rest of his life, Luther would blame the philosopher Aristotle for these theological errors. He was the one who formulated what a person was capable of, and because the humanists relied heavily on his work, Luther bemoaned, they believed everything he said. Luther did not have one good word to say about this Greek philosopher and instead called him a slanderer, a liar, and a clown who had fooled the church. If he had the time, he would have debunked "this actor who, with his Greek mask, had so thoroughly taken the lead in the church," and then he would have shown the world his shame.[16] In short, he felt there was too much Aristotle and too little Augustine. Luther wanted to get away from the great philosopher and instead go to the great theologian.

Luther first learned about Augustine during the winter semester of 1509–1510, when he lectured on two of the most comprehensive works written by this church father: *The City of God* (*De Civitate Dei*) and *On the Trinity* (*De Trinitate*). Being a monk in an Augustinian monastery did not necessarily mean that one would intensively study Augustine's works; it only meant that life in the cloister was regulated by the rules attributed to Augustine. When he had discovered Augustine, however, Luther learned from him about the essence of God and the essence of mankind and that there is no access to God through man. Augustine led him to distance himself even more forcefully from Aristotle, as he stated several years later: "All of Aristotle compared to theology is like a shadow is to light."[17] Around 1515, Luther delved into the anti-Pelagian writings of Augustine. He was impressed by his view on sin and grace and how this church father proved the powerlessness of mankind with arguments from the Bible. In Wittenberg he successfully convinced others to abandon Aristotle, as he wrote to Lang on May 18, 1517:

> Fortunately, our theology and Augustine's are making good progress and through God's intervention are now decisive for our university. Aristotle is on a downward slide and will soon be in ruins. Students have developed an aversion to lectures on the *Sententiae*. You really will not get a student audience unless you lecture on the new theology, that is to say, lectures concerning the Bible, Augustine, or another teacher with ecclesiastical authority.[18]

His colleague Carlstadt initially had difficulty accepting Luther's position and delved into Augustine himself to counter him. Things changed, however, because when he read what Augustine had written, he had to agree with Luther.

Turmerlebnis

Many books and articles have been written to address the question whether Luther's reformational breakthrough occurred in 1514 or 1518. Some experts maintain 1515, and others claim 1516 or 1517. There are even some who think that this happened a few years later. It doesn't really matter. Instead of choosing an earlier or later date, it is probably better to speak of a reformational development that began in 1513 and was completed by 1518. In the preface to his Latin works, Luther himself said that not until 1519 did he discover that the term "God's righteousness" in Romans 1:17 meant not that God *demands* righteousness but that he *imparts* righteousness.[19] It is clear that Luther gradually and more frequently questioned the prevailing theology and ecclesiastical practices.

Through the reading of Augustine, among others, Luther progressively understood that the human will is totally incapable of achieving anything in the context of eternal salvation; it depends completely on God's righteousness. Almost hopelessly, he searched Paul's letters for the meaning of God's righteousness: "I hated that word, namely, 'God's righteousness'; . . . indeed, I did not love God, but I hated this righteous God who punishes sinners."[20] He could not understand why God first condemned the sinner through the law and then also threatened him again in the gospel with righteousness: "I raged with an angry and thoroughly confused conscience, and unrestrained I went to Paul concerning this text, because I had a burning desire to know what the holy Paul would say about this."[21] Not until he had thought day and night about the relationship between the two words "God" and "righteousness" did he come to a conviction that this relationship was radically different from what he had always been told: "The gospel reveals the righteousness of God, namely, the passive, through which God the Merciful justifies us through faith, as is written: 'The righteous will live by faith.'" The hatred toward God immediately changed into love: "I felt completely newborn, and it was as if I had gone through the open gates into paradise itself."[22]

Luther at first appeared completely unaware at that time that this new insight would close the gates of Rome and that his perspective would be in conflict with the church. In the first place, it was a personal discovery, and what this would mean for other believers and the church as a whole was beyond his purview. Luther did not have an agenda for the Reformation, and "reformer" was not his career choice. Nor did he set out to cause a breach with Rome. True, he wanted reforms in the church, but many with him and before him wanted the same—that was not unique. Only when he learned that Rome considered his ideas heretical did he become aware of the threatening conflict. Luther wanted nothing more than a return to the Bible as the only norm. If this meant breaking with traditions, so be it. But Luther was not out to break with traditions either. His objective was not "reformation" but new attention to the message that grace is sufficient. Now that he had found the proper relationship between the law and the gospel, according to Luther, it was fundamental not only for him but also for all theology: "The one who knows how to properly distinguish between the gospel and the law can thank God and realize that he is a theologian."[23]

For some time there was no doubt about the actual place where Luther had come to his insight: his cell in the monastery. That cell was in the tower, and therefore, many spoke about Luther's *Turmerlebnis*, or "tower experience." He was very attached to that place and became annoyed when the elector wanted to fortify the city walls in 1531–1532 and demolish part of the monastery—the same section where the tower was. Luther heard about the plans and wrote, "If I live for another year, then I will have to leave my cell, while it was out of this place that I stormed the papacy. Therefore, this room is worthy of eternal remembrance."[24] There is a little problem, however. That little tower where Luther claimed he stormed the papacy was not built until 1519. Consequently, Luther's *Turmerlebnis* must have happened somewhere else in the cloister: it was an *Erlebnis* (i.e., an "experience") but not a *Turmerlebnis*.

Luther's protest was only partly successful: the elector built a new fortification wall around the tower, a wall that Luther thought was unnecessary. He also feared that the court was more preoccupied with planning for war and defense strategies than the spread of the gospel. Luther retorted that if you think you can defend faith with a wall, then you've not understood very much about faith.[25] After 1830, the tower was finally demolished and a real cloister garden made, which did not exist in Luther's time.

Procession

By 1515, Luther had not yet arrived at the point that he could see Christ as Deliverer and Savior. If what happened during a particular procession is any indication, in fact, the opposite was true. On the day of the sacrament in June 1515, Luther participated in a procession in his native city, Eisleben. This event was being held in honor of the consecration of the new Augustinian monastery. In the procession, Christ was shown to the village and the city in the form of the consecrated host in a "monstrance," or special vessel. At the same time, Christ's presence served to consecrate them. In this procession, von Staupitz carried the monstrance, but it was Luther who was afraid of walking too closely to Christ, whom he saw as Judge. After the procession, he immediately went to von Staupitz and confessed that during the procession he had been so afraid of Christ because it was he who condemns us. Von Staupitz told him that he was completely mistaken: "It was not Christ that scared you, because Christ does not incite fear but comfort."[26] Or as Luther repeated von Staupitz's words later, "Your shocking image is not Christ. . . . Christ is really the Deliverer who offers forgiveness of sins to people."[27] If Luther was concerned about the question whether he was elect or not, von Staupitz said that he should direct himself to the wounds of Christ, "because it is there that you will find predestination."[28] The worry about election was frightening for Luther: "When I think about that, I forget everything, what God is and what Christ is, and even arrive at the thought that God is a malicious being. . . . When we think about predestination, we forget God. Then praise ceases, and we begin to curse."[29] That is why von Staupitz said that it was better to avoid thinking about election altogether: "Imagine Christ before your eyes, and immediately the issue of election has disappeared."[30] Luther needed von Staupitz so that he would not descend totally into a depression, because he was well on his way.

More compelling than asking if he did enough for God was asking if what he did was good enough. Can I do something good? Luther asked. If not, every attempt to find God would be senseless. In the deepest sense, this concerned the doctrine of predestination. If God has not elected me, then every good work, every prayer, and every form of devotion is totally senseless, and I am and will remain a lost person intended for hell. A few years later he described his state of mind at this time using the words of Paul from 2 Corinthians 12:3:

> I know a man who claimed about himself more than once to have sustained such punishment, even though it was for only a short while. But these were so great and so hellish that no tongue could speak about them, no pen could describe them and no one, unless he has experienced it himself, can believe it. It was so terrible that if it had lasted only half an hour or a tenth of an hour, he would have been totally destroyed, and all his bones would have become ash. Here God shows himself as terribly angry and all creation with him. Then there is no escape, no comfort, not within nor from without, because then really everything blames you. . . . [I]t is strange to say it, but at such a moment the soul cannot believe it will ever be saved.[31]

According to Luther, it was particularly von Staupitz who taught him to direct his attention not to God's hidden will but to God as he has revealed himself in the crucified Christ. Therefore, Luther said that his insights began with von Staupitz: "Von Staupitz began with this doctrine."[32] A few years before he died, he wrote that von Staupitz "was my father in this doctrine."[33]

Vicar

In the meantime, Luther's ecclesiastical career steadily continued, and in 1515, when he was only thirty-one, he was appointed district vicar. In this function he had to supervise eleven monasteries, thus adding considerably to his workload. The manner in which he described this busyness was clear evidence that he had much more to do than pray and confess sins all day:

> Actually, I need two secretaries or recorders. All day long I hardly do anything else than write letters. Therefore, I often do not know whether I have written the same things. . . . I am the monastery preacher; I preach at the table, and every day I am also requested to preach in the City Church. I am dean; I am vicar, that is to say that I am prior eleven times. . . . I give lectures about Paul, I collect materials for lectures about the Psalms, with that in addition to what I already mentioned: the work writing letters requires the most time. Seldom do I truly have enough time to pray the regular prayers without interruption or to finish them; and then I also have to cope with the temptations of the flesh, the world, and the Devil. What a lazy person I am! . . . Tomorrow I will begin with the letter to the Galatians, but I fear that the presence of the plague will interfere with the continuation (of the lectures). It has cost us two or three people (altogether, not per day). The son of the smith opposite us, was healthy yesterday, was buried today, and another one is infected too. What must I say? The sickness is here, begins suddenly, and proceeds roughly, especially with the youth. Johannes Lang advised me to flee. But why? I certainly hope that the world will not implode if Brother Martinus blows out the candle. If the plague persists, I will send the brothers out into the countryside. But I have been placed here, and obedience forbids me to flee, until that obedience demands something different from me. Not that I do not fear death (I am after all, not Paul, but only his commentator!), but I hope that the Lord will deliver me from my fear.[34]

In addition to all these tasks, Luther was also appointed to a committee mandated with evaluating the university. The university had operated for fifteen years, and the elector had received complaints that the professors in the law faculty did not always take their lectures seriously. Therefore, the whole university was subjected to scrutiny to determine where they could improve. Luther began this task in September 1517 and did not complete it until December. A comprehensive package of proposals was sent to the elector, including a program to improve the content of the courses, plus a proposal to increase the number of professors. Fortunately, the elector had already said that he would make money available; it was important to him to have a good university.

Righteousness

In the fall of 1516, Luther's new perspective on righteousness made greater inroads. Erasmus had played a role in this development by bringing the Greek New Testament to the market. This was revolutionary because the church used only the Vulgate, the Latin translation of the Bible. The Vulgate alone was authoritative. As a humanist, Erasmus wanted to go back to the original source, and the original source of the New Testament was Greek. He also intended to bring a new, purer Latin translation to the market, but in order to show how he had come to this new Latin text, he published it alongside the original Greek text. Indeed, when his publication appeared, it was clear that the translation the church used did not properly correlate to the original text.

Luther noticed this especially in John the Baptist's appeal, "Repent, for the kingdom of heaven is at hand" (Matt. 3:2). Instead of the term "repent," the church's translation said that one must "do penance," and it spoke about penance as if it referred to all the church's rules for confession. But Erasmus's text spoke about repentance (Gk. *metanoia*) not as an act but as an internal change. We mustn't simply do things differently; instead, something must happen that will change us within. Only then will we change on the outside. Luther became convinced that the sequence of sanctification and righteousness had to be different. We are not righteous because we sanctify ourselves, but we sanctify ourselves because we have been justified:

> Therefore, it's not the way Aristotle maintained, that we become righteous by doing righteous deeds. That remains only an appearance of righteousness, a sham. Only those who become righteous and who are righteous, do righteous acts. First the person has to change; only then the works will follow.[35]

The church taught that Christ's righteousness meant that Christ enabled us to become righteous. Luther's growing conviction was that the righteousness of Christ means that he has made us righteous. In essence, those statements were two very different things. People who try to live so that they are acceptable to God "do not understand the righteousness of God, because that was given to us completely, and free in Christ." Whoever tries to do it himself shortchanges Christ:

"If we, with our own efforts and torments, had to bring peace to our conscience—indeed, why did he actually die?"[36]

In addition to the work of Erasmus, another book also confirmed Luther's insights. Earlier, he had become acquainted with the sermons of Tauler, and these had really left an impression on him. In 1516, he came across another writing that appeared much the same as that of Tauler. The author was unknown to him, but the contents were deemed to be so important that Luther decided to publish them himself, partly in 1516 and then completely in 1518. The title was *Eyn deutsch Theologia* (A German theology), but subsequently, this work was known as *Theologia Deutsch*. For Luther this booklet was reckoned among the top three, after the Bible and Augustine: "Besides the Bible and Augustine I have not come across any other book from which I learned more about who God, Christ, mankind, and what all things are."[37] In terms of content, Luther's explanation of the penitential psalms (Psalms 6; 32; 38; 51; 102; 130; 143), published in the spring of 1517, followed the same line of thought. These concerned self-examination, humiliation, and an abandonment of self-righteousness. Those who bow humbly before Christ's throne of grace receive forgiveness. Christ sits not on the judgment seat but on the throne of grace. In this particular booklet, however, Luther still emphasized personal conduct.

In his lectures and publications Luther also criticized ecclesiastical wrongs. The clergy did not do what they were supposed to do, and what they did they didn't do from the heart or reverently. They were lukewarm in their faith life and careless with the sacred things of God, evident in how they dressed, celebrated mass, read from the Bible, and prayed. They seemed to want to live in luxury and were more concerned about their own affairs than the eternal well-being of the members of their congregation. They revered the relics of the cross but refused to carry a cross. Their lifestyle was a poor example for the congregation. Underlying this criticism was Luther's conviction that in a church service everything concerned a relationship with the holy God. If that consciousness were lost, church would become sloppy, irreverent, and dangerous for the soul.

At this point, Luther wanted to have a discussion about his new perspective. He chose to do that in a fashion common to the university by having a disputation on a number of theses. The "Ninety-Five Theses" that Luther posted on October 31, 1517, are more well known than the "Ninety-Nine Theses" he published two months earlier on September 4. Nevertheless, the "Ninety-Nine" are far more radical than the "Ninety-Five," because in these Luther clearly challenged the prevailing scholastic theology. For some time it was thought that there were ninety-seven theses in this document; a later inquiry determined that there were indeed ninety-nine. Luther drafted these theses for the promotion of Franz Günther on September 4, 1517. It was customary that the professor would draft the theses, which the doctoral graduate would then have to defend to demonstrate his erudition. Luther demolished Aristotle, who according to Luther had to shoulder the blame for the notion that we are capable of commending ourselves to God. Luther turned this formulation around and therefore turned everything on its head. He also criticized Peter Lombard in these theses because he had taught that people have some merit of their own that offered hope of God's grace. Luther countered that this was wrong because people cannot possibly prepare themselves to receive God's grace. He attacked the theological authorities but in such a way that he would stay within the boundaries of church dogmas: "In all these things we do not say, nor have we said, that we believe something that is not in agreement with the Catholic Church and with church doctrine."[38] That sounded nice, and no doubt, he was sincere; Luther indeed wanted to remain a faithful child of the church of Rome. Yet what he began to say here did not simply disagree with Catholic doctrine but completely undermined it.

5

Theologian (1517–1519)

Indulgences

When Protestants hear the word *indulgences*, they tend to get uncomfortable. That's unfortunate, because indulgences were not really meant to be offensive. An indulgence was just an ordinary piece of paper telling you that you had met the requirements of the penance that the church had imposed on you. When someone became convicted of sin, he or she would confess that sin to the local priest. Then, on behalf of God, the priest could forgive the sin, but he would also insist that a particular form of penance would be necessary. It amounted to, "I forgive you, but you will be punished," a normal rule that would be familiar to many children even today. The penitent had to bear this punishment either in this life or otherwise in purgatory after this life.

The medieval church believed that purgatory was a place between death and heaven. In purgatory people had to do penance for sins that went unconfessed in life. This was the place where one had to bear the ecclesiastical punishments left over after one had died. Either someone did not have enough time to finish penance or had not done it properly. Purgatory was not hell, but it was considered a place of punishment and purification. Fear of this place drove people to do good works and to purchase indulgences. Penance or punishment could possibly involve a pilgrimage, for example, and proof was needed that the pilgrimage had actually been completed. To this end, a pilgrim would receive an indulgence, a written declaration that he or she had been absolved of guilt. It all sounded logical and was even defended using the Bible.

The situation went sideways, however, when parishioners would receive indulgences after someone else went on a pilgrimage on their behalf or when they would simply pay directly to the church whatever such a pilgrimage would have cost. People could even buy indulgences to pay for sins they would eventually commit in the future. When some people in the church recognized the business advantage of indulgences, the situation got really out of hand. A supply of indulgences was prepared in advance, and orders could be placed. People developed the thought that an indulgence could not only save them from punishment but could even absolve them of guilt. Furthermore, indulgences could be purchased for family and friends who had died and thus deliver them from purgatory more quickly. An institution that was established with noble intentions became a lucrative system of spiritual treachery and deceit. In effect, the church took advantage of people who wanted salvation. For more than a century, critics complained that this system made sinning easy and grace cheap. Sovereigns and other governing authorities had an additional objection: money from the sale of indulgences was drained from their economy and flowed instead to Rome. In short, with the exception of the church, which benefited from all this income, everybody was disturbed by the sale of indulgences (see fig. 5.1).

Tetzel

The combination of the term *indulgence* with the name Tetzel is infuriating for Protestants. But this man did nothing more than the task he was given and was otherwise a fine gentleman. Luther accused him of leading an immoral lifestyle, but there is no proof for that accusation. He was paid very well for his work, but good pay in and of itself is not necessarily sinful. Johann Tetzel (ca. 1460–1519) was a Dominican monk, belonging to a religious order that specialized in preaching (see fig. 5.2). He was appointed an indulgence preacher, which meant that he was expected to preach in such a way that people would flock to buy indulgences.

This special task was given to him when Albrecht of Brandenburg (1490–1545), archbishop of Magdeburg, was chosen to become

Figure 5.1 *A Question to a Mintmaker*. Woodcut of an indulgence seller by Jörg Breu the Elder, ca. 1530. Kupferstichkabinett, Berlin.

Figure 5.2 Johann Tetzel (ca. 1460–1519). Artist unknown, 1717.

archbishop of Mainz as well. This dual responsibility would have been an attractive opportunity since at that time these functions came with power and money and had little to do with spiritual leadership. According to the ecclesiastical rules, a person was not allowed to hold two of these functions. However, Rome had a financial motivation in allowing this arrangement since by it the pope could procure money needed for the construction of St. Peter's Basilica. If Albrecht paid Rome a hefty sum, he would be allowed to keep both offices. Only part of the money would go to Rome, however, because the other part went to the deeply indebted archbishopric of Mainz. How would Albrecht acquire the money? He brought a new kind of indulgence to the market that was proclaimed by the pope as Peter's indulgence. People who bought this indulgence received forgiveness for themselves or for others, and at the same time, they supported the construction of St. Peter's. It was seemingly a win-win. Pope Leo X proclaimed this indulgence on March 31, 1515, and openly declared that both pastoral and financial concerns were combined in this effort. It was not until the beginning of 1517, however, that the sale of these indulgences really began.

Tetzel received the mandate to preach the promotion of this sale in the archbishopric of Magdeburg. Thus, he began his circuit of preaching in the spring of 1517, accompanied by personnel from the Fugger banking house, which had made business arrangements with the pope. A large wooden box also accompanied Tetzel in which they put the money paid by people seeking their salvation. (This wooden box still exists, though the money has long disappeared.) The well-known rhyme "As soon as a coin in the coffer rings, a soul from purgatory springs" was not a form of anti-Roman propaganda but was actually used by Tetzel & Co. as an advertising slogan. Clarifying that an indulgence also required contrition and genuine confession would have complicated the issue and would have resulted in fewer proceeds. Tetzel therefore said that an indulgence provided complete absolution of sin: "Greater grace is not possible because people are sinners, and because of that, they lose God's grace. But by means of this absolution of sin, you will again be received into God's grace."[1] That was not true at all, because indulgences were to deliver people from the punishment for sin, not from the guilt of sin. Nevertheless, this misdirection was good for sales. Tetzel also proclaimed that punishments suffered by the dead in purgatory could be reduced by the prayers of the pope, to be purchased by money. Tetzel was not received enthusiastically everywhere, but in general his affairs ran well until he arrived in the neighborhood of Wittenberg.

Competition

Wittenberg was outside the archbishopric of Magdeburg, but it was close enough that the people in Luther's city heard about the deal they could get from Tetzel. Citizens in Wittenberg crossed the border to buy indulgences from Tetzel when he came to Jüterbog to set up his indulgence kiosk, a journey of about twenty-five miles. This showed how anxious people were about receiving surety for eternal life for both themselves and their posterity.

In the meantime, two people in Wittenberg worried about competition. Luther considered indulgences competition for Christ. Elector Frederick the Wise deemed Tetzel a competitor in the indulgence trade that he himself conducted. In the course of time, Frederick had assembled an enormous collection of 18,870 relics. He had managed to gather everything imaginable, and visiting this collection could earn forgiveness for many sins. Those who looked at each relic with an appropriate attitude, according to Frederick's calculation, could receive 1,902,270 years of indulgence. In 1517 alone, more than 9,000 masses were conducted, and 40,932 candles were lit. It was no wonder, then, that Frederick, who remained Catholic all his life, was nonetheless an ally to Luther. Not only was Luther his trump card in his power struggle with the pope and the emperor, but also Luther's action against Tetzel's indulgences supported his own collection—even if inadvertently.

Though Tetzel's trade brought Frederick into financial problems, it confronted Luther with a spiritual problem. He struggled with guilt and forgiveness and had just begun developing a focus on the biblical concept of *penance*. In the meantime, he was faced with members of his congregation who had traveled to Tetzel and returned with an indulgence yet appeared to exhibit neither remorse nor repentance. Tetzel's claim had generated this attitude, he believed. Tetzel asserted that indulgences provided reconciliation between God and mankind and that this was effective without proper penance.[2] Luther also directed concern about this issue to Albrecht of Mainz. Because this bishop was responsible for Peter's indulgence, Luther wrote him an extensive letter in which he explained his objections. On account of the conduct of the preachers promoting indulgences, "people think that they can be sure of their eternal salvation as long as they have bought an indulgence and additionally, that souls leave purgatory immediately the moment they have thrown their financial contribution into the box."[3] According to Luther, they went so far as to say that there was forgiveness through these indulgences "even if someone had raped the holy Virgin Mary, the mother of God, or impregnated her."[4] Luther wrote that he had no other recourse than to inform the archbishop about this, to prevent "that someone would arise who would oppose them and the directives about indulgences in such a scathing fashion that your highness would suffer great damage."[5] Though Luther added that he would be appalled by that prospect, he did not sound very convincing. The letter actually communicated a brief but terse message: if Albrecht didn't do something, Luther would.

Theses

Luther had long had problems with indulgences. In his first lectures on the Psalms, given in 1514, he already complained that the practice of indulgences made the road to heaven easy and made grace cheap.[6] At other times he expressed his concern about the whole trade in indulgences. How could money and guilt be connected with each other in such a destructive way? Luther maintained that people bought indulgences because they were afraid of punishment, while in actual fact they should be afraid of sins.[7] Indulgences provided people with a false sense of surety and strengthened self-love. Those who purchased them were concerned not about living to God's honor but only about how they could escape God's punishment. Indulgences created the wrong impression that punishment is the problem, rather than guilt before God. Though the original intention of indulgences meant that only the truly remorseful benefited from them, Luther argued that the truly remorseful do not require an indulgence. Luther's quarrel was not that German money went to Rome or that it was used for St. Peter's or that people spent so much money on indulgences even though they had so little to begin with. He was likewise completely unconcerned that Tetzel's indulgences were bad business for Frederick. For Luther it involved something far more fundamental: that people were being offered a kind of false insurance policy. Indulgences did not provide forgiveness of sins, and they did not help restore a relationship with God. Indulgences didn't create the remorse and repentance required by God. By making grace a financial transaction, grace became external and cheap, and indulgences, a temptation to people to sin. Whether an indulgence was even necessary at all was questionable, in light of what Christ had done on the cross.

With these questions Luther undermined the foundations of a system that held enormous economic consequences for the church and made an equally enormous claim on people's consciences. He was not at all concerned about the economics, but the burdening of people's consciences concerned him greatly—not least because his own conscience had struggled so intensely with the questions of guilt and forgiveness.

Luther was not the first person who protested about this issue. As far back as 1215, the Fourth Lateran Council had already sounded a warning concerning the misuse and overuse of indulgences. In subsequent years many theologians had complained about them and the false hope that these scraps of paper gave people. Unfortunately, the sale of indulgences generated too much money for the church, and the complaints were not taken seriously. By attacking this practice, Luther was posing a threat to the income of the church, as well as the whole ecclesiastical system. If what Luther said was true, many people would not buy indulgences anymore, and that meant that many masses and a lot of ecclesiastical personnel would become superfluous.

10.31.1517

Did Luther actually post the "Ninety-Five Theses" on the doors of the Castle Church in Wittenberg or not (see fig. 5.3)? Wouldn't it be rather unfortunate if that were not the case? What will we do with all those pictures that show a man decisively and courageously hammering the nails into the door? We've always believed this story, until a Roman

Catholic historian, of all things, claimed that this was probably not true at all.[8] Luther never mentioned this event, and the first person who did, Philipp Melanchthon, did not even live in Wittenberg at the time. Lutheran historians were not going to let Catholic historians rob them of this beautiful story. In the meantime, new research has changed their doubt into certainty (at least near certainty), because the door in question was the public bulletin board on which academics posted their theses whenever they wanted to invite their colleagues to a disputation. The actual posting, however, was done not by the professor but by the beadle of the university. In other words, not Luther but the beadle of Wittenberg should be pictured in all those illustrations. That this actually happened on October 31 is also logical because the following day was All Saints' Day, a holiday and therefore a good choice to host an in-depth theological debate. This disputation was not to be a normal one but one that also invited written reactions from colleagues who could not attend.

How everything actually transpired isn't as important as the fact that Luther wrote and published these theses. He made a public statement, but he did not seek publicity, demonstrated by the fact that the theses were published in Latin. The disputation would also be conducted in Latin, which meant that it was not intended for the common people. Despite this, the people were able to read the disputations fairly quickly because they were soon translated into German and distributed. Luther himself sent the theses to the bishop of Wittenberg, Hieronymus Schultz, as well as to Albrecht of Brandenburg, since Luther was subordinate to his authority as archbishop of Magdeburg. Albrecht referred to him as "a monk from Wittenberg who dares to say quite something" (*vermessenen Mönch zu Wittenberg*). Nevertheless, he did order that they had to be more guarded in the way they recommended these indulgences. Albrecht seemed to underestimate the explosive power hidden in Luther's theses. By the time he realized this power, it was too late to do anything about it. It seems that Luther himself saw this event as a deed of liberation because he signed the letter to Albrecht not as Luder or Luther but as *Eleutherios*, a derivative from the Greek word for "freedom."[9] The word could mean either "liberator" or "liberated"; perhaps Luther meant both.

Figure 5.3 Doors of the Castle Church in Wittenberg. In 1858, the doors were replaced with bronze doors that display the text of the "Ninety-Five Theses." Photo courtesy of Touristoffice Wittenberg.

The Theses

In the "Ninety-Five Theses," Luther did not reject indulgences but argued that they should be restricted to temporary punishments. He warned against the false idea that buying indulgences offered grace. In thesis 62 he discussed the treasure chest of the church, referring not to a wooden box or chest with money in it but to the treasure (box) of the extra good works of the saints. This virtual box, so to speak—which was controlled by the pope alone—contained all the credits earned by the saints, over and above what they themselves needed to be saved. The idea was that if, for example, you needed a hundred points to go to heaven, and you had actually earned one hundred sixty points, you had a credit of sixty points. Those points would accrue in the treasure (chest) of the church, and then the pope could hand them out to those who had earned them—usually someone who had paid for them. It was problematic that no one actually knew how many credits there were in the "box." Everyone realized, however, that this holy treasure chest was closely connected to the less holy treasure chest into which all the money from the indulgences went. That meant that Luther's criticism of the holy treasure of the church was also a criticism of that less holy box.

Though these theses were definitely not meant to precipitate a breach with Rome, they clearly highlighted the search for an understanding of the relationship between faith and grace, penance and forgiveness. This search was driven by the conviction that the actions of the church on these issues were unacceptable.[10] At this time, Luther was also convinced that the pope agreed with him and that he simply did not know what was being done in his name. As late as 1541, Luther stated that at the outset he did not object to indulgences but that he protested against their abuse.[11] He said as well that he had not anticipated the tremendous resonance the theses would have with the public. He had not anticipated that God would direct him in that one direction:

> God put blinders on me the way one would put these on a horse when it has to run a race on a racetrack. . . . And I said in my heart, that if God wants to start such a race with me, he should do it himself and preserve me that I do not meddle with that. . . . Well, he has heard that prayer mightily.[12]

Printing

The theses spread incredibly quickly, in both German and Latin. The rather recently developed printing press made Luther into a well-known personality, even a media celebrity, and his critics knew he couldn't be pushed aside too easily. The reactions to his theses required Luther to write a separate publication to explain what he actually meant in the first place. Luther did not have an agenda, and he did not have a system of theology. He had a thesis: that God gives grace and does not require merit. The consequences of that thesis were so enormous that they ultimately led to a different Europe.

Luther had intended that these theses would initiate Latin discussions among academics in Wittenberg. But quite quickly they were used for discussions in German among people at large. Soon the discussion was not merely about indulgences but also about the authority of the pope, the authority of God's Word, and the meaning of the sacraments. In a society in which the church, religion, and politics were so narrowly interrelated, Luther's vision had an enormous impact. If he was right that God's Word rather than the church was decisive, and not merit but grace provided people with peace, then the powerful position the church had over everyone, from cradle to grave, was unjustified. Society would be completely reordered. Luther had not expected that his theses would create such a tumult. He had to accept this and did so, even when accused of arrogance: "If I am more arrogant, then the piety as such will not become worthless because of my attitude." It was not about him but about the spiritual well-being of the people and about doing what he thought God required of him: "I do not want that whatever I do is done through human ambition or human insight but through God's ambition and insight. Because if what has now happened is from God, who will hold it back? And if it is not from God, who would be able to carry it on?"[13]

Doubts

Not until February 1518 did Luther notice what his theses had brought about. The theses had elicited many reactions, such as that from the Dominican Silvester Massolini (ca. 1456–1523)—who was born in the city Prierio and was therefore known especially as Prierias. He was one of the first to write against Luther, who was stunned: "O God, is it going so far that the pope is going to become involved in this issue?"[14] Luther feared that he would be on his own in Wittenberg, though in reality he had significant support. Nevertheless, Luther said years later that in the first three years there was no one who stood by his side,[15] a man standing alone, as in fact it had always been. Also for that reason, Luther began to question whether events were unfolding properly. On March 5, 1518, he wrote that the "Ninety-Five Theses" were distributed throughout the whole country,

> but it was not my intention, nor my wish to distribute them. Initially, I wanted to debate them with a number of people in my

> surroundings to hear the opinions of others, namely, if they were to be rejected and discarded or if they would be approved and published. Now they are, beyond all my expectations, printed so frequently and distributed so widely that I regret that I wrote them. It's not that I am not in favor of making the people aware of the truth—that is exactly above anything else what I want. But I do not think that this is the right way to instruct the people, because I still have doubts about some issues, and I would have said many things differently or more emphatically, or left them out altogether, if I had expected this.[16]

It was time for Luther to write in German. The common people of his country should be able to read what he meant. Therefore, he began to write a booklet about the value of indulgences, to explain to everyone "what I wanted to express with my theses."[17] That publication appeared under the title *Sermon on Indulgence and Grace* and was soon printed many times over. Within two years it had gone through twenty-two printings and had been translated into Danish, Dutch, and Czech. No copyright restrictions meant that every printer and publisher could reproduce Luther's book at will, which they did, as Luther's work proved to be quite profitable. All his life, he never signed any contracts because he was only concerned that people would read what he had written.

Printing had become advanced, resulting in a media revolution. Publishers would establish numerous printing shops and bookbinderies close to universities, since there they could find both writers and customers for the books; Wittenberg was home to a number of such businesses. Most printers also had a bookshop so that they could sell products directly to customers. Luther became famous, and the equally famous painter Albrecht Dürer let him know that he would be eager to make a copperplate portrait of him, a permanent remembrance of the man who had delivered him from great fear.[18] As much as Luther was pleased to have helped him, he seriously wondered whether he was equal to the task that he had begun. He himself did not even have a clear, definitive picture concerning the meaning of indulgences. People had unrealistic expectations of him.[19] Moreover, he had a strong feeling that he had to fend for himself, to slog it out with those papists.[20]

Tetzel's Countereffort

In March in Frankfurt am Oder there was a disputation of theses that defended Tetzel's indulgences. According to Luther's account, it was a fiercely fought debate: "The indulgence preachers fulminated against me from their pulpits; they cannot come up with enough ominous epithets. The one threatens me with the stake within fifteen days, another within a month; they publish antitheses; they will burst at some time with anger."[21] Those antitheses were clearly formulated against Luther. Apparently, they had hoped that these theses would isolate him, but things went quite differently than they had expected, as Luther wrote to Johann Lang:

> I'm warning you in advance in case rumors reach you about the burning of Tetzel's theses, because it could be that—as usually happens—they add all kinds of things to the story, and therefore, this is how it really happened: the students here, out of aversion to the study of the sophists, and out of a desire to study the Holy Scriptures, and partly out of sympathy for me, went up to a man who had come from Halle, sent by Tetzel, the author of the theses. They scared him and asked him how he dared to bring such things here. They bought a few copies from him, confiscated a whole pile of them from him, and the rest, almost eight hundred copies, they burned, after they announced that anyone who wanted to witness the burning of Tetzel's theses had to come to the market at two o'clock. All of this happened without the knowledge of the elector, the senate, or one of us. Similar to others, I am unhappy about the wrong that was done to this man by our people. Truly, I am innocent, but I am afraid that I will be blamed for all of it. People are making a big deal out of this event everywhere, but the indignation is greatest among the opposition, and not unjustly so. Where this will lead, I do not know, but the danger is greater for me as a result.[22]

Von Staupitz as well had informed Luther that he was worried about how it would go with him now that there was so much criticism. But Luther defended himself, saying that he could do little about it:

> I believe it right away that my name has a bad sound with many people. Many of those good people have accused me for some time

> already that I condemn the rosary, prayers of the rosary, psalms, and more prayers, indeed that I condemn all good works. . . . My doctrine is this: that people should not trust in anything else than in Jesus Christ alone, not in prayers, merit, or one's own works, because we are saved not by "our running" (Rom. 9:16) but through God, who is merciful. But I did not set out to acquire a good name or a bad name, and that will not deter me either. God will see it.[23]

Heretic?

Because Luther's work spread so quickly and had so many readers, it became more apparent to the leaders of the church that something was happening. It wasn't long until the question was raised whether Luther was a heretic and whether the church should intervene quickly. On February 3, 1518, Pope Leo X ordered Egidio da Viterbo (ca. 1469–1532), general of the Augustinians, to take the necessary measures: "I want, namely, that you take care of the problem of Martin Luther, a priest in your order. As you no doubt know, he propagates unheard-of new ideas and teaches our people in Germany new beliefs. . . . If you accomplish this quickly, according to me, this flame can still be extinguished."[24] At the same time, in Rome the first preparations were made for a heresy trial, meaning that Luther would have to go to the Vatican to give account.

Besides Luther, however, the church leaders faced another problem. For centuries the church and the political powers had been in conflict, because both wanted the last say. Rulers and popes squarely confronted each other regularly, not only with words but also with military might. From Germany, century after century, a stream of lengthy complaints had rained down on the roof of St. Peter's, expressing anger that the church had acquired so much worldly power. Magistrates had tired of the church's meddling and the tax money that went to Rome, though the situation was not as bad as they claimed. Elector Frederick the Wise led the charge with these complaints and had absolutely no inclination to allow "his" Luther to go to Rome, so he arranged that the first hearing would take place somewhere in Germany. The pope agreed to his request because he had no desire to offend Frederick—he needed him for a crusade that he was planning against the Islamic empire, known at that time as the "Turks," who were a growing threat.

In the fall of 1518, another diet was to be convened in Augsburg with all the rulers in Germany gathered together. This was deemed a good opportunity to have an ecclesiastical discussion with Luther. He did not have to go to Rome, but he would have to answer to a representative from Rome. Cardinal Tomasso de Vio Cajetan (1469–1534), the papal legate, conducted a debate with the rebellious monk, but that discussion resulted in nothing more than a mutual entrenchment of positions (discussed in more detail below). Luther's new perspective on sin and grace could finally spread, however, when Emperor Maximilian I (1459–1519) died in January 1519. The issue of who would succeed Maximilian was of enormous importance, both for the government and for the church. Each of the several candidates was perceived as a threat for the others and for the power of the church. The discussions about these issues were deemed so important that the problem about Luther was set aside. It could wait. Meanwhile, Luther's thoughts did not lie dormant but spread like a bushfire. More priests, monks, rulers, city administrators, intellectuals, students, and common people started to agree with him. This development came about not only because Luther had a spiritually refreshing way to state his case but also because his criticism had exposed sensitive issues concerning the power of Rome and the German money that ended up going to Rome.

Heidelberg

Before these events took place, Luther received an opportunity to explain his position in the Augustinian monastery in Heidelberg in April 1518. Officially, he had to attend the meeting to discuss their policies, but unofficially, it was seen as a good opportunity to have a thorough discussion with friar Martin about the issues he had raised. On April 9, Luther left Wittenberg on foot, as was customary for monks. While on his way, he heard that Emperor Maximillian had obtained information about him and had stated that they should not ignore the issue of the theses.[25] From the city of Würzburg, where he arrived on April 18, he was able to take a carriage and arrived at Heidelberg three days later. Together with a few other monks he was given a tour of the fortifications and was shown the castle and the relics in the Castle Church, after which they ate and drank to their heart's content. Nothing is known about the policy discussions. However, a great deal is known about the disputation that Luther held there.

It was fascinating for some, offensive for others, and remarkable for all. Luther presented forty theses that outlined his theology of the cross (*theologia crucis*): "True theology and genuine knowledge of God are to be found in the crucified Christ."[26] God reveals his wisdom in the foolishness of the cross; in this fashion he provides life for the dead, namely, through the death of Christ. With this theology of the cross, Luther also made a connection to speaking about the hidden God (*Deus absconditus*), who in his will, his way, and his wisdom is hidden to us; he hides himself as a child in the manger and as the one condemned on the cross. Luther placed the theology of the cross over against what he termed the theology of glory (*theologia gloriae*). According to him, this latter theology considered mankind able to achieve salvation in Christ himself. The theology that Luther presented in Heidelberg was the theology of a new, young generation, a generation in which Luther had put his hope.[27]

One of the younger people there was Martin Bucer (1491–1551), a Dominican monk from Strasbourg (see fig. 5.4). He was very impressed and was won over to Luther's way of thinking. Bucer would play an important role in the Reformation, especially by trying to establish bridges between the different parties. Through his influence on John Calvin, he would have a great impact on the theology and church life of Calvinists. That impact began in Heidelberg, where he first heard and saw Luther.

At this time Luther was quite conscious of the fact that his vision of grace countered the positions of the scholastic theologians:

> But also from the circle of theological doctors, I encounter hatred, because I give preference to the church fathers and the Bible, and they cannot handle that. I read the scholastics with an open mind and not with closed eyes, as they are used to. That is also commanded by the apostle: but test everything; hold on to what is good (1 Thess. 5:21). I do not reject everything of theirs, but I do not accept everything either. Those talkers make something big

Figure 5.4 *Portrait of Martin Bucer* (1491–1551). Engraving by Jean-Jacques Boissard, 1599. Herzog August Library, Wolfenbüttel.

> from something small, from a spark they make a fire, and from a mosquito, an elephant. With God's help I will ignore those empty words.[28]

Luther had appreciation for almost everyone with whom he had discussions in Heidelberg:

> Furthermore, the doctors of the Heidelberg faculty gave me complete freedom in my disputation and discussed it with me in a controlled fashion. As far as that is concerned, I have come to appreciate them a lot. Even though they found my theology a bit strange, they contested it sharply and purely, with the exception of one, who was the fifth one to receive a turn and belonged to the group of junior doctors. He had everyone laughing when he said, "If the farmers were to hear this, they would stone you for sure."[29]

This "number five" would eventually discover that he had incorrectly estimated the "Luther effect," because the farmers, especially, eagerly accepted Luther's message. However, they did so in such a fashion that they were the ones who were "stoned."

From Heidelberg Luther went straight home, but several things transpired during that journey:

> Finally, Saturday after Ascension Day, I arrived again in Wittenberg. I returned in a wagon, even though I had left on foot. I was simply compelled by the majority, and so I rode initially with the Nurembergers, almost to Würzburg; afterward, I traveled with the Erfurters, and after Erfurt with those from Eisleben. Those people had me brought to Wittenberg at their cost using their own horses. During the whole journey I felt great, eating and drinking, enjoying it so that some people said that I had become fatter. Von Staupitz, Lang, who is now the district vicar, and I were heartily received by Landgrave Wolfgang and Magister Jacob Simler, as well as by Steward Hazius. The discussions among us provided us with much joy. We ate and drank and were shown the treasures of the church, the armory, and, to finish it off, all the art of this illustrious court.[30]

In Erfurt Luther visited one of his former professors, Jodocus Trutfetter, who was not happy with Luther's thinking: "The Erfurters really hate my theology, and especially Trutfetter, who drove all my opinions into the ground in a letter in which he denied all my knowledge of dialectics, let alone of theology!" Luther would have liked to have had a disputation with the professors in Erfurt but was given no such opportunity. He did visit Trutfetter for a personal discussion, but that yielded nothing: "My effort was in vain! They hold fast to their own way of thinking in all kinds of distinctions, even though they admit that they do not have any other authority than 'natural understanding.' But their understanding is the same as ours, namely a dark chaos."[31]

Summer 1518

On October 31, 1517, Luther still put a heavy emphasis on the message that a person had to humble himself before God and acknowledge that he is a sinner. As a result of the pressure that arose from the discussions around the theses, and because of the intense involvement in activities in preparing for his commentary lectures—that is, his time spent in

Bible study—Luther arrived at the insight that we cannot justify ourselves before God but that it is God who justifies. Only then did the emphasis change to saying that we cannot do anything but that God does everything. The breakthrough of that particular insight, and the last step to come to the heart of the reformed message, happened sometime during the summer of 1518. Then arose his understanding of the stressful balance between agreeing with God about my condemnation and praising God that he acquits me of guilt.

Luther did not make this discovery in one moment such as some people portray, as if in one day Luther made the transition from one theology to another. Earlier he had already indicated that he was "not one of those people who from nothing became perfect and have insight in the Scriptures."[32] For him it was not abrupt but was rather a gradual process. It probably had something to do with the realization, when it dawned on him, that his theology would have major consequences—consequences as substantial as a new church and a changed society. Priests would no longer be approaching God with Christ's sacrifice on behalf of the congregation. But on God's behalf, they had to become preachers who had to bring the message that Christ's sacrifice made them free. The system of merit on which all ecclesiastical and societal life rested would gradually be replaced by a lifestyle of grace.

On Palm Sunday, March 28, 1518, Luther preached a sermon on what he called "double justification." He maintained that there are two kinds of righteousness, an active one and a passive one. The first one requires a person to put forth effort to become righteous before God, while in the second one, God makes a person righteous by means of faith and grace. For Luther this difference was clear: either I do it, or he does it. Either I achieve righteousness myself, or I am made righteous. If I have to do it, that will be my destruction. If he does it, it becomes my salvation. And fortunately, God does it. In this way, through all the discussions, through all his study of the Bible and the church fathers, through almost endless deliberation, Luther came to the conclusion that God was different from the God whom he had been taught since childhood. He had searched for God for such a long time, and he thought he had found him. That God is wrathful is a reality, but that is not God's character: "The wrath of God is in reality a strange work of God that he is forced to exercise by the evil of people, perforce but contrary to his nature."[33] Luther had always been afraid of God's strange work, but now he had discovered God's true nature.

After his return from Heidelberg, Luther also preached about excommunication and especially about the cavalier manner in which the bishop had used this action to manipulate people. If the bishop needed money and people did not want to give it, he would quickly threaten with excommunication, though that action was really intended for spiritual well-being. This sermon only further annoyed the ecclesiastical leaders. What did this man want, and what could they do to oppose him? On July 25, when Luther visited the Augustinian monastery in Dresden, Jerome Emser, chaplain at the court of Duke George, invited him for a hospitable dinner. His ulterior purpose was to hear Luther out and find out what he thought about excommunication and indulgences. A Dominican monk had been posted at the door so he could overhear the discussion and make a report.

Cajetan

Rome decided to take action. On August 7, 1518, Luther received the order to come to the holy city to give an account to the authorities. This writ really scared Luther,[34] so much that years later he would still remember the date, as he mentioned on August 7, 1540: "Today it is twenty-two years ago that I was summoned to Rome, and seventeen days earlier that I was condemned."[35] He knew that he was suspected of heresy and that a process had been initiated against him. He had been ordered to recant within sixty days; otherwise, they threatened him with excommunication. He had recently preached and written about this issue, and it already appeared that he would become a victim. For someone who was only looking for the truth in relation to a few select issues, and who for the rest remained a faithful child of the church, this was a great shock.

Luther did not want to go to Rome. That was not only on account of his first journey, which had been more than revealing for him, but also because he was afraid that he would not live to tell about it. Via Spalatin he informed the elector that this issue concerned the honor of the city and the University of Wittenberg. He asked the elector to try to keep him in Germany. At that time the elector also received a letter from Rome telling him not to worry about letting Luther go, because if it turned out that Luther was innocent, he would be able to return home in safety. The elector, however, did not have such a high opinion of Rome. Recently, together with his German colleagues he had protested against a new Turkish tax, an extra tax levied by Rome to finance the war against the Turks. Frederick was quite fed up with sending more money to Rome only to see it disappear. He also knew how much money lined the pockets of many clerics.

Rome decided not to push its request because the pope preferred to see Elector Frederick become the new emperor instead of Charles, the king of Spain. The Habsburger Charles had large territories in Italy and was seen as a threat to the Papal States should he become emperor. The pope also had valid concerns over Francis I, king of France. At the end of the day, Rome caved in and gave permission to have Luther heard in Germany. This hearing would be conducted by the papal legate Cajetan, an erudite theologian who had closely studied what Luther had said and written. He thoroughly understood not simply that this dispute was about a new theology but also that this theology could lead to a new church. According to Luther, Cajetan was a reasonable man. Yes, he supported the notion that the pope had supreme authority, but Luther also knew that as a theologian he wanted to discuss the issues from a biblical perspective.

Augsburg

At the end of September, Luther again set out on foot, this time for Augsburg. The elector provided him with twenty guilders for the journey. Luther was afraid to die a heretic's death: "Along the way I thought: Now I will die! And in my mind I already saw the stake prepared before me and said: O, what a shame that would be for my parents."[36] On September 29, he reached Weimar and preached there against hypocrisy and works righteousness. Overnight he had stayed with the Franciscans, who warned him not to continue the journey, to keep him from being burned at the stake.[37] Also in Nuremberg, where he arrived on October 4, he received this warning, but Luther continued on. "Even if Martin dies, as long as Christ lives," he wrote to his friends in Wittenberg.[38] Together with his friend Wenzeslaus Linck (1483–1547), who had given him a new habit,[39] he traveled the last distance in a carriage because he had stomach problems and felt dead tired.

After he stayed at the St. Anna Carmelite monastery, he revived somewhat and was strong enough to be engaged in a discussion with Cajetan. These discussions took place from Tuesday, October 12, to Thursday, October 14, in the Fuggerhaus, where Cajetan lodged. Soon it became quite apparent that they had not only a theological problem but also a personal one. Luther was offended by the authoritarian behavior of the cardinal. Cajetan thought that Luther's eyes looked so strange that he must be deranged.[40] As far as Cajetan was concerned, the discussions did not have to last very long.

At the outset Cajetan had three demands, and if Luther agreed to those, then they would be finished quite quickly. Luther only had to return to the bosom of the church, recant his errors, and promise that never again would he utter such bizarre things that caused confusion in the church. Luther immediately clarified that he did not come all the way to Augsburg to recant, because he could have done that just as well from home. He had come to debate a number of essential issues. After he had recovered from his disappointment with Cajetan's attitude, Luther tried to initiate a discussion by asking the cardinal if he would show him where he erred. Cajetan was willing to tell him that, but he did not want to debate with Luther. After some talking back and forth—and some shouting—Luther received permission to set out his vision on paper. That was Wednesday. On Thursday he received an arrogant response, and then the discussion was ended at the end of the morning. Cajetan argued exclusively on the basis of the authority of the church and tradition. Luther argued exclusively from Scripture. There was no middle ground.

On Sunday, October 17, Luther had a letter delivered to Cajetan in which he stated that perhaps he had been too heated. He suggested that they mutually agree not to discuss indulgences. On Monday Luther sent another letter, but when by Wednesday, October 20, he had still received no response from Cajetan, Luther left the city at night. Though the city gates had already been closed, one of Luther's supporters let him out of the city through a small door. After three days of discussion with Cajetan, Luther had had enough. Clearly, Cajetan did not want a substantive discussion but only wanted Luther to recant. When he heard that there was also a letter from Pope Leo X stating that Luther had to be imprisoned if he did not recant, he quickly made up his mind: "They're becoming afraid of me in Rome. They aren't so sure about their business, and they're looking attentively for subterfuges."[41] On a horse that had been loaned to him by a friend, he galloped off in the direction of Wittenberg. Making several stops along the way, he arrived back in Wittenberg on October 31, tired but safe. A year after he had posted the "Ninety-Five Theses," Luther was a well-known German and was on the road to becoming branded a heretic.

In the meantime, von Staupitz had informed Luther that he had relieved him of his vow of obedience. That gave Luther more latitude, but it also meant that von Staupitz would no longer be compelled to deal with Luther's alleged heresy. Even before Luther had returned to Wittenberg, a letter to the elector had arrived from Cajetan with the request for Luther's extradition. Luther had prompted this by his pronouncements concerning the authority of the pope. Frederick requested an explanation from Luther. The monk wrote him a frank and detailed letter,[42] in which he provided an account of the events in Augsburg, stating that he had not received an opportunity to discuss the issue for which he had gone in the first place. The elector wouldn't accede to the request to send him to Rome because Luther would not survive that, and Frederick would not be party to the shedding of innocent blood. Luther stated that he was willing to go into exile to relieve the elector of a problem and to avoid blemishing his good name. He knew that Frederick could end up in the midst of huge ecclesiastical and political problems if he protected a suspect and, possibly soon, someone who had been excommunicated. At the conclusion of the letter, Luther said goodbye to the elector and thanked him for everything he had done for him.

In subsequent weeks, Luther lived in anxiety over when the letter of excommunication would arrive. Excommunication meant a prohibition to write and speak publicly and meant he would be cast out from the church and, essentially, from society as well. Additionally, someone who was excommunicated from the church had no right to salvation.

Like Abraham, who did not know where he was going, Luther was prepared to leave. Of one thing he was firmly convinced: "God is everywhere."[43] On December 1, he had a kind of farewell gathering, but while they were still together, a message arrived from the elector that Luther should stay. For Luther all these events were confusing, as he wrote in a letter to Spalatin:

> If I had not received your letter yesterday, I would have left yesterday. Even now I am prepared to do both, stay or leave. My friends are very concerned about me, actually more than I am myself. Some of them have strongly urged me to have the elector imprison me! He would then have to lodge me somewhere, and then he should write to the papal legate that he is holding me captive but that he is prepared to have me give account in a safe place. Whether that is good advice, you can judge better than I. As far as I am concerned, I am safe in God's hand and in the hands of my friends. One thing is sure: everyone believes that the elector together with the whole university stands behind me. I recently heard this from someone who is absolutely reliable.[44]

Luther was happy with the message from the elector, but he did question whether the elector could continue to support him. Additionally, he feared that he would not be able to move around and express himself in Wittenberg freely: "If I stay here, I am afraid that I will lose a great deal of my freedom to speak and write. If I leave, I will be able to say everything, and give my life to Christ."[45]

Frederick informed Cajetan on December 7 that Luther would stay. Luther was indispensible to the university, but the moment someone provided proof that Luther had erred, Frederick would immediately put him in a coach and send him to Rome. Rome, however, did not react. That was the moment to excommunicate Luther, but the church remained silent because they needed Frederick. At this time, politics were more important than theology; leverage was more vital than the church.

Karl von Miltitz

Cajetan managed to elicit a papal proclamation concerning indulgences. He understood that Luther had some justification in claiming that the church had not clearly formulated its dogma concerning indulgences. Therefore, the issue arose for good reason, and there had been legitimate room for debate. But now that the church had established her dogma, the pope and Cajetan thought that it was time for Luther to desist. Luther was quite willing to stop if that would serve the cause, but recanting his views about indulgences and everything related to them would only happen if they could show him from the Bible that he was mistaken.

The pope attempted to address the issue in a different fashion. He decided to award Frederick the Wise a Golden Rose of Virtue (*Tugendrose*). This award had the shape of a perfumed golden rose and was presented to a ruler as a reward for his efforts on behalf of the church. This rose, besides giving a sweet-smelling aroma, was made of gold, and it came with extra indulgences, plus rights of confession that could be used by the ruler. This was certainly an appropriate gift that dovetailed well with Frederick's love for relics, indulgences, and confessional practices. The papal nuncio Karl von Miltitz (1490–1529) was commissioned by the pope to present the Golden Rose together with a letter in which he highly praised Frederick for everything he had done for the church. The letter also included the message that someone so devoted and faithful to Rome should also make sure that the church would be delivered from heretics like Luther. Luther also heard that von Miltitz was on his way to visit the elector and had on his person "three papal letters to arrest me and hand me over to the pope." He had to be prepared for every eventuality because they could put him to death, imprison him, or banish him to France. "To prevent an unprepared death or oppression by means of punishments," he wrote to Spalatin, "I have made arrangements and now await whatever God decides about me." He had informed his congregation that "they should not let the papal punishments that rage against me scare them, but they should leave this matter and other things to God."[46]

Von Miltitz was underway for three weeks, but the closer he came to Wittenberg, the more he noticed that the issues were far more complex than the people in Rome had thought. He saw that Tetzel had indeed messed up the situation with his indulgence show and that Luther was tremendously popular among the people. He realized that he would have to amend the papal tactics if Rome wanted to pacify Luther and keep Frederick as a friend at the same time. Luther was definitely prepared to accept a solution and composed a letter in which he declared that he was not against indulgences per se but against the improper use of indulgence practices. He also wrote that he had been too heated in his language against the pope and would dearly like to submit to him. He added that he had no objections against purgatory and the veneration of saints, provided they were invoked for spiritual reasons. But again, he clarified that he would not give a thought to recanting.

Subsequently, some discussions were held between Luther, von Miltitz, and Spalatin. Von Miltitz complained that Luther "had won over the whole world" and had "estranged them from the pope." Luther related his encounter with von Miltitz:

> In every inn he [von Miltitz] discovered that out of five people there were hardly two or three who favored Rome. From court circles I heard later that he had come here, equipped with seventy apostolic letters about this issue, and through these he was authorized to take me prisoner to that cut-throated Jerusalem, that purple Babylon. When that intention was deemed impossible to implement, he tried to make me feel bad: I had to give back to the Roman church what I had taken away; I had to recant. I then asked him to explain to me what exactly I would have to recant, and finally we agreed to entrust the issue to a few bishops. For that purpose, I suggested the bishops of Trier, Salzburg, and Friesling. After I had agreed to that, we had a pleasant meal, and finally he kissed me goodbye. I acted as if I did not see through his Italian show. In Leipzig he had Tetzel summoned and scolded him and accused him of appropriating a salary of ninety golden guilders every month in addition to a wagon, three riders, and compensation for all costs. Tetzel has disappeared, no one knows where, except perhaps the brothers of his order. . . . In Leipzig they have finally agreed to a disputation with Eck. They accused me that I wrongfully wrote that they refused this disputation, and now they demand that I set the record straight. But I know for sure from a remark made by Duke George that they refused. I told them twice that the dean had turned down my request at an earlier stage, and he did that. Those are the strata-

> gems they use to prevent this disputation, but Duke George is really pursuing this.[47]

The discussions produced no results. The pope's proclamation concerning indulgences, made on the advice of Cajetan, was of no consequence for Luther because the document spoke mostly about the authority of the church but hardly at all about the Bible. He also differed in his view of good works from that of the pope. The righteous do good works, but good works do not justify a person. The two sides made no progress, and the matter remained jammed when Cajetan started meddling in it again in May 1519. The elector was fed up with it, because despite the past efforts, he still did not have his Golden Rose. On June 8, he wrote to Cajetan to ask him what was holding up this rose. He was an obedient son of the church, and he would remain that way. Therefore, there was no reason why they shouldn't give him this rose. Frederick finally received his rose in October but not personally. As Luther reported on October 3, "The Golden Rose that he had wanted to bring to Wittenberg with much pomp von Miltitz finally dropped off in Altenburg, where the elector received it in absentia."[48]

A New Emperor

The election of Charles V as the new emperor was essential to the position of Luther and the development of the Reformation. He became the successor to his grandfather, Maximillian I, who died on January 12, 1519, right around the time that von Miltitz was in Wittenberg urging Luther to return to the fold and promoting friendly relations between the elector and Rome.

Nine electors, who had to judge whether certain individuals were suitable to be emperor, elected emperors. One became emperor only after first being chosen as king of the Holy Roman Empire. The descriptor *Roman* had nothing to do with the church but referred to the old Roman Empire. Once that title had been acquired, one was entitled to seek the emperorship. Electors were influential heads over parts of the empire and certainly wanted to retain power and influence. The two most important candidates were Charles of Luxembourg, born in Ghent, but better known as Charles V, and King Francis I of France.

The pope preferred Frederick the Wise because he was seen as less hostile to Rome's power. Frederick, however, had no desire to become emperor. Consequently, two candidates remained. Also, in those days it was customary to buy votes, and therefore, Charles and Francis both threw bags of money at this campaign to win the support of the electors. Because Charles had offered the most money, he was chosen as king of the Holy Roman Empire, on June 28, 1519. Charles was only nineteen years old, but he had already become king of the Habsburg Empire and king of Spain. His father, Philip, the son of the Habsburger Maximillian, was married to Joanna of Castile, queen of Spain and the Netherlands, among other territories, including the colonies in America and Asia. Philip died in 1506; Joanna was not well either, with the consequence that she has gone down in history as Joanna the Mad. Charles became the ruler over an enormous empire, and when he became Holy Roman emperor, he became emperor with a long list of titles:

> *Charles, by the grace of God, Holy Roman Emperor, Forever Augustus, King of Germany, King of Italy, King of all Spains, Castile, Aragon, León, Navarra, Granada, Toledo, Valencia, Galacia, Mallorca, Sevilla, Cordoba, Murcia, Jaén, Argarves, Algeciras, Gibraltar, the Canary Islands, King of the Two Sicilies, of Sardinia, Corsica, King of Jerusalem, King of the Western and Eastern Indies, Lord of the Islands and Main Ocean Sea, Archduke of Austria, Duke of Burgundy, Brabant, Lorraine, Styria, Carinthia, Carniola, Limburg, Luxembourg, Gelderland, Neopatria, Württemberg, Landgrave of Alsace, Prince of Swabia, Asturia, and Catalonia, Count of Flanders, Habsburg, Tyrol, Gorizia, Barcelona, Artois, Burgundy, Palatine, Hainaut, Holland, Seeland, Ferrette, Kyburg, Namur, Roussillon, Cerdagne, Zutphen, Margrave of the Holy Roman Empire, Burgau, Oristano, and Gociano, Lord of Frisia, the Wendish March, Pordenone, Biscay, Molin, Salins, Tripoli, and Mechelen.*

With such a title it was no wonder that the two other great heads of state, Francis I and the pope, felt threatened. The electors felt as well that Charles had an awful lot of power, but at the same time, they considered how much money they had received from him. In short, when such a "jammer" as Luther arose, he was seen as a welcome instrument to strengthen the electors' own positions, even though they did not all agree with him. Their reasoning was quite logical: if the emperor troubles me and Luther troubles the emperor, Luther may be useful to me. The emperor could reason, if Luther is useful to people who are a bother to me, I shouldn't make things too difficult for Luther. At bottom, the matter of the Reformation had the advantage that all of them were a bother to each other.

Melanchthon

In the meantime, the work at the monastery and the university proceeded as usual. Luther was not always preoccupied every day with the aftereffects of the theses. Luther's elector, Frederick, became sick after his return from the election of the emperor. Having heard this, Luther wrote for him a kind of comforting message for the sick, which he published in February 1520 under the title *The Fourteen Consolations: For Such as Labor and Are Heavily Laden*.[49] The number fourteen was not randomly chosen but referred to the fourteen saints whom the church told people to invoke to help in times of distress. Each saint was assumed to have his own specialty. Luther maintained the number fourteen and divided those into seven distressful situations such as sin, fear, danger, and temptation. Over against these he described seven deliverances. But only one—namely, Christ—can provide deliverance when we are besieged by death and hell. In the place of the fourteen saints he substituted one person: Christ.

As far as the university was concerned, the objectives of both Luther and the elector fit together nicely. Frederick wanted his university to succeed, providing high-quality, comprehensive education, and Luther realized that renewal of the church and preaching should begin with the renewal of theology and scholarship. A works-based faith had generated much anxiety and dread of God and was closely connected to the way the instructional program had been composed. A healthy church would begin with a healthy university.

In March, a new plan lay on the table for the philosophy faculty, that is, the first part of the university study program, which included the important subjects of grammar, logic, and rhetoric. Frederick had allocated money for a solid scholarly institution and had made sure that chairs for Hebrew and Greek would be possible. Philipp Melanchthon (1497–1560) was appointed to the Greek chair and arrived on August 25, 1518, to begin his career (see fig. 5.5). He was only twenty-one years old but was already renowned as a scholar who had much to offer. Luther was impressed by his inaugural presentation on August 28, 1520:

> Before an audience of approximately five hundred listeners, Philipp held a brilliant first theological lecture on the letter to the Romans. Everyone had really been looking forward to this event, which turned out to be a great success. May God perfect this vessel that he has begun. I am convinced that shortly the whole Christian world will drink the purest theology from this spring. I believe that in the past thousand years the Scriptures have never been discussed so clearly and that his gifts approach those of the apostolic period.[50]

Melanchthon's inaugural presentation made a great impression. In beautifully articulated language, he made a plea for a thorough study of Greek and for the modernization of university studies. Luther sat in on his lectures, as Melanchthon did with Luther's lectures on theology. Luther had great esteem for him, even higher than for himself. "That little Greek chap is better in theology than I," he had to acknowledge.[51] He recognized as well the essential importance of good language skills and sound scholarly methodology. He had no problem being corrected by Melanchthon: "My Philipp Melanchthon, agewise he is still young, but in terms of wisdom and insight he is old, serves me as my Greek instructor, and does not allow me to think that way."[52] Melanchthon represented many Martins. He was a strong enemy of the Devil and of scholasticism. He was acquainted with their nonsense, but at the same time, he knew the Rock, Christ.[53] Melanchthon would become Luther's most important colleague and would try to bring order to Luther's theology.

In Wittenberg they lived only a few houses down from each other, but their characters were miles apart. Luther's relationship with Melanchthon was intense and had a very unique character, so much so that it is questionable whether one can speak of friendship. Melanchthon was regularly overworked and suffered from sleeplessness on account

Figure 5.5 *Portrait of Philipp Melanchthon* (1497–1560). Painting by Lucas Cranach the Elder, 1537. Staatliche Kunsthalle Karlsruhe, Karlsruhe.

of his worries about the church. He was also sometimes at his wit's end because of the recklessness of Luther's behavior, and he suffered under this as well, as he confessed after Luther's death. The "little Greek chap" was calm, mild, and constantly looking for ways to make peace. Luther was completely different. Melanchthon's credo was "We were born for speech," while Luther was especially born to debate, and that caused friction.[54] Luther himself saw that contrast in their behavior:

> I was born to wage war against sects and devils, and that is why my books are so stormy and combative. I have to root out stumps and branches, cut out thorns and hedges, fill up the holes, and therefore, I am the great woodcutter who has to forge a path, and therefore, I have to destroy so much. But Master Philipp proceeds calmly and neatly, he builds and plants, sows and waters, and does so with pleasure, totally employing the gifts that God has given him for this.[55]

Melanchthon had his share of trials. For one, it really troubled him that he did not have any friends in Wittenberg. Also, one of his sons died in August 1529. Luther tried to comfort him, but it was a difficult task.[56] He also comforted Melanchthon when he struggled with his faith. For example, in 1521, when Luther was in the Wartburg, he wrote, "Sin strongly, but ever more strongly you should believe and rejoice in Christ, who has overcome sin, death, and the world." With this I don't mean to suggest that you should sin, Luther wrote, but that you realize that as a human being, you are sinful. If you do not have a sense of sin, then you will not have a sense of grace, and then you do not need Christ. "If you do not feel your sins," he explained, "then surely you are completely dead in sin, and sin rules fiercely over you."[57] All in all, Luther and Melanchthon formed a unique pair.

In the spring of 1521, the Hebrew chair was finally filled, by Matthias Goldhahn (Latinized to Aurogallus), a renowned scholar. This appointment came at a crucial time, as the university greatly needed someone to teach the students how to read the Old Testament.

Support and Opposition

Luther received support from several sides, including a group of people known as humanists. They were happy with Luther's criticism of the wrongs in the church and with his appeal to return to the original sources. The Latin publication of his collected works in October 1518 at Basel became important for the dissemination of his thinking. The printer was Johann Froben, who had also published works by Erasmus (see fig. 5.6). The printing was soon sold out and found its way throughout Europe. The printer mentioned to Luther that six hundred copies had even been delivered to Spain and France. Some copies went to England, Italy, the Netherlands, and Switzerland, where Huldrych Zwingli (1484–1531) was one of the buyers. Erasmus was less enthusiastic with this publication. Soon he was associated with Luther's works, and some suspected that he had actually helped publish these works. Erasmus quickly defended himself and attempted, as he always did, to avoid making any choices, keeping all his options open. Repeatedly he said that he had not read Luther's works but that he had great respect for the person. Instead, he appealed to Luther to calm down

Figure 5.6 *Portrait of Erasmus* (ca. 1466–1536). Painting by Hans Holbein the Younger, 1523. National Gallery, London.

and advised his opponents not to judge Luther without reading his works. At this time he didn't feel compelled to distance himself from Luther, but both the humanist and the reformer understood that they were not on the same wavelength on every matter.

The reactions from the ecclesiastical side, such as from Tetzel, were very unfavorable, but real discussion did not begin until Johannes Eck (1486–1543) from Ingolstadt became involved in the conflict (see fig. 5.7). This exceptionally erudite theologian initially agreed with Luther's reconsideration of the issues around faith and church. But this agreement was short lived. Once he became acquainted with Luther's "Ninety-Five Theses," he seriously wanted a debate with Luther, and he drafted a document that countered Luther and labeled him rebellious, rude, and heretical. Luther reacted, and with this reaction the contrasts became even more transparent. By this time, it was not so much about indulgences anymore but about the pope, tradition, and even the Scriptures themselves.

Figure 5.7 Johannes Eck (1486–1543). Artist unknown. Liebfrauenmünster, Ingolstadt.

Eck, who had always maintained good relations with the people in Wittenberg, wanted to limit the discussion, similar to Luther, to prevent it from becoming a public debate. Such a debate could confuse people in the church. Carlstadt was of a different opinion. He involved himself publicly in the discussion between Eck and Luther, and as a result, there was also a debate between Eck and Carlstadt. They agreed that they would meet in Leipzig to exchange their views in an academic but, nevertheless, public disputation. The theological faculty were not in favor, but Duke George of Saxony, who as landlord was overlord of the university, insisted that it should happen. He hoped that this debate would create clarity in the theological discussion that had become so heated. The theme was very important, and moreover, he felt that such a discussion would serve the public image of the university well: our university makes it happen. The theologians were thus compelled to show their expertise. Additionally, by means of this debate, the truth would finally come to light.

In the prelude to the disputation, it appeared clear that Eck was less concerned about Carlstadt than he was about Luther, and therefore,

Luther proposed to Carlstadt that he would also contribute to the debate. Luther would have to engage Eck in a discussion, and he realized that that would not be easy, because Eck was not only recognized as a brilliant theologian but was also known as an expert in canon law.

In the meantime, the main theme had become *authority*, specifically, the primacy of the pope. This meant that there was an even more pressing question: "If it grieved Rome already when the indulgences began to die out, what shall it do when all her decretals perish?"[58] The church of Rome proclaimed that she was the head of all other churches, but that idea was only four hundred years old. During the eleven hundred years before that, a different picture came to light, according to Luther. Luther's colleagues were not very happy with this remark. Luther countered by saying that this was just the beginning. Friends may have thought that he had become crazy, and like the disciples in Gethsemane, they may desert him, "but if this matter is from God, it will continue on, with or without Luther." Rome was destroying the church, and if they did not do something against that, they might as well stop pursuing theology. The fact that the pope had authority was not even the problem, but the fact that the papacy twisted the whole Bible around to defend it was a problem.[59]

In anticipation of the debate, Luther prepared himself thoroughly in the decisions of canon law and was shocked at what he found. On March 13, he confided in Spalatin, "Christ, that is to say, the truth about him, is so twisted and crucified in the decretals that I don't know anymore whether the pope himself is the Antichrist or his apostle."[60] As such, Luther had nothing against the pope, as long as he did not act as if his position were derived directly from the Bible and as long as he did not misuse his power. Rome was not really the mother of all churches, and that the bishop of Rome was head over all the other bishops rested only on human agreements. The manner in which Luther now used the Bible over against the tradition was new and revolutionary in its consequences. One consequence was that he would declare the pope a heretic, someone who would misuse the Bible and still proclaim heresies. Luther had not yet reached that point, but it wouldn't be long before he went that far. The disputation with Eck would serve to create more clarity for both sides.

Disputation

The disputation attracted lots of interest from all parts of the empire. It was quite clear that something important was going to happen. On June 24, the delegation from Wittenberg arrived in Leipzig, with Carlstadt in the first carriage. He had taken along a substantial number of books to use as proof. In the second carriage were Luther, Melanchthon, and the rector of the university, Duke Barnim von Pommeren. Two hundred armed students from Wittenberg surrounded their carriages, thus making it very clear that, if necessary, they were prepared to draw weapons to defend their professors. This show of force was not completely superfluous because the people in Leipzig plainly supported Eck. "The people of Leipzig do not greet us or visit us but treat us like their worst enemies," Luther recorded.[61]

After several discussions about procedures, the disputation began on June 27 with a church service in the Thomas Kirche; it would last three weeks. After the service, they formed a procession and walked to the castle, where the disputation was to take place. Because such a large crowd had gathered, the university lacked a space large enough to accommodate everyone. Two lecterns were placed over against each other. The professor of Greek, Petrus Mosellanus, delivered an opening oration in which he appealed to the debaters to be honest and frank and to seek the truth together without becoming strident. That was the style of God's children. When the oration was finished, they all kneeled and together sang the prayer "Come, Holy Spirit." Later on, Mosellanus provided a description of the three debaters: Eck, Carlstadt, and Luther. Concerning Luther he said,

> Martin is of medium height, and gaunt as a result of worrying and studying so that you can almost see his bones. He's at a manly and young age, with a clear and powerful voice, but is full of scholarship and knowledge of the Bible so that he can quote from memory. He knows so much about Greek and Hebrew that he is able to properly evaluate the explanations of others. He has no weaknesses because he has a large vocabulary and knows a lot. Concerning his life and manners, he is courtly and friendly and in no respect is he surly or unpleasant but rather flexible. In company he is funny, jolly, lively, and always in a good mood.

> He always appears spry and radiant, even when his opponents threaten him, so much so that it would be unimaginable that he could persevere in these important matters without God's help. But he has a weakness that everyone admonishes him about, and that is that he is sometimes too rude and too sharp, as does not befit someone who embraces a new theology and who is a theologian.[62]

On request of Duke Barnim, Luther preached on Sunday, June 29, the so-called St. Peter and Paul Day. Originally, it was the intention to have this take place in the Castle Church, but because there were so many people, they had to resort to the great hall of the Pleissenburg in Leipzig, the same hall where the disputation was to take place. In accordance with the preaching roster for that Sunday, Luther was supposed to preach on the text Matthew 16:13–19. Clearly, that was no coincidence. He preached on the question of how a person could be justified before God, and he connected this to the role of the church and specifically to the role of the pope. According to Luther, the keys of the kingdom of heaven, to which the text refers, were to be used not as a means of excommunication but as a means of proclaiming grace: "Indeed, it is correct that he gives the keys to St. Peter, yet not to him personally but as a representative of the church. And therefore, these keys are given to me and to you as comfort for our consciences."[63] Luther's appeal for a council dovetailed with a discussion that had been ongoing for a century. That discussion centered around the question whether a council or the pope had the highest authority in the church. Did the pope have the last and the highest word, or was a council consisting of cardinals and bishops a higher authority?

The Account of the Disputation

On July 4, 1519, the disputation began in the great hall of the castle. During the first week, Eck and Carlstadt debated. In the second week, it was Eck against Luther, and finally, Eck had two more days against Carlstadt. The theses that Eck had drafted concerned grace and free will, penance, and the absolute primacy of the pope. Those became the essential points of discussion. Luther understood that the deliberations in Leipzig could become crucial. Eck had organized the debate in a shrewd fashion so that his opponents were not given room to maneuver. From the beginning the meetings did not bode well because the participants disagreed over who should receive the account of the proceedings to determine who had won the disputation. Eck had also decided that he would deliver the closing address. "We are in a fix," Luther related to Spalatin, "because in either situation we will end up being discredited, be it that we refuse to debate, or that we are forced to submit to the referees who are not honest."[64] Because an accurate record was being made by a team of four secretaries, the discussion progressed slowly and with difficulty. (The advantage to us today is that we know exactly how the talks transpired.)

Both sides, as was the custom, first made a solemn pledge that they did not want to deviate from the Catholic faith and were willing to let the pope correct them. Eck and Carlstadt debated free will, but the most important theme in the disputation was between Eck and Luther, namely, the question about the primacy of the pope. The fact that this theme could be discussed publicly or even discussed at all was unique. Eck began with a number of Bible texts that he claimed undergirded the dogma of papal primacy. Those appeared to be convincing texts, but Luther tried to prove from church history that the pope was never the head of Christendom. When Eck concluded that Luther asserted that the pope's authority originated not with God but rather with man, it put Luther into an even more suspect position. The critical moment in the deliberations came when Eck accused Luther of embracing the views of John Hus (ca. 1369–1415). Eck's tactic was to unmask Luther as a heretic and thus have him condemned. Eck's strategy succeeded when Luther acknowledged that Hus had good things to say, such as his assertion that it was not necessary for one's salvation to believe in the primacy of the pope. Luther then questioned the correctness of the decisions of the Council of Constance. That view in itself placed Luther formally outside the fellowship of the church. This matter became completely evident when Luther was forced to admit that according to him, councils can also err. With this admission, he had embraced the view of Hus, the man who was burned as a heretic by the Council of Constance. From that decisive moment, Luther was known as a heretic. What's more, Hus was also the name associated with the costly rebellions that had lasted for many years known as the Hussite Wars. With this tactic, Eck was able to label Luther not only a heretic but also an insurgent, a revolutionary.

At this point, they spoke about purgatory and indulgences, but these issues had become anticlimactic. Officially, the Universities of Paris and Erfurt had to decide a winner, but that was only a formality. Everyone present at the disputation had heard what had happened, and as a result, stories soon spread all over. Representatives from Bohemia, Hus's homeland, went home with enthusiasm, but those siding with the papacy were deeply annoyed, because for many years they had tried to win Bohemia back to the church.

On July 20, Luther arrived back in Wittenberg. The preceding weeks had been unique and stressful. Jerome Emser, the former secretary of Duke George who was now employed as the court chaplain, published his own account of the disputation. As he related, Luther had said that he did not belong with the Bohemians and yet that the primacy of the pope was based not on divine but on human right. Luther's extremely passionate reaction demonstrated how fully he understood that he had ended up in the thick of problems. Occasionally he wrote in a friendly style, then in a crude fashion; sometimes he was conciliatory and then implacable. In the meantime, he had also researched the work of Hus and could not come to any other conclusion than this: "Up to now I have unknowingly learned and accepted everything from Hus."[65] He even went further: "Without realizing it, we are all Hussites. Yes, in fact, Paul and Augustine were also Hussites."[66] It was clear to him: the pope erred, the church had degenerated into an institution of power, and now was the time to oppose them.

From all sides Luther received support, especially from the side of the humanists, of which a number actually joined him. But from the side of von Staupitz, it was quiet, very quiet. Luther was deeply saddened by this.[67] Von Staupitz was really conflicted himself; he doubted and was worried, so much so that in early 1520 he resigned his position as head of his order.

The disputation in Leipzig became a kind of model. Many cities asked supporters and opponents of Luther to debate each other, and then these cities would decide whether they would stay with the pope or join the Reformation. The publications that followed delved into the differences and contradictions.

After Luther had initiated the discussion on the primacy of the papacy, Eck broke off all contact, which he had established earlier. He felt he could no longer associate with someone who had placed himself outside the fellowship of the church. Luther was deeply affected by this breach. Eck also initiated measures to have Luther condemned by the church. It was now clear to Luther. His view on the papacy had made a significant transformation: "Here [in Wittenberg] we are convinced that the papacy is the seat of the true and living Antichrist. For the sake of the salvation of many souls, we maintain that everything is permitted to oppose his lies and deceit."[68] At this point, he spoke of the papacy as an institution, but before long, Luther would declare the pope himself the Antichrist and a "murderer of souls."[69]

Rejection

While the Universities of Paris and Erfurt failed to provide a judgment on the disputation, the Universities of Leuven and Cologne did so with fervor. In Leuven they made a list of heresies from Luther's works, as those had recently been published. For the purpose of an audit, they sent the list to Cologne. On August 30, the latter university condemned a list of Luther's views. Leuven followed suit on November 7. In the fall of 1519, Eck wrote a letter to Rome because he thought it was high time that the church should take measures against Luther. In pursuit of his objective, he departed for Rome himself on February 10, 1520. It was abundantly clear how seriously relations had been disrupted: Eck had gone to Rome to have Luther excommunicated; Luther asserted that Eck had gone for *chrysos* ("gold") and not for Christ.

Another rejection came from Augustine Alfeld, a Franciscan monk from Leipzig. On April 7, 1520, he published a book in which he thoroughly defended the primacy of the pope over against Luther, stating that it was entirely biblical. Alfeld appealed not only to Christ, who was assumed to have made Peter head of the church, but also to the high priesthood of Aaron. Luther thought this work was so obtuse and crude that he asked a student to write a reaction. Alfeld reacted again from his side with a booklet that irritated Luther so much that he grabbed the pen himself: "We should fatten that swine for the Lord God so that he can come to slaughter it himself."[70]

At the end of June, Luther's *Concerning the Papacy in Rome* was published.[71] Luther had completely rounded off his thinking about the papacy and wrote passionately and fiercely. Their appeal to divine right didn't mean much to him, he said. Did they also call sucking Germany dry a "divine right"? Luther did not believe at all that they attacked him on account of matters of faith. The only reasons they attacked him were the threats to their financial benefits and their interests in power. According to the Bible, the church looks completely different. Christ is the Head, and he does not need a vicar on earth. Indeed, the church has an exterior, and therefore, it needs an organization. As far as he was concerned, this could also be a structure in which the bishop of Rome provided leadership. If so, then he should do that as it was meant to be when bishops were appointed, that is, serving and not ruling, a service that is focused on saving souls and not on the good of his own stomach and wallet:

> If we punish thieves with hanging, bandits with the sword, heretics with fire, why don't we use all the available weapons and grab these masters in destruction, these cardinals, these popes, and the whole manure pile of that Roman Sodom that causes endless ruin to the church of God and wash our hands in their blood, so that we liberate ourselves and everyone with us from this widespread and fatally dangerous fire?[72]

Luther realized that he was now in constant danger: "The bishop of Brandenburg apparently said that he did not want to lay his head down in rest until he had thrown Martin into the fire just like the piece of wood that he just had in his hands and threw into the fire. In this way the Ecksian wind inflates this miserable windbag."[73] But support and hope came to Luther from outside the country:

> I would really appreciate it that a few more suitable brothers would be sent to us. Both priors from the Low Countries, Jacob and Henry,[74] wrote me full of concerns and despair and begged whether anything could be done through their vicar. They say that they will send brothers or even that they would come themselves,

but that will probably not happen because their letter was written on Easter, and they have still not arrived. I just received letters as well from Prague in Bohemia from two priests of the Utraquists,[75] who are very familiar with the Holy Scriptures. With one of the letters there was a booklet written by John Hus, which I have not yet read. They urge me to be steadfast and patient because the theology that I teach, they say, is pure.[76]

6

Architect (1520–1521)

New Building

Luther soon realized that his insights were to lay a new foundation of Christian theology. Even so, Luther determined to leave it to others to build on what he established. What Calvin had built in Geneva looked different from what Martin Bucer had done in Strasbourg, and the structure in the Netherlands was different from the one in Scotland. But the foundation and the building materials were the same. This new understanding of the relationship between God and people had far-reaching consequences for the church, society, and every individual person. This was more of a revolution than a reformation. In a sense, October 31, 1517, could be called the birthday of a new world, a world in which life looked different in every context for those who followed Luther's lead. A society that was based on the conviction that people have to restore their relationship with God changed radically when a new foundational conviction emerged: that God in Christ accomplished everything. God's justice was no longer the threat that drove someone to pursue a morally upright lifestyle, but rather, it was a gift that motivated people to gratitude. This theology, this new relationship between God and people, removed the logical basis of the mass, pilgrimages, veneration of relics, celibacy, monastic life, purgatory, preoccupation with the salvation of the dead, and the all-encompassing and supreme position of the church. Luther's theology brought something totally different from what previous attempts at reformation had sought. The fact that God provided righteousness instead of requesting it made it necessary to reconsider the church, preaching, lifestyle, marriage, education, politics, heaven and hell, death, and the Devil.

In 1520, Luther initiated a season of producing an enormous amount of written materials on these topics; he was constantly writing sermons, letters, books, and brochures. He worked day and night and thought he should have been doing even more: "I know how to tackle the issues, and I have a good memory that does not require me to rack my brains. It comes easily, and yet I do not do enough."[1] He was unable to do certain things anymore, even though he thought they were necessary:

> For my sermons on Matthew, I haven't even been able to prepare a single word for printing yet. . . . I simply do not have time. Additionally, I have made no progress with my commentary concerning the period from Advent to Lent, and with respect to Lent itself, I have not even begun. And if you want to know why that is, I simply don't get around to it. There is a desire to do so, and by God's grace, I do not lack the strength, but it is the work on the Psalms that I can barely handle.[2]

Also, time and again people came to visit, and friends asked if he could spare just a moment to do something for them. It was often "just a moment," but it cost him time and divided his attention. "Yesterday I again lost half a day to reply to Meissen's ban,"[3] he recorded. "I can write quite quickly, and I have a strong memory that produces even more as the pressure for writing increases. And yet, that is not enough. I actually wonder how people who are slower than I, do it."[4]

His work at the university increased, and as a result he also had to be involved in internal issues, such as the discussion whether students who were not associated with the university should be permitted to carry a weapon like a dress sword. In a sermon on July 15, 1520, Luther tackled this issue, which had dragged on for some time already. The students of the university thought that the students of the painter Cranach should not have the right to carry a weapon. According to them, this age-old right had been established only for university students. The conflict about this matter became more acute each day, and in his sermon Luther labeled this dispute the work of the Devil. Isn't this what the Devil wants, Luther asked, that confusion reigns and people disagree with each other? In this way the advancement of the gospel will be disturbed, he said.[5] After the sermon, the students cried out, "If that little monk has another sermon like that, we'll strike him in church on his monk's head with a stone."[6]

Sacraments

The biggest impact of Luther's insights concerned the place and function of the sacraments. The Catholic Church had seven sacraments. Erasmus had already publicly wondered if those seven sacraments could all be traced back to the Bible. Erasmus asked the questions, as he always did, and Luther provided answers. According to Luther, only three of the seven were found in Scripture: baptism, the Lord's Supper, and penance. He changed not only the number but also the contents, publishing a sermon on each of the three remaining sacraments.

In his *Sermon on the Holy, Highly Esteemed Sacrament of Baptism*,[7] he stated that baptism is not just a moment when original sin is eliminated but is the moment when God enters into a covenant with us. That moment becomes the beginning of a lifelong process of dying to sin and being resurrected to new life. Baptism was changed from being an event to a process, from a momentary event to an attitude toward life, rooted in the divine promises given in baptism. This meant that baptism was not to be seen as a one-time event but something for every day.

Luther's sermon about the Lord's Supper created controversy. In it Luther also proposed that it would be good if a council were to decide that laypeople should receive not only bread but also wine. His use of the word "chalice" caused a stir, since the word was often associated with the rise of the Hussites. Duke George of Saxony appealed to Frederick to finally take action against Luther. Some priests openly declared that it would not be a sin to kill Luther since he was a heretic. Spalatin thought that Luther should have expressed himself with greater restraint. Luther admitted that he had been too sharp, but he was resilient, insisting that his stance concerned God's affairs and that he could not be silent when his enemies were not.

In his sermon about the sacrament of penance, Luther stated that much had to change: "Nothing in the church needs a reformation more than confession and penance, because it is here that all laws, greed, violence, tyranny, heresy, dangers, and endless evil for all souls and for the whole church flourish vigorously."[8] The heart of confession is not self-examination and not the accusation of the conscience, Luther said, but the promise of forgiveness, the word of grace. That is why it does not concern remorse but concerns the faith with which the penitent embraces the word of forgiveness. Therefore, it is the Word, not the priest, that forgives. This means, Luther reasoned, that every Christian is permitted by God to forgive the sins of another. Forgiveness depends not on the measure of one's understanding of sin but rather on whether he believes in forgiveness. Luther did not want to abolish confession because he believed it was necessary that people be able to confess their sins to talk about their guilt and hear about forgiveness. In January 1519, Luther wrote *A Brief Manual about How People Should Confess*.[9] This work was distributed initially as a brochure and a year later in a more extensive format as a small treatise. Luther wanted to liberate confession from nervous tension and from endless self-examination, but he wanted to retain the sacramental character of the confession. In 1522, he still spoke with appreciation about what he had derived from confession: "Yes, I would long have been strangled by the Devil if confession had not kept me standing."[10] By this Luther referred to a brotherly discussion in which one can unburden one's conscience. It was that personal aspect that Luther wanted to retain in confession, not the idea that confession was a good work.

Around the same time that Luther wrote these sermons on the sacraments, he penned a sermon on good works. These themes were all related to Luther's doctrine of justification by faith alone because they concerned the question of what God does and what humans do. Critics of his doctrine of justification by faith claimed that people would now no longer be focused on living a sanctified life. Luther disputed this criticism with his *Sermon on Good Works*:

> The "Sermon on Good Works" is now flowing from of my pen. However, it is not going to be a sermon but a booklet. That is how

> this work is growing during its writing. If it continues like this, it will become—according to me—the best work I have published up to now. At the same time, I realize that whatever is pleasing to me in my work does not please everyone because it happens to be infused with that yeast.[11]

The yeast Luther referred to was his new theology on grace. Good works do not cease with grace but should begin there. Luther made his clearest statements about this in his lectures on Genesis, delivered during the last years of his life: "We know that faith is never by itself, but that faith is accompanied by love and many other gifts."[12] It is by faith alone (*sola fide*), but faith is never alone (*fides numquam est sola*). Faith is crucial, because believing is the only good work that we have to do. Everything that does not originate from faith is sin. In this way, Luther wanted to articulate a vision of Christian obedience that was devoted to God but not weighed down by the demands of the law.

Excommunication

Luther was busy, and he realized that Rome was likewise busy:

> I've read the letters from Rome, numb and defeated, now that I have to confirm with my own eyes that there is such sinful dullness in control in the top offices of Rome. I am afraid that consciences and the truth are so muddled there that there is no room for another opinion or other feelings. First they condemn my work, but then they acknowledge that it has scholarly quality and is well thought out. And then they say that they didn't read it and that they never wanted to read it. May the Lord have mercy on all of us.[13]

Luther did not know quite what to do, but he was convinced that he did not choose to be embroiled in this issue:

> What advice must especially I give to the elector to his response? . . . My books witness that it was not my desire but was against my will that I ended up in this business. I crave peace and tranquility. If they also agree to that, I would love to be silenced. Surely everyone knows that Eck enticed me into this discussion concerning the pope for no other reason than to bring my name, and the name of

> the university, into ill repute! Now everyone sees that God thwarts this, and now people accuse me of conceit. And what kind of honor would I be seeking? What would I want other than rest and no public attention?[14]

Nevertheless, he said that he was not afraid of the consequences:

> Good, let them take my office away, burn my books, fine! But as long as people do not free me from my teaching position and from my ministry of the Word, I will continue to observe my office in all freedom. I have enough sins, and I do not want to add something unforgivable such as neglecting the office with which I have been entrusted and thus be found guilty of a sinful silence at the cost of the truth and of so many souls. I am always ready to step down as long as the truth of the gospel does not have to step down! They can get anything they want from me as long as they keep the way of salvation open for Christians. That is the only thing I request, nothing more. And otherwise, let them relieve me of my office, and let me live and die in a small corner. I do hope the elector will write back in such a way that the Roman heads understand that up to the present, Germany is oppressed, not by her own but by the Italian crudeness toward God's secret counsel.[15]

That was strong but necessary language. Rome tried again to force Luther to recant or else have him silenced. Pressure was put on both the elector and von Staupitz, but these efforts were in vain. Consequently, Rome made preparations for excommunicating Luther. With the election of Charles V as emperor, there were no longer any political reasons for Rome to give special consideration to Frederick. After discussions in various committees, the papal bull was established on June 15. It was published in Rome on July 24 and posted at St. Peter's Basilica and by the papal office on the Campo de Fiori. The official title of the bull was *Bull against the Heresies of Martin Luther and His Followers*, though it is more commonly known by the first words of the bull: *Exsurge Domine* ("Arise, Lord"). These are words from Psalm 10:12, in which God is urged to arise against the enemies that threaten his people; also, the bull uses imagery of a swine that is attempting to destroy the Lord's vineyard (Ps. 80:13–14). In the bull Rome described how heresies had arisen in Germany like those of John Hus, even though Germany had opposed Hus earlier. It summarized forty-one theses, of which forty were taken directly from Luther's work, addressing the issues of indulgences, penance, the pope, and the mass. Under the threat of excommunication, every believer, every church organization, and every university was forbidden to agree with any of the theses. Luther himself was commanded to stop preaching and writing, to burn his writings, and to recant his heresies within sixty days. If he ignored this demand, no one was allowed to associate with him, and every person and every city was asked to take him prisoner and send him to Rome.

On September 26, Aleander, the papal ambassador responsible for implementing the papal bull, arrived to meet the emperor who was staying in Antwerp at that time. Two days later, Charles V made a proclamation that in the Netherlands all of Luther's books had to be burned. A little more than a week later, the first official burning of Luther's books took place in Leuven. Cologne and Mainz followed in November. Rome's pressure on Frederick to do the same in his region fell on deaf ears. He adopted a clear position: if Luther had taught falsely, he would have immediately taken action against him, but Luther was entitled to a fair hearing in Germany first. The bull was directed not only against Luther but also against some of his followers, including Carlstadt. Copies of this bull were shared widely and were posted by order on the churches in Saxony. Though Luther was aware of the preparations they were making for the bull, he did not see the actual contents until the beginning of October.[16] He realized that Eck was the force behind this bull, and he had already determined that he would address these accusations as "deceitful" and "godless."[17] "Finally, the Roman bull that Eck brought along and about which many of us have written so many letters to the various rulers has arrived," Luther recorded. "I detest this bull and will attack it as deceitful, godless, and in every respect Eckish."[18] It was still only a threat of the bull and not the excommunication itself, but given Luther's response, that excommunication was certain to come. Luther informed Spalatin, and via him also the elector, that he had seen it coming. What about the burning of books? If anything should have been burned, then it should have been the books of canon law, something Luther would do later in the year. Luther felt supported, not only by people in his surroundings but also by many throughout the German Empire. He informed Rome that if they wanted him out of the way, many would arise to continue his work.[19]

Together with Spalatin, Luther wrote a lengthy letter to the emperor, still hoping to gain support for his issues. But the letter was not received enthusiastically. On October 11, 1520, Luther heard that the emperor had torn up his letter, even though he had sent him two copies, in the hope that he would do something with them. With care, Luther had made clear that he was fully prepared to explain and defend his so-called new doctrine. But he would do that only if certain conditions would be met. The emperor turned this offer down and left Luther with little hope that he could salvage the situation:

> Nevertheless, I rejoice with all my heart that I must suffer for such an excellent matter. Actually, I am not worthy to be tested in such a fashion. In many things I feel freer, now that I am certain that the pope is the Antichrist and has clearly been revealed as the throne of Satan. But may God save his own, so that they may not be tempted by his unmerciful attitude. Erasmus writes that the court of the emperor is so totally controlled by the tyranny of the mendicant monks, that one does not have to expect anything from Charles. That is not a surprise: do not trust in rulers, children of men, because there is no salvation in them.[20]

Nevertheless, it had to be the emperor, "who must deal thoroughly with this matter, which is not just the matter of one person, but of God, of all Christendom, and of the whole German nation."[21] Luther stood against the pope and the emperor, and none of the three was planning to move aside or give in.

Eck

Eck looked after the distribution of the bull first posted in Meissen on September 21. From that moment it had legal force, initiating the sixty days. From Leipzig, where Eck was staying temporarily, he had several servants deliver the bull in Wittenberg, not daring to personally enter Frederick's territory. But even in Leipzig he was not safe. The common people threatened him; reports came that fifty students had left Wittenberg to deal firmly with Eck.[22] The university advised the elector not to let Luther go and to be careful, since there would be rebellions if something happened to Luther. The question was now, what would Luther do? Leave? Stay? Recant? At that moment, von Miltitz became active again because he understood quite well what was going to happen: "When the bull becomes effective, this will lead to a church schism."[23]

They agreed that Luther would once more write down what the issues were both in German and Latin and then clearly state that his critique was not personally directed against the pope. Luther did as requested, and he prefaced this statement with a pacifying letter to Pope Leo X, whom he wanted to acknowledge as an instrument of Christ: "I expect Christ as Judge, and using the Roman see, he will declare his judgment."[24] Luther still saw the pope as "a lamb in the midst of wolves and as Daniel in the midst of lions. And you live like Ezekiel between scorpions. What can you do against these monsters by yourself?"[25] This was a play on words, since the pope's name meant "lion." Here Luther made his last attempt at reconciliation; soon he would see the pope as a wolf in sheep's clothes.

In addition, Luther published several small works in which he reacted much more aggressively against the bull, including a booklet with the descriptive title *Against the Bull of the Antichrist*.[26] He saw the excommunication bull as a product of the Antichrist because it was directed against the truth. After all, the bull directed people to burn Luther's books, even those that did not have any of the alleged heresies. Luther eventually came to the conclusion that the pope, or at least the papal institution, was the Antichrist. But for the time being, he was willing to see the bull simply as a product of Eck. He accused Rome of coming with a bull when he had only asked for a discussion based on the Bible. Luther was convinced that the wrath of God would rain down on the papists as enemies of the cross of Christ and God's truth. Luther, like his opponents, declared an excommunication: "As they excommunicated me in their godless heresy, I excommunicate them for the sake of the holy truth of God."[27] This conviction would also undergird the notion that it was Rome that had departed from Luther, not Luther who had abandoned the church.

Successful Trilogy

In 1520, three of Luther's most well-known and successful works were published. In these three publications his thought continued to evolve concerning how things in the church and the world should or should not go. The three booklets became very successful. Also, all three were connected to the name *Eleutherios*; Luther felt that his reformational discovery had freed him, and now he wanted to free the rest of Christendom as well.

The first work was directed to the Christian nobility, titled *To the Christian Nobility of the German Nation, concerning the Reform of the Christian Estate*.[28] In June he had already announced that something like this was on its way: "The secrets of the Antichrist must finally be brought to light. . . . Therefore, I am planning to write a pamphlet against the tyranny and the worthlessness of the Roman curia directed to Charles and the nobility of all Germany."[29] The book was made available on August 12. Six days later, all four thousand copies were sold out, an unprecedented feat at that time.

In this booklet, Luther addressed the secular government, no longer accepting that the church had authority over the state. Also, rulers and burgomasters were seen as members of the church, and in that capacity, Luther addressed them concerning their responsibility. If the leadership of the church did not facilitate reform, then the members who have authority should. Every baptized Christian is a priest, and therefore, among Christians no one is higher or lower. He criticized the church of Rome for hiding behind three impenetrably thick walls. The first wall was Rome's teaching that the authority of the pope was higher than secular government. The second wall was the dogma that only the pope was qualified to explain the Bible. And the third wall was the belief that the pope had higher authority than church councils. No reformation or breakthrough would be possible unless the political leaders would intervene in this distressful situation.

Luther did not address the wrongs in the church, but he did believe the nature of the church was different from what he had been taught, just as he had discovered that the nature of God was different from what he was taught. In other words, another perspective on God means another perspective on the church. This booklet was a catalyst and made the Reformation into a national movement. It was certainly no coincidence that he chose to publish a booklet in the German language. The people finally heard a voice that dared to counter the power of Rome and correct the pope. The finality of *Roma locuta, causa finita* ("Rome has spoken, the matter is finished") was replaced by the view that the matter would only be finished after the Bible had spoken.

In October, Luther published his book *On the Babylonian Captivity of the Church* (see fig. 6.1).[30] He wrote this forceful volume in Latin since, more than anything, he wanted the clergy and scholars to read it. The core thesis of this book was that the church had been imprisoned by the doctrine of seven sacraments and that this doctrine had become a means for the clergy to exercise power. According to Luther, the church maintained that people needed the sacraments for their salvation and that only the priests could administer these. But the Bible stated something quite different. Luther said that the New Testament recognized only three sacraments: baptism, the Lord's Supper, and penance. Marriage was not a sacrament but belonged to the civil order. Extreme unction, the ordination of priests, and confirmation were, Luther argued, deceitful inventions of the papal church.

DE CAPTIVITATE
BABYLONICA
ECCLESIAE,
Præludium Martini
Lutheri.

Vuittembergæ.

Figure 6.1 Original title page of *On the Babylonian Captivity of the Church*, 1520. Lutherhalle, Wittenberg.

Luther also eliminated the difference between the clergy and the laity by positing that every baptized person is a priest, "because that which has crawled out of baptism may glory in the reality that it has already been ordained to be priest, bishop, and pope."[31] This priesthood of all believers meant that everyone who has been baptized stands directly before God's face. No longer does a person have to approach God via a priest because everyone who has been baptized is a priest. The difference exists only in that everyone in the church and in the world has his or her own task and calling, but in faith there is no difference in level or standing. "We are all Christians, all priests," Luther explained. "Those whom we call priests are our chosen servants who must do everything in our name. Their priesthood is only a service."[32] As another shock to the wall between clergy and laity, Luther attacked clerical celibacy, asking where the Bible prohibited monks and nuns to marry. With this question, he struck a blow at the basis of monastic life and inspired many nuns and monks to leave the cloisters and monasteries.

Similar to the three walls mentioned in *To the Christian Nobility of the German Nation*, Luther spoke of a threefold prison that binds the consciences of church members. Papal withholding of the wine from the laity in the celebration of the mass was the first prison. The dogma of transubstantiation, the belief that the bread and wine are changed into the body and blood of Christ, was the second prison. And the third prison was the belief that celebrating mass was a good work and a sacrifice.

These charges showed how far reaching the consequences of Luther's vision had become. Where the first booklet dealt with relationships in the church, the second concerned the doctrine of the church and specifically a totally new view of the mass. Luther indeed had turned everything on its head. The mass is certainly a good work, Luther said, but it must be seen as a good work that God does for us. In the mass the priest does not approach God on behalf of the congregation with Christ's sacrifice. Instead, via the priest God comes to the congregation with Christ's sacrifice. In the mass there is no sacrifice, but the sacrifice is proclaimed. In this way Luther transformed the priest into a preacher. Book printers, quickly realizing that something sensational had been written, hurried to market a German version, which likewise sold out immediately.

In mid-November 1520, Luther's third booklet was published,

Figure 6.2 *Portrait of Pope Leo X and His Cousins . . .* (1475–1521). Painting by Raphael, 1517. Uffizi Gallery, Florence.

a booklet about Christian freedom "that includes a summary of all Christian life."[33] In a letter that served as a kind of preface but was published separately, Luther addressed Pope Leo X (1475–1521), who, regardless of all the threats he had made, was addressed as "most holy father in God," even though Luther had stated earlier that in the papacy he saw the Antichrist (see fig. 6.2).[34]

Luther still had the impression, or at least the hope, that the pope was unaware of all the things that were done in his name, and he hoped that if the pope would read this little booklet, he would come to a different insight. Luther added that at least he himself would not change his opinion. If someone would think that he would recant, then he could only say, "That is not going to happen; no one ever should consider that possibility."[35] It is simply impossible to bind God's Word to human rules. This letter was Luther's last attempt to reach agreement now that he knew the excommunication bull was in the making. This awareness caused Luther to employ some deceitfulness himself;

he dated the letter September 6 even though he wrote it in the beginning of November. Luther wanted to give the impression that at the time of writing this letter, he did not know that the papal bull had been published (which took place on September 29) in the diocese of Brandenburg, of which Wittenberg was a part.

In his booklet on freedom, which was published almost at the same time in both Latin and German, Luther provided a new definition of faith. Faith is not an accomplishment but a gift. I do not simply believe whatever the church believes, but I personally believe what God has revealed to me in his Word by grace. Faith liberates. The source of that freedom and the meaning of freedom Luther illustrated with a somewhat older image of the miraculous exchange (*der wunderbare Tausch*), which he applied to the relationship between the bridegroom, Christ, and the sinner, a harlot. In that marriage, implemented with community property rights, Jesus took upon himself mortality, sin, and the wrath of God, while sinful humanity received righteousness and glory from him. Luther's freedom did not mean that people were free to do whatever they wanted, but rather, Christian freedom was the freedom to want only what Christ wants. Luther articulated this freedom as a formulation that was meant for every Christian life:

> A Christian is free, lord over all things and subject to no one;
> A Christian is a willing servant of all things and subject to everyone.[36]

He did not articulate a list of things that were or were not permitted but rather defined freedom as the freedom to constantly do what Christ requires and to avoid everything that may injure my neighbor. In this way, Luther sought to liberate people's consciences from the permanent fear that God would see, weigh, and ascribe (or deduct) points for every deed, every word, and every thought. God's grace in Christ meant, in Luther's view, that God judged people according to what they intended to do and not according to what they eventually managed to do.

Luther had formulated his three walls with the intention of freeing the church and Christianity from the chains that had imprisoned them. He had substantial support for this call. Luther's productivity resulted in complaints from the printers in Wittenberg that they had difficulty keeping up with his writing. Luther, however, felt that he had to continue writing because "the time to be silent has passed and the time to speak has come." The printers did not have much reason to complain, since Luther's booklet to the Christian nobility had an unprecedented printing of four thousand copies, and soon they had to prepare a reprint. Their good earnings benefited from the fact that Luther did not ask for a cent in royalties. Luther hardly had time to check the printer's proofs, because the printers almost plucked them straight from his hands so that they could keep up with the demand.[37] People were eager to read Luther because he spoke to them and about issues relevant to their lives. He made optimal use of the new media and presented himself as a young, straightforward, and enthusiastic clerical leader who knew what was on the minds of the people.

Fire

On June 28, 1519, the Spanish Habsburger Charles V, grandson of Maximillian, was chosen as emperor, but his coronation did not take place until October 1520. By the time the new emperor and the pope finally turned their attention to the controversy around the "Ninety-Five Theses," the events of October 31, 1517, were already three years old. There could be no way to hold back the consequences. The papal legate Aleander reported to Rome, "All of Germany is in an uproar. Nine-tenths shout out the battle cry 'Luther,' and the remaining ten percent, if they are indifferent to Luther, express the slogan 'Death to Rome.'"[38] On June 15, 1520, the Roman curia had already published a bull in which Luther was threatened with excommunication, but Luther had reacted in a novel manner. Instead of recanting his views, he just burned the bull. On December 10, after exactly sixty days, when the excommunication bull went into effect, Melanchthon posted an announcement for people to come to the Chapel of the Holy Cross, just outside the Elster Gate, at 9:00 p.m. There they would burn the books of canon law and books of scholastic theology. The students especially had been invited to observe this pious spectacle, because this would be the historical moment when the Antichrist would become visible.

Because no theologians wanted to donate any of their books to be burned, the books of scholastic theology were spared. As a consequence, only the books of canon law were burned. The manual for conducting confessions disappeared into the flames, as did a few works written against Luther by Eck and Emser. When everything was burning, Luther himself came "with fear and trembling"[39] and threw in the excommunication bull. Afterward, he went home, but the students stayed and had a party, which included a parade and the singing of satirical songs.

Whether they all understood the implications of this evening is not known, but the following morning Luther explained the meaning of the event in his lectures. Now was the time to make a choice against the pope and for Christ, even if that would create danger for one's own life. For the common people he wrote the booklet *Why the Books of the Pope and His Disciples Were Burned by Dr. Martin Luther*.[40] It is notable that Luther addressed himself as doctor in the name of this book. He wanted his audience to recognize him as a teacher in the church: "I am a sworn doctor of the Holy Scriptures, and in addition to that, someone who preaches everyday. It is part of my title, and it belongs to my position, my oath, and my office to defend against and destroy false, tempting, and un-Christian teachings."[41] He saw it as his task and calling as doctor to intervene now. Once more, Luther listed all his arguments, and then the conclusion was clear: canon law made the pope to be God on earth; such an unbiblical thought had to come to an end. He had been "trembling and in prayer" but added, "Finally I rejoiced about this action more than any other deed in my life, because these [i.e., the papal works] are even more poisonous than I think."[42] He informed Spalatin,

> On December 10 of the year 1520, at nine o'clock in Wittenberg at the eastern gate by the Holy Cross, all papal books . . . and the bull from Leo X . . . and other writings from Eck and Emser and additionally whatever others dragged in were burned. In this way those Italian murderers will notice that not much energy is needed to burn books that they cannot defend. That is the news for now.[43]

Luther was quite conscious of the fact that the burning of the bull and the books of canon law had created a definite breach with Rome.

To him that meant that he had broken with the whore of Rome and had returned to the church of Christ. Rome, for its part, had had enough. On January 3, 1521, Luther was excommunicated. The severity of excommunication is not to be underestimated; it was customary that the political authorities would follow the lead of the church, which meant exile from the empire. Fortunately for Luther, a number of rulers already did not want to yield to Rome. Some were touched in their hearts by Luther's message or at least by his efforts to reform the church. Others saw his action as a convenient opportunity to sever their ties with the pope and emperor. For some, both arguments were important. Frederick the Wise was able to strengthen his position by demonstrating his independence. That is why he and his colleagues were able to prevent Luther from having to go to Rome. Luther would give account to the emperor at the imperial Diet of Worms, and even though he had been excommunicated, he was promised safe conduct. In addition to Frederick's strong position, there was still another reason why he made a special effort on Luther's behalf and thus annoyed Rome even more. Frederick had wanted to marry Margaretha, the daughter of Emperor Maximillian. But he needed permission from the pope for that. Two times he had asked, and both times the pope turned down his request. Being forbidden from marrying the woman he really wanted was simply another good reason for Frederick to thwart the papacy.

Worms, 1521

In modern-day Worms an important monument commemorates Luther's visit to the 1521 diet. The monument is very detailed, depicting many figures as predecessors and fellow fighters with Luther. Luther stands on top alone, looking determined, just as he stood before the emperor. In the days preceding that event, the situation was quite a bit different. Luther experienced self-doubting, especially as to whether it was possible that he could be the only one in church history to know what he knew. It would have been quite something if he had been the only one in all those centuries who saw that the church had corrupted its message and forsaken true Christianity.

On March 29, 1521, Luther received a letter in which the emperor asked him to come and give an account at the imperial Diet of Worms.

Sometime earlier Luther had understood that the authorities hadn't agreed with each other how he should be treated. Some feared that a public process would bring Luther even more publicity and support. The advisers to the emperor, however, recognized that it was politically better not to have a discussion with him behind closed doors. At the diet, too many sovereigns who supported Luther would be present. Originally, the Luther issue had not been put on the agenda of the diet. The pope's side hoped that the excommunication would be endorsed by the diet, making a hearing redundant. Frederick the Wise, however, managed to convince the emperor that Luther should be invited to give an account and should be guaranteed safe travel to and from Worms for twenty-one days. The emperor felt compelled to accommodate this request because he realized that an increasingly large number of people had joined Luther, including many political rulers. They did not necessarily support his theology, but they did support his criticism of the wrongs in the church. Nevertheless, the invitation lacked clarity as to why Luther should come to Worms in the first place. Was it to recant? Was it to explain? The emperor kept the door open to both the pope and the rulers. Luther himself clearly understood that the journey to Worms was dangerous, but he wanted to go:

> At this time we should not consider danger or health. On the contrary, we must be sure that the gospel with which we began is not left to the mockery of the godless, and that we do not give opponents an opportunity to gain strength by saying that we do not dare to declare publicly what we have taught and that we would be afraid to shed our blood for that. May our gracious Christ keep us from such a cowardly attitude and spare us from the glory of others. Amen.[44]

With this attitude Luther departed on April 2 for Worms. In accordance with a rule in the Augustinian order that a monk should never travel alone, friar Johannes Petzensteiner was asked to travel with him. Luther did not have a particularly high opinion of this man, because "when he has had quite a bit to drink, he tries to be more learned than all of us."[45] The city had provided a horse and a covered wagon, and the university had given him twenty guilders in travel money. In addition to Petzensteiner, Nicholas von Amsdorf (1483–1565), the jurist Justus Jonas (1493–1555), and the nobleman Peter von Suaven, a representative from the students, accompanied Luther. Melanchthon's responsibilities at the university prevented him from going. Indeed, Luther himself didn't have time to go to Worms, because he had started lectures on the Psalms again. Luther felt it was necessary to go through the Psalms again because he had grown in his understanding of the Scriptures. More than five years had passed sincc his earlier lecture series, and what he had learned since then had challenged his previous thinking. He had just gotten into his series of lectures when he received the summons to Worms. He wondered whether he would be able to get back to them afterward.

Regardless, he was determined to go to Worms and even maintained that a sickness would not prevent him from appearing before the emperor.[46] Nevertheless, he dreaded it. Constantly, he thought of John Hus, who received safe conduct but ended up being burned at the stake in Constance. When he was traveling, his companions asked him early one morning whether he wanted to continue the journey after seeing the imperial notices along the way with the condemnation of his views. He responded that he would remain steadfast but that he did so trembling.[47] He also made it very clear, "If I will have gone only to recant, I wouldn't have gone." It must now be declared publicly: "According to the doctrine of St. Paul (1 Cor. 5:13), it is now the time before the eyes of the whole world to admonish the public evildoers," so that in this way we can drive this grievance out of God's kingdom.[48] As he explained to Spalatin,

> Now that I see that they do not have any argument against me other than that I, according to them, have written against the practices and traditions of the church, I will certainly not retract anything. I will answer Emperor Charles that I won't come if I have been asked to come only to recant. That would be the same as if I had gone and had returned already. If I must only retract, then I can do that from here as well. If, however, he has invited me in order to kill me and because of this reaction he sees me as an enemy of the empire, then I will offer to come. Because with Christ's help I do not want to flee from the battle or abandon the Word. I am quite certain that

> those bloodhounds will not rest until they have killed me. And I would like the papists to become guilty of my blood only if I could accomplish that. It's clear that we have been made into heathens, as we were before Christ. In this way the scheming Antichrist has held kingdoms imprisoned in his hands for centuries. The will of the Lord be done.[49]

In the meantime Luther was informed that von Staupitz had distanced himself from Luther and had submitted himself to the papal policies. This news devastated Luther. Deeply disappointed and indignant, he wrote von Staupitz an extensive letter: "Truly, this submission has deeply affected me. It showed me a different Staupitz than the one who was once the preacher of grace and the cross."[50] Luther felt terribly abandoned by his former father-confessor.

Journey

The Luther question had soon become one of the most important political issues in Europe. For many in Germany, he had become a hero, and for everyone, he was a spectacle. Luther's journey to Worms might be compared to a papal tour today. Everywhere people were standing along the road wherever he came, in every city, every village, lining every street. In some places he was hailed, and in others city authorities tried so hard to ignore him that the interest only increased. In Leipzig no one paid him any attention, and in Nuremburg someone rebuked him as a heretic, but in Erfurt it was a completely different spectacle. The rector of the university, Crotus Rubeanus, met Luther outside the city with forty knights to lead him into the city in a stately and formal fashion. The next morning, when he preached in the Augustinian church, it was so full that people panicked; several who were sitting upstairs broke the windows to get out more quickly. Luther calmed the people and blamed the Devil for the panic. Churches in Gotha and Eisenach were likewise packed.

Along the way, however, Luther was anxious with fear and temptation. He became so sick that they resorted to bloodletting. His intestinal issues plagued him again: "During the journey I had a feeling that, indeed, I now shall die. And I imagined the stake that had been prepared for me and often told myself, 'Oh, what shame am I bringing on my parents!' In this was the physical that made me afraid."[51]

On April 14, they arrived in Frankfurt, and the next day they went to Worms. Luther trusted that he "would enter Worms also against the will of all the gates of hell and the powers of the air."[52] Instead, he first heard a trumpet sound. When Luther and his companions approached the city gates on April 16 around ten in the morning, trumpets from the church tower announced his arrival. In front of the city gate, a delegation of the Saxony nobility waited to lead him to the place where he would be staying. Along the streets approximately two thousand people greeted him loudly, much to the annoyance of the papal delegation. Pictures of Luther sold so well that printers could not meet demand. There were even pictures of Luther with a dove above his head, as a sign of the Holy Spirit, who was leading him. People wanted to touch him, as if he were an image of the saints or a relic. The entry into Worms, according to critics, was so well organized that most people would have been reminded of Jesus's entry into Jerusalem.

Luther was lodged at the Johanniterhof, where part of the Saxon delegation lived. The emperor would have preferred to have him lodged in the neighborhood of the Habsburgers, to keep an eye on him, but the Saxons believed that was too risky and enforced their own wishes. Because of the imperial diet, the town lacked sufficient accommodations for all the travelers, and Luther had to share his room with two others. Almost immediately, he was visited by several rulers, such as the young Philip of Hesse (1504–1567), who would become quite important for the cause of the Reformation. On the morning of April 17, Luther was informed that at four o'clock in the afternoon he was expected at the palace of the bishop near the church tower, where he would appear before the emperor. He was told no more, because at that time it was still not clear how they were going to deal with this point on the imperial agenda. He hoped that he would at least have an opportunity to explain his vision about justification and discuss the points of disagreement. Because there was still ample time before his four o'clock appointment, he decided to first carry out his pastoral responsibilities and paid a visit to Hans von Minkwitz, a nobleman from Kursachsen who was seriously ill. Luther first heard his confession and then celebrated the Lord's Supper with him. While he was personally against the individual celebration of the Lord's Supper if no congregation was involved, he sometimes made exceptions, as in this situation.[53]

The Hearing

As they had arranged, one of the emperor's chamberlains picked up Luther at noon. Because the streets were full of people who wanted to see him, he was led via small gardens and alleyways to the emperor (see fig. 6.3). The beginning was awkward; Luther entered with a cheerful expression on his face but soon realized that such behavior contravened protocols for being in the presence of the emperor. Luther was also surprised when Johannes Eck, who was actually in service to the archbishop of Trier but spoke here on behalf of the emperor, asked if all the writings on the table were his. Luther then requested that they be named one by one. When that was done, he acknowledged that he had indeed written them. Immediately, he was asked to retract them. Luther requested time to give this demand consideration, "because it concerns God's Word, and that is after all the highest in heaven and earth." Luther did not want to fall under the judgment of Christ, "who said that whoever is ashamed of me on earth, I will be ashamed of him before my heavenly Father and his angels."[54]

When he stood before the emperor and appeared to have some doubt, his request for some time to reflect was not surprising. He was standing before the most powerful man in the world, who was surrounded by a large group of powerful people from both the church and the empire. The emperor had just made it clear that for his own health, for that of the entire church, and for that of the whole empire, it would be better if he would quickly recant and then act normally again. Additionally, Luther realized that everything he had ever written would have to be retracted with one statement.[55] The lack of communication only increased tensions. The emperor spoke only Spanish and French, while Luther spoke only Latin and German—there was little to say. In reaction to his request for time for reflection, Eck told Luther that he did not have the right to make such a request, because he should have known in advance that he was called here to recant. But the emperor

Figure 6.3 Luther at the Diet of Worms before the emperor, April 17–18, 1521. Woodcut, artist unknown, 1557. Underneath is written, *Hier stehe ich, ich kann nicht anders, Gott helfe mir. Amen* ("Here I stand, I can do no other, God help me. Amen"). From Ludwig Rabus, *Historien der Heyligen Auserwählten Gottes Zeugen* (Strassburg, 1557).

wanted to be merciful and granted him time for reflection until the next day at noon.

Afterward, he immediately left and heard from supporters that his performance had not been impressive. It had been difficult to hear him, and he had not shown a strong defense. When he returned to the inn after his first hearing, toward late afternoon, he wrote a letter, which was as much as he could do since so many people wanted to see and talk to him.

Fortunately, that evening several people dropped in to encourage him for the following day. The next day, Thursday, April 18, was better. In the morning he received a few more visitors, who mentioned that he appeared spirited and healthy again. Around and inside the building where the diet was being held, there was again such a mass of people that Luther had to push himself through them. When he was finally given permission to speak, he excused himself for his behavior the previous day. He explained that he "had not grown up in the courts of rulers but had grown up among monks." He offered apologies to all those whose position he had not properly respected. Whether he was actually as innocent and simple as he maintained is questionable. In the immediately preceding years, he had had substantial contact with highly placed officials, so that he probably could have known how he should have behaved. Nonetheless, Luther opted to show humility. Subsequently, he explained in German—and afterward, to accommodate the emperor somewhat, in Latin—that it was impossible for him to recant. He added that if he could be "convinced from the Scriptures, from the evangelists and the prophets," that he was wrong, he would eagerly retract.

Concerning the question whether he would retract all his books, Luther responded by dividing his books into three groups. In the first group he included works of edification on faith and personal piety. Those topics were good for every Christian, and therefore, he could not retract those books. That was also the case with respect to the second group of books, those against the papacy and the wrongs in doctrine and lifestyle in the church. If he would retract those books, he would be reinforcing impiety and supporting godlessness. For a long time already Germany had protested against these problems.

His third group of books had been directed against individuals who supported the papal tyranny. He admitted that here and there he had been too vehement and sharp, but after all, it concerned the name of Christ, and therefore, he could not retract these books either. Luther would not recant any of his work. A comprehensive reaction from Eck followed, which ended in a renewed appeal to retract. Subsequently, they heard Luther's renowned response:

> If, then, I am not convinced by testimonies of Scripture or by clear rational arguments—for I do not believe in the pope or in councils alone, since it has been established that they have often erred and contradicted each other—I am bound by the Bible texts that I have quoted. And as long as my conscience is captive to the Word of God, I cannot nor do I want to retract anything when things become doubtful. Salvation will be threatened if you go against your conscience. May God help me. Amen.[56]

The words "Here I stand, I can do no other" fit nicely with this address, but they appear only in a later publication. Luther stated, "I am completely willing to retract all errors, and I will be the first to throw all my books in the fire," but he would do this only if the authorities could provide evidence from the Bible that he had erred.[57] He added that he was bound by his conscience and simply could not retract if he did not want to go against God's will. After that, the hearing was ended.

Outside there was loud cheering among the people, but no one was sure what would happen next. As for Luther, he was so tremendously relieved that he felt like he had won a contest. Once he was back at the inn, he threw his hands in the air like a sprinter who was the first one to cross the finish line and cried out, "I am finished! I am finished!" Several nobles came to visit and thanked and encouraged him. The city, however, was restless. Spanish soldiers in service to the emperor had shouted, "Into the fire with Luther," which led to fierce protests from the people.[58]

Whether Luther actually spoke the words "Here I stand, I can do no other" is not terribly important. It was clear that even without these words, there was no way back. The one church would be divided; the one empire would be divided into many states. Banishing Luther from the empire on May 8, 1521, and declaring Luther an outlaw did not change anything either. Many rulers had pledged their support for him, and none of them had any desire to capture Luther. In the meantime, the emperor feared the growing numbers of knights and princes who threatened to revolt. Luther also feared this and was completely opposed to the notion that "force and killing would be used fighting for the gospel."[59] He was convinced that "the world is conquered and that the church is safeguarded only by the Word, and through that Word the church will again be strengthened. The Antichrist will be demolished by the Word, and that without lifting a single hand."[60]

What Now?

It was still unclear what was going to happen to Luther, but everybody was certain that the emperor would take action. As early as April 19, he had a declaration read to the representatives of the diet that he had written down immediately after the hearing. In this he declared that "he was certain that one monk erred in his vision, a vision, namely, that conflicts with more than a thousand years of Christianity and with the one of today, because otherwise it would mean that all of Christianity had continually erred up to today." As the one called by God as "defender and the lord protector of the catholic faith," he regretted "that he had hesitated so long before implementing anything against Luther's false doctrine." The emperor ended with unequivocal language: "I am determined no longer to listen to what he says, . . . but I will deal with him as a notorious heretic."[61] Luther responded with a letter to the emperor in which he again explained why he would have liked to retract but why, because of the Bible and his conscience, he could not.[62] He appealed to Charles in the name of all Christendom not to take any measures against him and his supporters. Luther realized, however, that his letter would probably do little to stop him.

The emperor wanted action, but first, several high church officials held private discussions with Luther in Worms. These ended up being futile because the officials could not convince Luther to change his mind. They insisted on one thing: Luther's retraction, which they believed would maintain unity in the church. Luther consistently answered that not even for the sake of peace could he accept another view: "Christ is the stumbling block, and I cannot make Christ different from anything God himself has made him."[63]

Luther departed for home. The safe conduct was also valid for his return trip to Wittenberg, but during his journey, he was prohibited from preaching, writing, or doing anything that could cause tumult among the people. He could only react with, "As the Lord wills; the name of the Lord be praised." They shook hands and departed.

While Luther readied himself to return home, the emperor still had to discuss with the rulers what should be done with the man from Wittenberg. After many days of deliberation, the resulting Edict of Worms was made public on May 25. Because the diet had already technically ended, the edict was backdated to May 8 to make it an official decision of the diet. Luther was now formally under the ban of excommunication and was declared an outlaw and a heretic. He had already been placed outside the church, but now he was officially placed outside society as well. The words of the edict were clear and unambiguous, stating that everyone must view "the aforementioned Martin Luther as an estranged member of God's church and as an obstinate schismatic and as a notorious heretic." No one was allowed to eat or drink with him or provide shelter, and everyone was ordered to take him captive and deliver him into the hands of the emperor. The edict declared prohibitions concerning the works "that have been published by this obstinate heretic to buy, to read, to possess, to write about, to print, or to have them copied or printed."[64] For ten years this edict would serve as a heavy-handed instrument to oppose Luther's supporters and followers. But for those rulers who disagreed with the edict, their principalities freely continued developing reformational thought. Frederick the Wise chose to ignore the edict completely, and Charles V didn't dare take action against Luther. As this reality became clearer, Luther could calmly develop his theology and shape the practical aspects of his reform program.

During the evening before his departure, Luther and a small group of individuals were introduced to a plan to have him temporarily disappear from the public eye. This was to enable his guardians to take him into protection. To Cranach he wrote, "I'm allowing them to hide me, but I do not know where."[65] The next morning, April 26, Luther and his travel companions left the city accompanied by twenty horsemen sent by a friendly supporter, the knight Frans von Sickingen.

The riders were offered as protection for him for the first part of the return journey. The travel did not proceed very quickly; along the way many people wanted to see or speak to Luther. On May 1, he stayed overnight in the monastery near Hersfeld, where the abbot asked him to preach the next morning. Though the emperor had forbidden him to preach, Luther proclaimed that the Word cannot be bound. On May 3, he preached in Eisenach and visited several family members who lived in the area. In the meantime, the number of travelers had diminished to three, and only von Amsdorf and Petzensteiner were with him. On May 4, in the forest near the Altenstein Castle, they were suddenly overtaken by raiders. The coachman was compelled to tell the attackers whom he was transporting; Petzensteiner fled on foot and raised the alarm. Pro forma, von Amsdorf (who knew about the attack ahead of time) protested vigorously. Luther was dragged out of the wagon, grabbing his Hebrew Bible and Greek New Testament in the process. Subsequently, he was forced to walk beside the horses, but as soon as

Figure 6.4 The Wartburg near Eisenach.
Photo courtesy of Touristoffice Eisenach.

they were out of the coachman's sight, he was given a horse, though he could hardly ride. That night around eleven o'clock he was delivered at the Wartburg Castle (see fig. 6.4).[66]

The Wartburg

The news of the kidnapping came like a thunderclap in a blue sky. Among the common people the rumor spread that the emperor had broken his promise of safe conduct and that Luther had died in the attack. The well-known painter Albrecht Dürer (1471–1528), who was in the Netherlands, wrote in his diary,

> Is he still living, or did they murder him? I don't know. . . . O God in heaven, . . . if we lose this man who wrote with more clarity than anyone before him . . . to whom you gave such an evangelical spirit. We pray to you then, heavenly Father, that you give your Holy Spirit to someone else who will unite your holy Christian church. O God, if Luther is truly dead, who will then proclaim the holy gospel to us so clearly? O, all you devout Christians, help me to weep intently for this man who was led by God's Spirit, and let us pray to him that he will send another enlightened man.[67]

Figure 6.5 Luther's room in the Wartburg. Photo courtesy of Touristoffice Eisenach.

Luther was actually quite alive and was disguised as a knight named Junker Jörg, with a beard and normal hairstyle:[68]

> When I look in the mirror, I hardly recognize myself. I have had to exchange my habit for knight's clothing, my monk's tonsure I have had to grow out, and I have even grown a beard. I think that even my friends would not recognize me now that I am no longer Brother Martin but have become Junker Jörg. The advantage is that I can move around unnoticed, and without fear I can leave the castle from time to time and go to Eisenach.[69]

Luther was given a small living area with a separate bedroom (see fig. 6.5). The castle was managed by Hans von Berleph, who looked after his "captive" well. Luther was relieved to hear from Spalatin that the elector was paying for his keep at the Wartburg. Luther said, "I wouldn't stay here an hour longer if I knew that I was using up his money and goods, even though he gives it to me eagerly and with joy." Thankfully, he did not need to feel concerned about his host. "That is my nature that I am afraid to be a burden, even though that may not actually be the case," he wrote. "But okay, it's only proper that a normal person worries about that."[70] Von Berleph even took him along one time to go hunting, though Luther did not really appreciate this:

> Last Monday [August 12] I went along hunting for two days to learn about this bittersweet pleasure of heroes. We caught two hares and a pair of skinny partridges; indeed, an activity that fits with people who don't have anything else to do. Between the netting and the dogs, I sat thinking about theology, because, regardless of how much pleasure this scene gave me, it was mixed with pity and guilt when I observed this secretive flushing out of animals. What does this image mean other than that the Devil who through his persecution and through those godless teachers with their dogs (namely, bishops and theologians) hunt these innocent little animals. This very sad and hidden connection with simple and believing souls is obvious. There was an even more gruesome interpretation added to this event. I had managed to save a little hare's life. I had hidden it in the sleeves of my coat and walked a short distance. The dogs found the poor hare anyway. Right through my coat they broke his right rear leg and bit through his throat. Well, that is how the pope and Satan carry on, so that even the souls that have been saved are killed, and whatever I try to do to prevent that doesn't bother them in the least.[71]

This experience was actually symptomatic of his stay in the Wartburg. It was a complete change after three years in the center of ecclesiastical and political discussions. Figuratively and literally, that was behind him now, and Luther had to live in tranquility and rest. But Luther's physical troubles remained. His diet as a knight was much different from what he had eaten as a monk, so much so that his intestines didn't accept it and went "on strike": "My bottom has become angry."[72] On May 12, 1521, he wrote,

> The Lord has afflicted me in my backside with great pains. My stools are so hard that I have to push them out with such force that I break out in a sweat. The longer I put it off, the worse it gets. Yesterday, after four days I had one bowel movement. Therefore, I didn't sleep all night and got no rest. It is a visitation from the Lord who does not want me to live without a cross.[73]

He felt surrounded by devils and forsaken by God. Associated with this season of life is the well-known Luther legend that he vented his anger at the Devil by throwing his inkpot at him when he supposedly saw Satan standing before him. The stain has been carefully preserved and is touched up regularly because it was something that drew many visitors who wanted to touch it. Luther never spoke about it, but he did say that he had met the Devil in various forms. Once this was even in the form of a dog, which he threw out the window. Considering the location of the Wartburg, Luther would have been the last one to see this dog alive. The legend of a flying inkpot is surely more palatable to modern people than that of a flying dog. It is problematic, however, that the ink stain was not discovered until the middle of the seventeenth century and that in Luther's time inkpots didn't exist; ink was instead kept in a small bowl. If he had thrown that, the whole wall would have been splattered with ink stains.

Luther did not throw bowls, even though initially there was little else for him to do at the Wartburg: "I sit here the whole day doing nothing. I feel bloated, and I have headaches."[74] Something had to happen, and therefore, he took it on himself to find tasks: "I shall write a German sermon about the freedom to do confession. Additionally, I will continue the work on the Psalms and on the postils as soon as I receive what I need from Wittenberg. Included among those materials is also the *Magnificat*, which I started already."[75] The situation made him productive, and he wrote a so-called postil, a sort of commentary on Bible texts that was intended for preachers to use as an aid to write sermons. These were also meant for personal use. In the course of several years, Luther would publish more of these postils. In the summer, the first installment of Luther's postils was published. Two years earlier he had begun to help preachers with their sermon preparation when he noticed that not everyone understood what the gospel actually says. The guidelines he prepared addressed this matter for preachers especially well. In this way he could also help prevent that "everyone preaches whatever he wants" and that "instead of preaching about the gospel, they would preach about little blue ducks."[76] Luther named this "the very best book I ever wrote,"[77] and indeed, many people used it immediately. He couldn't preach as he had been used to doing, but through his writing, he turned the Wartburg into his pulpit. He called the Wartburg his

Patmos,[78] comparing himself to the apostle John, able to perceive what was happening and what would happen. He also knew who belonged to the whore of Babylon and who belonged to the bride of Christ.

With these distinctions in mind, Luther continued to write polemics against Rome. The method of arguing, however, raised questions here and there. When Albrecht of Mainz agreed to connect a special indulgence to the relics that could be visited in Halle, to help relieve some of his financial distress, Luther reacted with a vehement little work that he sent to Spalatin. He asked to have it published but was denied. Spalatin wrote, "The ruler [elector] will not allow you to write against the man from Mainz." "I can understand his concern," Luther replied, "but for the sake of Christ's sheep, one should oppose this terrible wolf with all one's strength, also as an example to others." Those politicians in Saxony may have been concerned about the political peace, but far more important, Luther held, was "the eternal peace of God that is disturbed by that godless man and his practices that dishonor God."[79] A treatise would eventually appear, he said, and Luther already knew what he was going to call it: *Against the Idol of Halle*. This was a fitting title because the collection of relics was considered an idol, which "deprives these poor, simple Christians of their money and their souls."[80] The elector forbade the publication.

The threat that Luther felt from Rome intensified his vehemence: "The pope will attack everyone who stands behind me." But Luther did not believe that this would yield very much fruit, "because God brings many into action and also the people's hearts. But if they begin to oppress the matter with violence, it will become ten times worse, because Germany has many farmers.'"[81] Nevertheless, he did not want a riot or a revolt, because that would only cause problems for the progress of the gospel: "In the gospel we do not find a command or advice that gives us that right. After all, the gospel is a law of free-willed and free people. That is to say, of people who have nothing to do with the sword and the justice of the sword."[82]

Confession and Vows

There were two more topics that urgently needed thorough contemplation: confessions and spiritual vows. Luther's reforms began with the issue of confession, and in fact, this issue would emerge again at the end of Luther's life. He consistently held on to confession as a sacrament, that is, as a sign of God's promises and grace. The personal conversation in which a sinner could confess his sins to another Christian, who could then provide the promise of forgiveness on behalf of God, was something he would not relinquish. But it had to be done differently. Thus, he rejected the thought that forgiveness could only be granted for sins that had been confessed. These thoughts encouraged people to examine their consciences so that they would be sure not to forget sins. God also forgives sins that one has forgotten, because God is concerned about uprightness of heart, not about the completeness of one's list of sins. That had also been Luther's objection against compulsory confessions. In Christ we have been freed of obligations, and that is especially the case with confession. If it becomes an obligation, there is a danger that it will no longer be a matter of the heart, whereas God's concern is that people have their hearts broken by their awareness of sin. All these aspects were articulated in Luther's *On Confession*, in which he also underscored his view that confession is not only confession when it takes place before an office bearer or cleric. Everyone who has been baptized is a priest, and therefore, confession can find a place among brothers and sisters in the Lord.

The second important issue was the question about the validity of spiritual vows. Luther's criticism of celibacy in his booklet *To the Christian Nobility of the German Nation* had already led in May 1521 to the first marriages of priests. One of them was Bartholomew Bernhardi, a student of Luther's who was priest in Kemberg near Wittenberg. Luther heard about it and sent him a note of congratulations. But he was concerned about the wave of priests getting married throughout the land. From Wittenberg he heard that Carlstadt and his ilk had pressured all clerics to get married. Luther himself did not want to think about marriage: "Dear God, are our Wittenbergers also going to give wives to the monks? They will certainly not compel me to get married."[83] When they accused him of turning everything in the church on its head so he could marry, he immediately rejected that: "I hope . . . that God grants me the grace to remain as I am."[84]

Because he did not know if everyone realized why clerics and nuns broke their vows of chastity as well as their monastic vows, he wrote a hefty book to explain everything.[85] He stated that it would not be acceptable for people to break their vow because they simply said they could not keep it. Then that situation would have to be valid for all the vows made to God. The issue concerned vows that people had been compelled to make that they could not keep. That included vows motivated by the belief that people could make vows to earn their salvation. Such vows were deemed to be ungodly and were invalid before God, because Scripture says in Romans 14:23 that everything that does not come from faith is sin. Moreover, Luther reasoned, in Christ we are free, and therefore, we have the freedom to serve him in a celibate state or not. It was not Luther's intention to empty the monasteries but to relieve the consciences of monastics. The question was not whether vows had to be kept but rather what was a true vow according to God. There is actually only one vow that truly counts, Luther said, and that is God's vow to us in baptism. That vow frees us from trusting in our own works and therefore frees us also from compulsory celibacy.

This treatise began with a remarkable preface: an open letter to Luther's father. Luther confessed that his father had been right to protest the way his son took monastic vows, and at that time his son had sinned against the commandment to honor his father and mother: "You are still my father, and I am your son. And all those vows are not worth a nickel. On your side stands paternal authority, on my side only human temerity."[86] From the perspective of his new insights, Luther had settled with his past and gradually restored a right relationship with his father. And in the process, he had laid a foundation for a reformation structure that would develop in various, though often unexpected ways.

7

Reformer (1521–1525)

Turbulence in Wittenberg

While Luther had to stay in the Wartburg, far from all the activities, beyond the castle everything was changing. In Switzerland, a reformation had begun under the leadership of Huldrych Zwingli (1484–1531). At the same time, civic authorities were enacting policies that manifested the practical consequences of Luther's ideas. Everywhere it gradually became visible that the Reformation was a movement of renewal and change. That also happened in Wittenberg and in such a manner that it caused Luther concern.

Since Luther was absent, Carlstadt had assumed leadership, but he was too eager. On July 19, 1521, Carlstadt published a number of theses, which among other things stated that it would be a sin if someone celebrating mass took only bread. Luther disagreed with this view, primarily from a pastoral perspective. He understood how difficult it was for someone to take wine when he or she had been brought up since childhood with the belief that wine was the blood of Christ and that only the priest was allowed to drink it.[1] Compelling people to drink wine would unnecessarily damage the conscience, as if the efficaciousness of the sacrament depended on one's drinking. Moreover, a Christian was to be free from such imposed laws. For centuries the law had forbidden the people from drinking wine at mass; now a new kind of law almost forced them to drink it.

At the end of September, the discussion about the mass came to a head. At home, Melanchthon celebrated mass with his students, using both bread and wine. In Luther's monastery, only a few doors down, the prior forbade the mass because the monks there wanted to celebrate it with both bread and wine. The elector did not want to change anything at all, not only out of conviction but also because he realized that the disappearance of the mass was going to cost him money.

From the Wartburg, Luther attempted to intervene with a treatise about the mass that he wrote in both German and Latin. He stated that the mass is not a sacrifice but a gift. The mass is not something that people do for God but something people receive from God. Mass was not about serving, since it was not something that I do but something that God does. In this writing it is clear that Luther was searching for what Christ's institution of the sacrament actually meant. That is also why he wanted another name for it too: "We can observe the mass as sacrament, or as testament, or thanksgiving, in Greek that is Eucharist, or supper of the Lord, or remembrance of the Lord, or communion, or whatever pious term that appears to be appropriate."[2]

Luther had also heard that his monastic colleague Gabriel Zwilling had preached against the mass in Wittenberg, demanding that the mass should be abolished and be replaced with the celebration of the Lord's Supper with both bread and wine. Zwilling had already developed a new liturgy, had divested himself of his monk's habit, and had begun preaching in normal clothes. As a result of his preaching, thirteen monks had left the monastery. In and of itself, there was nothing wrong with that, Luther said, but he felt that everything was going too quickly and without proper forethought. The tone of the preaching was also too aggressive. Luther heard about the situation in Wittenberg and thought that it was time to go and see everything for himself. From December 4 to 9, Luther went to Wittenberg in disguise, though someone in an inn still recognized him as the reformer.

He stayed overnight at Melanchthon's house, where the decision was made to create a German translation of the New Testament. It is telling that Luther was not dissatisfied with the situation in Wittenberg. "What I see and hear is exceptionally satisfying to me," he said,[3] even while several days earlier students armed with daggers had disrupted the celebration of mass in the City Church. However, he remained concerned how events would unfold in the coming weeks. Among the citizens and among the professors there was division; tensions were increasing.

Back at the Wartburg, Luther apparently came to the conclusion that the situation was a bit threatening and therefore wrote a short treatise in which he appealed to his readers to show consideration to the weak, while also continuing with preaching and renewal. According to him, they should begin from the inside and not the outside. People first needed to be instructed, so that they could accept change with conviction. Changes were good and also necessary, Luther held. If, however, these came not from the Word but were driven only by a desire for change, it would go awry. In *A Faithful Exhortation to All Christians to Guard against Turmoil and Anger*, he distanced himself from people who pursued extreme kinds of changes and identified their changes with him.[4] He also distanced himself from those wanting to define themselves by his name:

> People should stop using my name, and instead of calling themselves Lutheran, they should be willing to be called Christian. What is Luther? The doctrine is not mine. And I have not been crucified for anybody. . . . How would I, a bag full of maggots, come to the point that people, the children of Christ, call themselves after my unwholesome name?[5]

By the middle of December, matters escalated. The private masses were abolished, and Carlstadt celebrated mass without his priest's cassock, administering both bread and wine. Additionally, he read only the words of the institution of the sacrament and neglected the complete liturgical form. Before the mass, the celebrants had neither fasted nor done confession. They held the chalice with their own hands, and one of them had even dropped the host on the floor—shocking events that made the situation worse. Some had even broken a number of objects normally associated with the celebration of mass.

Escalation

Around the time that Luther had begun translating the Bible, the situation in Wittenberg became increasingly unruly. As it was, the changes in Wittenberg became a magnet for radical-reform-minded people. The best known were Nicholas Storch and Thomas Drechsel, cloth makers from Zwickau. This duo, who would become known as the Zwickau prophets, wanted—like many others before and after them—to realize the ideal church by abolishing everything that had to do with the organization of the church and its order. All those regulations impeded the work of the Spirit, they said. According to them, images were also such an impediment, and consequently, on January 10, they instigated the activity of violently removing all the images. Luther called them iconoclasts (*Bilderstürmerei*) and thus introduced a new and graphic concept.

Luther was strong in language. He was able to translate beautifully and rebuke powerfully. According to him, a group of people who went too far implementing the Reformation and spoke so much about the Spirit that they forgot the Word should be called *Schwärmer*, that is, hawk moth, referring to swarming, like that of bees (translated in English as "fanatics"). The goading sermons of Carlstadt and his treatise on abolishing images prompted the former Augustinian monks to bring the images and altars out of the monastery and burn them in the courtyard. Luther feared that the governing authorities would intervene the moment the Reformation began to look like a revolution. Carlstadt's sermons against academic knowledge and scholarship even prompted a large group of students to leave the university, while others had already left because of the turmoil or because their parents called them home. Luther, however, needed well-educated people to build the church and bring the Word.

The matter was further exacerbated when the prophets from Zwickau arrived. They had been influenced by, among others, Thomas Müntzer (ca. 1489–1525), who had been a priest and then a reformer but who wanted much more radical reform than Luther's (see fig. 7.1). These men, Storch and Drechsel, had come to the conclusion that infant baptism was unbiblical, that sermons and sacraments were only externals, and that the inner word of the Spirit was much more important. Together with Markus Thomae (also called Stubner), they visited Melanchthon, who was immediately impressed by their apocalyptic visions, prophetic enthusiasm, and godly inspiration. Luther heard

Figure 7.1 Thomas Müntzer monument in Zwickau at the Katharinenkirche. Photograph courtesy of Tilo Hauke (CC BY-SA 2.0).

about it and wrote on January 13 that he shouldn't allow himself to be so easily impressed, especially when it concerned infant baptism. Nowhere did the Bible say that only adults are to be baptized, but it did say that "in the time of the apostles small children were baptized."[6] Concerning the rest, Luther said that these prophets should prove that whatever God had revealed to them also agreed with everything that God had revealed in the Bible. If they could not do that, it would be clear that their vision was not from God but from Satan.

Return

At the end of January 1522, Luther decided that he had to return to Wittenberg. He could no longer stay in seclusion. He knew that the gospel did not depend on him, but he also realized that his absence from Wittenberg was causing distress. The elector advised him not to come because it was still too dangerous. Luther informed him that he, as a Christian and servant of the Word, must return. The elector was afraid that he would not be able to protect him sufficiently well, but Luther said that he did not have to be afraid of that because "my Lord Christ is more powerful than all my opponents and enemies, and if he wills, he can protect me and preserve me. And if that is not his will, also then his good will will happen."[7]

In mid-February, Luther left the Wartburg. In Jena he had an encounter with Johann Kessler, a student from St. Gallen who was traveling with his mentor to Wittenberg. In the Black Bear Inn, Kessler and his companion met a knight with a red hat, armed with a sword. The man had a booklet in front of him on the table and invited them to drink something with him; he then gave the students the advice to thoroughly study Hebrew and Greek. They in turn told him that in Wittenberg they wanted to see the man who had overturned the mass. After the man asked them what they thought of Luther in Switzerland and used a few Latin words, the students began to question whether this gentleman was an ordinary knight, especially after noticing that the book in front of him was written in Hebrew. When the innkeeper told them that the knight was Luther, they did not believe it until they actually saw him again in Wittenberg about a week later.

On March 1, 1522, Luther was back in Wittenberg. It was time to set matters straight, which he could do best by preaching. Therefore, Luther continued his task as preacher in the City Church and left his main task as professor until the summer of 1524. On March 9, he began a series of eight sermons, and because that particular Sunday was called the *invocavit* in the liturgical year, those sermons became known as the "Invocavit Sermons." In his first sermon, Luther began not with admonishing but rather with praising his audience. He told them that they had understood very well that they are children of wrath and that the work of people in itself is nothing. Those who trust in Christ receive acquittal from guilt and may be children of God. In Wittenberg they had understood these two core concepts, but that had been the limit of their understanding. The fig tree was flowering but there was still no sign of fruit.[8]

After this single sermon of reassurance, he delivered seven sermons with emphatic exhortations, instructions, and admonitions. Every day he delivered a sermon to clarify what was central to the Reformation.

In the "Invocavit Sermons," he appealed to his listeners to combine faith with love. That meant having consideration for the weak in faith and therefore not enforcing reform with compulsion. The images must be abolished, but first they should disappear from our hearts and then in the churches. Luther thus rejected iconoclasm; he believed "that images are not good or bad and that it is better to give people freedom whether they want them in their houses or not—as long as people do not believe in them or believe the delusion that we serve God with the making of images."[9] He did not approve of destroying images, and he hoped that "the iconoclasts would leave [him] a crucifix or an image of Mary . . . so [he could] wear it or see it, not to venerate but only to remember them."[10]

Luther also taught in the "Invocavit Sermons" that the Lord's Supper should be celebrated with both bread and wine but that no one should be compelled to drink from the chalice or hold the host with his or her hands: "I reject that masses are seen as sacrifices and as good works, but I am not going to forcibly go against this, and those people who do not want this, I am not going to compel."[11] Monks may abandon their monasteries, not to seek freedom but because one's conscience compels this decision. Some of the people thought that grace meant not having to do good works, so on Palm Sunday in 1523, Luther expressed his disappointment that the gospel appeared to bear such little fruit, that there was so little love and religious zeal among the people: "The longer I preach here, the worse it gets with your eating, carousing, and other sins."[12] The radicals had made the Reformation itself a goal. But for Luther, it was a means to an end—the restoration of the preaching of the pure Word.

As a result of these sermons, much of the spiritual renewal that Carlstadt had introduced was reversed. For the time being, Luther reintroduced the old format of the mass and continued to preach. Every Sunday and every holy day he preached from one of the Gospels in the morning service, and at noon he would preach from another book of the Bible. Most of these sermons have been preserved, especially because they were printed and distributed—sometimes with his consent but more often without it. To Luther's annoyance, often the printed copies of his sermons were unfaithful to the original. In any case, rest returned to Wittenberg, for which the people and city council were thankful. Out of gratitude, they rewarded Luther with an allotment of wine and beer and with material for a new habit. An unhappy Carlstadt left the city, but Luther would have to deal with him again many more times.

Bible Translation

At the Wartburg, Luther had started a work that would become his greatest literary accomplishment: the Luther Bible. At that time there were other German translations available, but these usually included only part of the Bible, and many were poor translations. Luther wanted to translate the whole Bible, and on Melanchthon's advice he began this work. The basis for his translation was the second edition of Erasmus's Greek New Testament, which had appeared in 1519.

There are at least four misunderstandings concerning Luther's translation of the Bible. In the first place, sometimes people speak about the Luther Bible as if it was his own version. On the contrary, Luther did nothing other than translate the Bible as it had always existed.

The second misunderstanding is that Luther was the first one ever to translate the Bible into German. In actual fact, there were at least eighteen German translations of the whole Bible when he began his work. The quality and success of Luther's translation, however, meant that the other eighteen translations were forgotten.

Third, it is commonly thought that Luther translated the whole Bible in the Wartburg and that when he left the castle, his translation was immediately for sale in every bookstore. In the Wartburg he completed the New Testament, but he did not wrap up the Old Testament until after he returned to Wittenberg. For the rest of his life he continued revising his translation. The Bible was never truly "finished."

The fourth misunderstanding is the belief that Luther's Bible translation brought uniformity to the German language. That process had started already before Luther. However, he did indeed have an enormous influence and was instrumental in developing new words that spread to other Germanic tongues, such as Dutch.

Luther continued his preoccupation with the Bible because he believed that it was essential for every person to be able to read and hear Scripture as clearly as possible. God himself "lives" in the Bible, "and therefore, worthy Christian: get in, get in!"[13] Luther believed that Christians must be engaged with the Bible. They must dig deeply into the Bible and become buried in it. Luther was convinced that he would have remained in error if he had not been continually working closely in the Bible.[14]

The plan to translate the Bible began when Luther had visited Wittenberg secretly for a week in the beginning of December. Eleven weeks later, the New Testament was already finished. Luther, however, needed the expertise of Melanchthon on some Greek concepts; the revisions would have to happen in Wittenberg. "On my Patmos," Luther noted, "I translated not only the Gospel according to John but the whole New Testament. Now Philipp and I have begun revising and fine-tuning. If God wills, it will become a beautiful work." In response to a request from Spalatin, Luther committed to "use simple words and not the vocabulary spoken in the court or in the surroundings of the elector. Simplicity, namely, should be the hallmark of this book."[15] Spalatin had gemstones from the elector's treasury delivered to him so that he could see with his own eyes the colors of the gems mentioned in Revelation 21. In September 1522, the first printing came off the press, and for that reason it is often called the "September Testament." The price was comparable to an average week's wages—not cheap but affordable. Luther did not ask for any royalties and was not offered any by the printers either, though they earned a good return on his work. Luther was annoyed, however, that as the author he did not get enough free copies.

It is striking that in Luther's publication the table of contents mentions separately the letter to the Hebrews, the letters of Jude and James, and the book of Revelation and that they do not have their own page numbers. Luther apparently wondered about the canonicity of these books. He was certain that the letter of James wasn't canonical. "If it is something that does not teach Christ," he reasoned, "it is not apostolic, even if Peter or Paul were to teach it. Once again, apostolic is only that which Christ teaches, even if Judas, Annas, Pilate, or Herod does that."[16] When Luther speaks about "what Christ teaches" (in which

Christ is the one teaching, not the one taught about), he means words that Christ taught in a way that Luther learned to know him. Luther made his theological insights normative for what belonged or did not belong in the Bible. In doing so, he at least gave the impression that he did the same thing he accused the pope of doing.

The book of Revelation was illustrated with twenty-one woodcuts made by Lucas Cranach, in which it was clear who, according to Cranach, the harlot, the dragon, and Babylon were. The publication was a great success. The first printing, apparently three thousand copies, sold out within two months, so that by December a new printing was released.

Old Testament

In the meantime, Luther had begun translating the Old Testament:

> In my translation work of the Old Testament, I have come to Leviticus. It is, in fact, unimaginable how much writing letters, issues, social responsibilities, and many other things have delayed me. But now I have decided to lock myself up at home and make haste, so that before the end of January the books of Moses can go to the printer. We will publish them separately, after that the Historical Books, and then, at last, the Prophets. The size and the price of these books compel us to publish them one by one.[17]

The first section, with the five books of Moses, came out around mid-1523, while the second section, with the books of Joshua through Esther, appeared on December 4, 1523. The third part was considerably more difficult because of the book of Job. Since they couldn't progress as quickly, a section was published in the fall of 1524 containing the books from Job to the Song of Solomon:

> We are doing our best to translate the Prophets into German. God, what a huge and tiring task this is to force the Hebrew writers to speak German. They do not want to abandon their Hebrew singularity to follow the barbarian German. It is something like the nightingale, who, after she has forsaken her lovely manner of singing, is forced to imitate the cuckoo, while she abhors its monotonous call.[18]

Luther had great appreciation for the Hebrew language:

> The Hebrew language is the best and the richest in words. She is pure and does not beg. She has her own color. Greek, Latin, and German have many composite words, while the Hebrew language does not have one. . . . The Hebrew language is simpler than other languages, and yet it is majestic and beautiful, simple and made of few words, but there is much hidden behind them, and no one can imitate that.[19]

Not until 1532 were the translations of the Prophets published. Appropriate to his less than modest character, Luther wrote that his translation of the Prophets was the best one that ever appeared.[20] Subsequently, Luther began the translation of the Apocrypha, but that task ended up being more challenging than he expected. He completed part of it and left the rest for others, not least because he did not consider these books as important as the Bible itself. Therefore, the 1534 publication received the title *Apocrypha: Are books that are not held equal to the Sacred Scriptures and yet are useful and good for reading*. In September 1534, twelve years after the publication of the New Testament, the complete translation appeared with 117 woodcuts, some of which were made under Luther's direction. In addition, this translation included an introduction to each book of the Bible and marginal notes that offered a complete profile of Luther's theology. This translation became a best seller and a lucrative project for the Wittenberg printers. In 1543, they were the three richest people in the city. Luther himself did not earn anything from this and did not want to earn anything: "Because I received it without cost, I am giving it away free of cost, and I do not want anything for it either. Christ, my Lord, has repaid me more than a hundred-thousand-fold."[21]

During Luther's lifetime alone, Wittenberg produced ninety-one printings of the whole Bible or parts of it. Despite warnings against the Luther Bible from ecclesiastical and political authorities, 253 editions were published outside Wittenberg. In total, during Luther's lifetime, half a million copies were sold, for that time an unimaginably large number. Luther continued to revise his translation and thus reworked the Psalms, for example, "so that David would speak better German."[22]

The last printing that Luther oversaw was the tenth, which appeared in 1545. To prevent illegal printings, official printings included two authenticating illustrations: the Luther rose and a lamb bearing the sign of the cross. Apparently, this safeguard was insufficient, because from 1541, Luther added a threat directed at unauthorized potential printers warning them of God's judgment against greed.

Commentaries

As concerns the interpretation of the Bible, Luther was convinced that the Word of God on its own was clear enough and that therefore it was unnecessary to have the position of a pope to determine how the Bible should be read. For Luther it was clear that

> the Bible itself is perfectly sure, easy to understand, clear, and open, and is her own interpreter [*sui ipsius interpres*], to test, to direct, and to enlighten through all human contentions, as is written in Psalm 119:130—*"The unfolding of your words gives light; it gives understanding to the simple."*[23]

The clarity of the German Bible did not mean that it was always clear what was in the Hebrew or Greek text. The Catholics viciously attacked Luther's Bible translation because in many cases he had not translated literally or had not stayed closely to the original text. That same criticism had been leveled since the appearance of his New Testament in 1522. Duke George of Saxony seized every copy he could lay his hands on. Jerome Emser published a list of approximately 1,400 Bible texts that Luther had translated incorrectly. Emser published his own translation, but shortly after its appearance, he confessed that it was a revision of Luther's translation. In Catholic circles, Emser's Bible had gone through at least thirty-eight reprints, so until the eighteenth century, many German Catholics, without realizing it, were using Luther's translation.

When others also said that Luther had been too free, specifically with his translation of Romans 3:28 (where he added the word "alone" to the phrase "justified by faith"), Luther felt it was time to respond. He published a booklet about translation and discussed how essential it was for him to be involved with God's Word. He quickly dispensed with Catholic criticism. It was evident that when criticism came from Catholics, he found it difficult to respond substantively: "It is my testament, and that is the way it should stay." For those who were not satisfied with that defense, he also added, "I can explain the Psalms and the Prophets, and they can't do that. I can translate; they can't." When he was asked why he translated so freely, his answer was quite simple: "Because Dr. Martin Luther wants to do it that way." That was also his argument concerning the word "alone," though it was not found in the original Bible text: Luther wanted it that way, and as doctor, he stood above all the doctors of the papacy—"and that is where we will leave it."[24]

In response to those who stood on his side, he was willing to explain how he had worked out his translation, noting that those who now read the Bible hardly had a clue how difficult this task was:

> Yes, my dear friend, now that it is translated and prepared in German, everyone can read and understand it. With your eyes you now can go through three, four pages without faltering, but then you don't notice the stones and lumps that were lying there. Like going over a nicely planed board, you pass over the places where we sat and sweated and asked ourselves anxiously how we could remove those stones and lumps so that access would be freed and you could easily pass over them. It's easy plowing when the field has been cleaned. But no one wants to begin clearing the forest and stumps to prepare the field.[25]

One of the hefty tomes of Luther's works includes a collection of short texts that Luther handwrote in the front of Bibles.[26] Those texts were taken from more than three hundred copies of Bibles that were saved, originally belonging to people who went to Luther with their copy and asked him to write something in them. Those texts reveal much about Luther and especially what the Word of God meant to him.

Politics

Gradually, Luther became more significant politically. George of Saxony especially did everything in his power to make sure that the decision concerning Luther would be implemented. In reaction to George's decision to confiscate all the copies of Luther's Bible translation, Luther wrote about the limits of secular authority, in *Concerning the Secular Authority and How Far They Must Be Obeyed*.[27] The ideas Luther formulated in this volume would eventually develop into what is now called a "two kingdoms" theology. The Christian lives in two kingdoms, according to Luther: the kingdom of the world and kingdom of Christ. The secular kingdom has power over external matters but not over the heart and soul. As a member of Christ's kingdom, I am free, but as a citizen of the world, I am bound to the laws of the government. The secular kingdom is ruled by the sword to restrain the sinful, unregenerate citizens who live there. Consequently, it cannot be ruled using the principles of love and forgiveness, because the world would become unlivable. Christians actually do not need laws but must live by civic laws on account of their unbelieving neighbors.

George paid no attention to this treatise and continued his efforts to negate Luther's impact, though he was constantly countered by the protection Elector Frederick provided Luther. The difficulty in dealing with Luther was related to the way Germany was divided politically. During Luther's time, Germany appeared politically like a colorful patchwork quilt, consisting of approximately 350 larger and smaller duchies, principalities, imperial cities, abbeys, and other kinds of territories ruled by an equal number of ecclesiastical and secular rulers. Only the most important ones among them could determine the kingship, but all the territories could make their own choice whether they would join the Reformation or continue their association with the church of Rome. For some the choice in favor of the Reformation was prompted by a desire for more independence, but many noblemen and rulers made their choice on religious grounds.

In any case, Luther was invited to come to different cities to preach so that he could teach the people about the new doctrine. From April 25 to March 6, 1523, he made a tour, going to Borno, Altenberg, Zwickau, and Torgau. The sermons, most of which have been preserved, dealt with well-known topics, such as good works, marriage, and infant baptism. This tour meant the end of the *stabilitas loci*, the basic principle that a monk stayed (*stabilitas*) in the place (*loci*) where he was. This would be the beginning of Luther's years of extensive travel to support and explain his doctrines. His point of departure usually remained that the local community should take the initiative. What he meant by that Luther explained in *The Right and Power of a Christian Assembly to Judge All Teaching and to Call, Appoint, and Dismiss Teachers, Established and Proven by Scripture.*[28] Judgment concerning doctrine belongs to the members of the congregation, not to priests or rulers. Cooperation with the local bishop was possible, but if the bishop declined, members of the congregation would have to take their own initiative. The congregation has the right to judge the preaching, as well as the right to call a preacher or depose him. This advice was eagerly received, so much so that Luther could say that already Christ was ruling in many places.[29] Luther also mentioned a desire to hear God's Word in Bremen, Hamburg, and Friesland.[30]

In Magdeburg, the city of the bishop, which had an imposing cathedral, the situation threatened to get out of hand. The city council demanded reformation, but citizens responded by attacking clerics who did not want to cooperate. The city quickly called on Luther to help. He arrived on June 24, 1523, and was lodged in the Augustinian monastery. Three times he preached in St. John's Church, and the riots were restrained. Together with the city council and representatives of the church, Luther made arrangements to write a new church order. On Luther's advice, Nicholas von Amsdorf was installed to carefully carry out the objectives of the Reformation, a task he enjoyed so much that he would persist in it for eighteen years.

In Wittenberg itself, a team of colleagues had formed around Luther that would work together to shape Luther's theology in the coming years. In March 1521, Johannes Bugenhagen (1485–1558), originally a humanistic teacher, arrived in Wittenberg (see fig. 7.2). His experience in teaching was very useful, and he could both study and teach. In 1523, he was appointed as preacher in the City Church and thus became Luther's pastor. In the summer of 1521, Justus Jonas arrived in Wittenberg from Erfurt to teach canon law. Some students remained after completing their studies to become teachers as well, such as Caspar Cruciger and George Major. Together with Melanchthon and Spalatin and a number of assistants, there was a considerable group that supported Luther.

Figure 7.2 *Portrait of Johannes Bugenhagen* (1485–1558). Painting by Lucas Cranach the Elder, 1537. Lutherhaus Wittenberg, Wittenberg.

International

Luther had become a problem for the church and for politicians, but he had also become famous throughout Europe. Johannes Dantiscus, a Polish ambassador, had been in Spain for some time and in 1523 stayed for three days in Wittenberg on his return journey. Already at that time, it seemed to him a kind of Protestant Rome: "You would almost think that if you've been in Rome and not seen the pope, and in Wittenberg and not seen Luther, you've not seen anything."[31] Luther was an attraction and an international consultant. Questions for advice and support came from France and the Netherlands. Luther responded with letters of comfort for those who suffered persecution for the sake of the Reformation, but he did not have a program for reform, believing instead that the Word of God would provide everything they needed to figure things out properly.

That did not mean that all would go well with those who wanted to follow the Word as taught by Luther. The first martyrs of the Reformation were from the Netherlands. They were confronted with the unmerciful action of authorities allied to Rome. According to Luther, God would not ignore that. The reformer had heard that

> in the Netherlands the minions of the emperor, those deluded sages, persecuted that same gospel with an unbelievable rage. But God has given them a sign of his judgment, so that perhaps they may come to insight and repentance. Near Harlem a sea monster washed up, a whale seventy feet long and thirty-five feet wide. According to a century's old tradition such a miracle is a sure sign of God's wrath; may the Lord have mercy on them and us.[32]

Despite the announcement of God's wrath, Luther was very concerned about his Augustinian brothers, especially when the monastery in Antwerp was closed amid accusations of pro-Luther preaching. In the spring of 1518, Luther's writings were already for sale in Antwerp. Jacob Praepositus (1486–1562), the prior of the monastery in this city, was very interested and decided to visit Luther in Wittenberg. After his return, Praepositus preached openly against indulgences and held up Christ as the only sacrifice for sins. This resulted in his arrest. Luther stated, "Jacob, the prior in Antwerp, has again been arrested. They think that he and two others with him have already been burned. It had been established as a given, namely that he would be killed because he refused to recant."[33] After his imprisonment, Praepositus openly retracted these beliefs in early 1523 but again preached in the spirit of Luther after his release, no more to return to Antwerp. In August 1522, the correspondence of Wessel Gansfort (1419–1489), who came from Zwolle in the Netherlands, was published. Luther wrote the preface for this publication explaining that before him there had already been witnesses of the gospel.

Hendrik Voes and John van Essen were two witnesses from Antwerp who were burned alive at the stake in the Great Market of Brussels on July 1, 1523, because of their Lutheran convictions. When Luther received news concerning these first Protestant martyrs, "he began to cry within himself and said, 'I thought that I had to be the first one who would have to die the martyr death on account of this gospel, but I have not been counted worthy of it.'"[34] Subsequently, he wrote a letter to "All Dear Brothers in Christ, So in Holland, Brabant, and Flanders"[35] and the song "A New Song We Are Raising."[36] The first stanza reads as follows:[37]

A new song we sing,
It rises up to God, the Lord,
We sing about what he has done
To his praise and honor.
In Brussels, in the Netherlands,
Through two young men has he
Made known his wonders;
He has adorned them richly,
With the most beautiful gifts.

In another stanza of this song, Luther wrote that Satan's persecutions were evidence that the Word of God was winning. He was not surprised that people were put to death, only that they were willing to endure death though given the opportunity to retract or live as a Nicolaitan. This song was an encouragement to a third Augustinian, Lambert Thorn, who was imprisoned and to whom Luther wrote a letter of encouragement.[38]

The fanaticism exercised against his followers made Luther concerned about his own safety: "Plans are being made to burn me as well. I irritate Satan and his mob every day, however, so that the day of Christ, who will destroy the Antichrist, will come more quickly."[39] A different sound came from England in July 1521, where King Henry VIII published his booklet defending the doctrine of seven sacraments (*Assertio septem sacramentorum*). As a result, the pope honored him with a unique distinction. But he also received a fierce attack from Luther, who had finally heard about this booklet in June 1522. Because Duke George was at this time promoting a German translation of Henry's work, Luther opposed it vigorously in his writing and showed absolutely no respect for Henry, calling him "that lying king of England." Luther did not want to enter into all the details of those sacraments because Henry had not based his arguments on the Bible. The main question, Luther wrote, was whether the mass was a sacrifice brought by people to God or a sign from God to people. Is the mass a good work or a word of grace?[40]

Luther's opponents and some of his allies alike believed that he had been too vehement in his opposition to Henry, and some suggested that he would probably have achieved more if he had exercised some tact.

Luther saw it differently: “Pope, bishop, priest, monk, kings, rulers, Devil, death, sin, and everything that is not Christ or in Christ must give way for the gospel that I, Martin Luther, have preached, and they will all suffer loss. Nothing and no one can help that.”[41] It had become his gospel, and he quickly assumed that criticism directed against Martin Luther was criticism of the gospel. This made him vulnerable, increasingly more unmanageable, and certainly militant. He wasn’t going to step aside for any pope.

As it stood, Pope Leo X, the man of the excommunication bull, had died December 1, 1521. After him there was actually some hope of restoration when the Dutchman Adriaan Floriszn Boeyens (1459–1523) was chosen as pope on August 3, 1522, called Adrian VI. The new pope wanted renewal, but his papacy was too short lived to accomplish anything. He died little more than a year later, on December 14, 1523, and was succeeded by Clement VII. The latter pope was uninterested in what was happening in Germany.

Visitation

Elector Frederick, who remained Catholic and cautious in implementing reform, died on May 5, 1525. On his deathbed he still celebrated the Lord’s Supper—on his request, with both bread and chalice. Luther was asked to preach at the commemoration service and at the funeral. His first meeting with the elector was also his last, and even then, with a dead elector.

Frederick’s successor was John the Steadfast (1468–1532; r. 1525–1532). He took firmer control and tried to reorganize the church and society. The monasteries had emptied, and many monks had married, but significant areas of social service had disappeared. Education also needed to be renewed. Elector John’s greatest concern, however, was the affairs of the church. Priests who had become ministers needed to be reeducated, and the councils and finances of the churches and of her ministers needed to be regulated. Luther and Melanchthon heard that some ministers had used the Reformation’s message of grace so they could continue their immoral lifestyle. Other preachers had not completely understood what Luther meant when he said that we are not saved by good works. They told their congregations that good works were even dangerous for their eternal salvation, a message that empowered the antinomianism of some. This indicated that it was time for Luther to visit the churches.

Luther was personally in favor of maintaining the independence of the local church, but he realized that the circumstances called for leadership. This suggestion was well received because for many centuries politics had gone head-to-head with the power of the church. As a result, a church structure evolved—the *landesherrliche Kirchenregiment*, or "land ruler church government"—in which the local ruler became a kind of director, an "emergency bishop." Beginning in 1539, Wittenberg formed a consistory, an idea that other cities copied as well. This consistory, however, was made up not of elders but of some officers, a minister, and a number of deacons, and it was responsible only for the organization of the church. This organization appeared to be more like a board of directors than a church council. Luther did not object, especially since he believed that Christ's return would happen during his lifetime anyway. He did, though, have clear directions for the regulation of church affairs:

> Making a law is truly a great and dangerous task, because without God's Spirit it will not yield anything positive. Therefore, to maintain a proper balance, this should happen in the fear of the Lord, and in humility before God. Short and effective, few laws but suitable ones, and then slowly but surely continue.[42]

Marriage

Luther's impact resulted in a massive emptying of the monasteries. His new insights on faith and grace also meant that compulsory celibacy for the clergy had to be discontinued. The reform-minded needed to reappraise and reappreciate marriage between men and women. For centuries it was believed that those who chose a life without marriage could serve God and the church much better than those who married. Moreover, sexuality was viewed as sinful and depraved, even within marriage. Therefore, those who sought to avoid sin were advised to avoid marriage. The best solution was to enter the monastery. Taking holy orders was seen like a second baptism, which provided a huge claim to grace. Luther's view on grace, however, meant a direct attack on the principles of celibacy and monasticism, and consequently, an upward appreciation of marriage and sexuality:

> Whoever is ashamed of marriage, is ashamed to be human and creates the impression that one can do a better job than the way God created it. Adam's children continue to be people and therefore must also bring forth children. . . . It's the god of this world, the Devil, therefore, who has demeaned marriage and made it into a shame.[43]

This new perspective also generated so many questions that Luther wrote to Bucer, "I have so many matters and issues pressing upon me, and then especially those concerning marriage and the priesthood, that I am hardly able to address all of them."[44] Not only had compulsory celibacy been too hard for many people, but for decades also the complex regulations in canon law were generally unclear and often impossible to follow with regard to consanguinity and valid engagements. In his treatise *The Estate of Marriage,* Luther addressed all these issues and discussed what would change in this area if marriage and sexuality were approached from a biblical perspective instead of a traditional one. This resulted in an increased appreciation for the position of women, restoration of honor for parents (since children would again be expected to request permission from their parents to marry), and a massive purging of all kinds of laws and regulations.

In other works he also responded to practical questions, such as the position of nuns and monks. Luther had three objections against monasticism. First, monasticism conflicted with faith because life as a monk or nun signaled a trust in poverty, chastity, and obedience rather than in God's grace. Second, monastic life conflicted with the universal command to love one's neighbor, because in a monastery that love was restricted to other monks or nuns. Third, Luther considered that monasticism conflicted with the biblical concept of freedom for all Christian people, because life in a monastery was regulated by rules and regulations made by people, not by God.

Concerning celibacy, Luther had also discovered clarity: "You have read in the Bible that it says that it is not good for a man to be alone. Not for nothing did God make two kinds of people."[45] When people heard that monasticism could possibly conflict with God's Word and that it would be better to get married rather than enter holy orders, thousands of nuns and monks abandoned their monasteries. Everywhere they heard what Luther had to say on this issue, including those in the cloister where Katharina von Bora (1499–1552) lived (see fig. 7.3).

Katharina

Luther's future wife was born in 1499 in Lippendorf, a small town near Leipzig. Very little is known about her youth. Her name indicates that she had roots in the landed gentry, but by that time the nobility had lost much of its property and esteem. When she was six years old, she lost her mother, after which her father brought her to the Benedictine cloister Brehna, near Bitterfeld. Her experience was like many daughters of noble origin, as well as children who were orphaned or partially orphaned. Enrollment in a monastery was free, and the monks or nuns provided clothing, shelter, and even education. That was seen as an ideal solution. Sometimes family members placed children in a monastery because they wanted to eliminate a number of heirs. Since monastics were not allowed to own property, they would not demand anything when an inheritance had to be divided.

In 1509, Katharina, at the age of ten, moved to the Cistercian monastery Marienthron, in the vicinity of Nimbschen. Perhaps it was comforting to her that the only sister of her father, Aunt Magdalena, also lived in that monastic community. In 1515, Katharina took her vows as nun, and so it appeared that at a fairly young age, the doors to her parental home and to the rest of the world were shut. The next eight years would be filled with singing, praying, reading, and silence. These were the same years that Luther also lived in a monastery, though he entered a bit earlier, in 1505, when he took vows in Erfurt. The following eighteen years were certainly more turbulent for him than for Katharina. Not until 1523 is anything more known of her.

Escaped

The nuns in Nimbschen also heard about the turbulence surrounding Luther, and despite their vows of silence, they eagerly shared his mes-

Figure 7.3 *Portrait of Katharina von Bora* (1499–1552). Painting by Lucas Cranach the Elder, 1526. Private collection.

sage with others. Some of the nuns did not appreciate Luther's doctrines, but many were enthusiastic about his views. It was unclear in any event what they could do with this knowledge. Leaving the cloister was difficult from a practical perspective, but even more distressing would have been the breaking of their vows. The latter was seen as a grave sin.

Luther had been made aware of the fact that a number of the nuns wanted to leave the cloister, and therefore, he cooperated with Leonhard Koppe from Torgau to develop a plan to help these women escape. Koppe was a merchant, and he also made deliveries to the monastery. On April 4, 1523, he brought a load of goods to the monastery. But this time he also took a lading of goods back from the monastery, namely, twelve nuns, nine of which ended up going to Wittenberg. As Luther wrote on April 8, "Yesterday I received nine nuns from their imprisonment at the monastery in Nimbschen."[46] The other three nuns could immediately go to family members. The story that they were taken in empty herring barrels is remarkable but probably a little too sensational to be true, though Koppe did often take back empties from the monastery. It is true that after this escape, Luther wrote a public letter and admitted, "I am the spiritual bandit who rescued these poor souls from human tyranny."[47] The fact that this activity took place on the eve of Easter was fitting, "because it was then that Christ delivered his own from prison."[48] Luther mentioned right away that as far as he was concerned, this did not have to be a once-only event: "If God would allow it, I would free all imprisoned consciences and empty out all the monasteries, in a similar or in another fashion."[49] And indeed, in September 1525, Luther would repeat this action by helping thirteen more nuns escape. As for the first group of nuns from Nimbschen who arrived in 1523, Spalatin asked Luther what he was going to do with them. Luther answered,

> I will first inform their families and ask if they will take them in. If they refuse, I will try my best to find accommodation for them. Several people have already offered. If possible, I would also like to marry a few off. The escaped nuns are called: Magdalena von Staupitz, Elsa von Kanitz, Ave Gross, Ave Schönfeld and her sister Margaretha, Laneta von Golis, Margaretha Zeschau and her sister Katharina, as well as Katharina von Bora. They are in such poor condition that they certainly deserve our help: the help we offer them is a service to Christ. In the meantime, they have been saved in a most wonderful fashion.[50]

Of the nine nuns who ended up in Wittenberg, none could be reunited with their families, either because they didn't have any or because their family lived in areas that remained Catholic, jeopardizing the nuns' safety. Nevertheless, Luther felt responsible for these ladies, and so it happened that the nun called Katharina von Bora came to live with the family of the jurist Philip Reichenbach and worked as a housemaid for the already famous and wealthy painter Lucas Cranach and his wife, Barbara. The painter was not only a good artist but also a good businessman, owning a printshop and an apothecary. There were constantly student painters in the house, and people came from near and far to visit; Katharina was exposed to an entirely different world. At this time she was twenty-four years old. For eight years she had had to practice silence but had not lost the ability to speak. She was soon well known for her outspokenness, even sometimes addressed as "Katharina von Siena," a reference to the fourteenth-century saint Catherine of Siena, who had apparently used her verbal forcefulness to exercise influence on popes and rulers.

Marriage

Luther believed that the best outcome would be to find appropriate husbands for the nuns. In this time marriage was often the only economic stability offered to women, and the nuns had neither family nor money. By the end of 1524, he had found husbands for most of the nuns. "There is one, however, whom I cannot get rid of," Luther wrote.

> Her name is Katharina von Bora, a young, noble woman who was brought to the monastery as a child. She's a zesty lady, and she is "proud and snooty." I would not know "what devil would want her." She's living in the house of Cranach, helps well, but she is very conspicuous because of her mouthpiece. I have a candidate for her, but if she doesn't want him, it will take a lot of time before another one comes along.[51]

At one point it looked like a fitting husband had been found, after, in Melanchthon's house, she made the acquaintance of Jerome Baumgärtner. This young man came from Nuremburg, the son of a leading citizen. Katharina and Jerome liked each other, but Baumgärtner's father recalled his son, possibly fearing the social cost of becoming the father-in-law of an ex-nun. Luther did not let the matter rest and a year later wrote a letter to Jerome: "If you still want Käthe von Bora, you will have to be fast before I give her to someone else who is waiting. Moreover, her love for you has not abated."[52]

It turned out to be a lost cause; there was no response from Nuremburg. The person who was waiting in the wings, according to Luther's letter, was Dr. Glatz. He wanted Katharina, but she did not want him. She still loved Jerome, and moreover, she did not find Glatz attractive. Nevertheless, she was moved that Luther had put so much effort into finding someone for her. She also realized her lack of income meant she needed a match quickly. Therefore, in March 1525, she took a somewhat unconventional initiative. Via Luther's friend Nicholas von Amsdorf, she informed Luther that he shouldn't bother her any longer with Glatz and that she was willing to marry either von Amsdorf or Luther. Luther was taken aback by this proposal, especially because he had not given marriage any consideration. Whenever he was asked why he didn't get married, he would reply that marriage was not for him. Of course he felt "carnal" interests, but since he saw "death and the deserved punishment for heresy before [his] eyes everyday," he believed marriage was unwise.[53]

There were factors, however, that made marriage for Luther quite desirable. In the first place, for many years he had maintained that marriage was a positive good and had tirelessly promoted the marriage of nuns and monks. Increasingly, many more people were asking why he didn't get married. The second reason was his father's wish. When his son had entered the monastery, his hope for posterity disappeared. Becoming a patriarch had become a bit more of a possibility after October 31, 1517, but if this hope was to become reality, his son would first need to have a wife. Satisfying his father was therefore a good reason to marry. At the end of April 1525, Luther visited his parents in Mansfeld, and they again encouraged him to get married. Luther could defend his marriage by appealing to the command to honor his father and mother.[54]

The third and most important reason was driven by the turmoil that engulfed the German Republic in 1525. Often called the German Peasants' Revolt, the name is somewhat problematic. It was not a revolt, it was not only peasant farmers who caused grief, and it did not take place only in Germany. In any case, laborers, peasant farmers, and other ordinary people who had embraced the Reformation and Luther's new views on freedom also saw in it a way to finally free themselves from unjust economic and social constraints, including high taxes. After peaceful protests failed to accomplish anything, they rebelled, for which Luther was blamed. Luther saw a great danger for the gospel. What Luther had meant by "freedom" had been twisted by leaders of the revolt, and Luther believed he saw the work of Satan in it. Though he initially had some understanding for the plight of the protesters, he did not want his message equated with revolution.

Luther chose the side of the rulers, and even suggested that they could "earn" heaven by killing a peasant here or there, a message the authorities took to heart.[55] But now, Luther felt the blood of the peasants on his conscience. He concluded that the Devil was trying to drive away all joy in his life.

Trying to defy the Devil, Luther considered getting married, assuming that marriage would make him happy. He perceived a nearing unhappy end: "Now then, when I am home again, with God's help I will prepare for death and await my new lord, that robber and murderer." But before that, he wanted to do something else: "If I can make it happen, I will defy the Devil by taking my Käthe in marriage before I die."[56] Because of the Peasants' Revolt, he was threatened by death on all sides and wanted to marry "so that at the end, I will be in the same state as when God created me, and as a result there will be absolutely nothing left of my papist life."[57] As there were arguments in favor of marriage, there were also arguments against getting married. As a married monk, wouldn't he be the target of mockery, and wouldn't they reproach him with the accusation that the ultimate purpose of his reform was so that he could get married? Also, here it is clear that Luther was looking for the best solution, seeking a way in which he could serve the concerns of the gospel. In his analysis, the "pro" arguments were much stronger than the "contra" arguments. He was aware of the mockery, and that would come too.

Käthe

Katharina became his choice, though Luther initially thought her arrogant and too outspoken. Apparently, others thought that as well; when he announced that he wanted to marry Katharina, his friends urgently advised that he should marry not her but someone else. Shortly before the wedding day, Luther himself said, "I do not love my wife, but I do appreciate her."[58] A somewhat bizarre sentiment to start a marriage with and not really nice to read, but the feeling did not last long, as is evident from the way Luther spoke about and to Katharina throughout their marriage.

Despite the advice of friends and Luther's lack of love, the ex-monk and ex-nun had their marriage solemnized in June 1525. The ceremony took place in the customary fashion. On June 13, at five o'clock in the afternoon, the bridal couple, family, and friends came together. Luther and Katharina made their vows, pastor Bugenhagen solemnized the marriage with prayer, and subsequently the "sleep in" took place in the presence of the wedding party and several guests. This seems to be a somewhat strange way to begin a marriage, but it was formally acceptable at the time. The bride and bridegroom, fully dressed, would lie down on the marriage bed in the presence of witnesses, and then, absolutely nothing else happened. By means of this activity, the marriage was official.

Two weeks later, following a public church service, public festivities were held. These events were postponed to June 27 so that family and acquaintances from outside Wittenberg could also attend. Luther's father and mother came, as well as Leonhard Koppe, Katharina's "kidnapper." Additionally, Lucas Cranach and his wife were present as witnesses, along with Johann Apel (who had recently married a nun as well), Justus Jonas, and Johannes Bugenhagen. From the city council Luther received twenty guilders to pay for the party. From Elector John the Steadfast, Luther even received one hundred guilders to set up house. Nevertheless, the party celebrations were modest. There had been criticism about this marriage. Some thought it was inappropriate to marry and party in such times of war and trouble. Others thought that with this marriage, Luther had succumbed to carnal love. Melanchthon was offended and further felt that the timing, namely, in the middle of the Peasants' Revolt, was totally unfitting. He was also of the opinion that Luther had allowed himself to be enticed by a former nun. But since it was now an accomplished fact, he hoped that this marriage would have a calming influence on Luther. As it turned out, that hope was in vain.

At first Luther enjoyed married life, especially the first weeks, called the "pillow weeks," in accordance with an old tradition in which the husband and wife would share one pillow. It was an adjustment for Luther to wake up and see two pigtails lying beside him.[59] He enjoyed it, as he indicated in a letter to Spalatin. He had been unable to attend Spalatin's wedding, but he did advise him to intimately wrap his arms around his wife in the marriage bed and kiss her passionately. In the meantime Spalatin was instructed to think, "Look at this person, the most beautiful little creature from God that Christ has given me. To him be all praise and honor." And then Luther would think and do the same on Spalatin's wedding day.[60]

In the end Luther was unimpressed with the criticism he received:

> I have silenced those who want to give Katharina and me a bad name. . . . Through this marriage I have made myself so disgusting and worthy of such contempt that I may hope that all the angels laugh and all the devils cry. The world and their sages do not understand this godly and holy work; indeed, because of me personally, they present it as godless and devilish. Therefore, it makes me feel really good that my marriage condemns and insults the opinion of those who continue with their ignorance of God's will.[61]

With his marriage Luther wanted to be an example. He continued to live in the monastery in Wittenberg, commonly called the Black Cloister:

> I myself live now like a normal family man, but I will continue to live in the monastery as long as Christ wills. Because I did not take a wife as if I still wanted to live for a long time (I even believe that my end is imminent, especially when I notice how the rulers and the people are haranguing me), but for the sake of the weak in faith, I wanted to leave my teaching, emphatically reinforced by my example—teaching that will soon be suppressed after my death.[62]

Lady of the House

The marriage between professor Luther and the sixteen-year-younger Katharina von Bora was a fact. From this time, Luther spoke only of his Käthe, an affectionate nickname, but his feelings did little to assuage the terrible financial hardship of the young couple. Luther had an annual wage of about eight guilders, and Katharina did not earn anything. They did receive many wedding presents, not all of which were obviously beneficial. For example, from the burgomaster of Wittenberg, they received a barrel of beer, and from the university, a silver beaker—an appropriate combination. Albrecht, the archbishop of Mainz, of all people, was in a somewhat reformed mindset again and gave the bridal couple twenty guilders, equal to two and a half years of salary for Luther. The gift was the occasion that led to their first marriage crisis, because Luther did not want to accept a gift from the man who had been instrumental in the sale of indulgences through Tetzel and who had Luther placed under the ban of excommunication. He demanded that the twenty guilders be sent back. Käthe was wiser and resolutely had no reservation about accepting money from her husband's opponents. Without Luther's knowledge, she made sure that the money remained in the family finances.

By living with Luther, Käthe had once again taken residence in a monastery. Their dwelling was a long, stretched building with narrow cells meant for the monks and only a few larger rooms for gatherings and meals. There was a brewery, as was the case with most monasteries. On the one side of the monastery, next to the chapel, was the graveyard, and on the other side, the city moat. In one of those cells, Luther had lived all those years (at least as far as one may call such an arrangement "living"). He himself said, "Before I was married, I did not make my bed for more than a year so that the straw was soaked with my sweat. I worked terribly hard from early morning to late at night, and then, dead tired, I would fall into my bed so that I didn't notice anything."[63] Elector Frederick the Wise had decided, while he was deathly ill, that Luther should receive the monastery and its gardens. He made the condition that if Luther wanted to sell it, Frederick would have the first right to buy it. John the Steadfast, with whom Luther had personal contact, confirmed this gift when he succeeded Frederick in 1525. Thus the monastery could grow into the Luther house that is still there today.

Käthe was immediately immersed in work. She had a wash facility built and took measures to counter the moisture from the adjacent moat. She herself turned over the soil in the graveyard and made a vegetable garden. Additionally, she had stalls built for livestock, including pigs, cows, goats, and chickens. After several years, Luther's salary was increased from eight to one hundred guilders. With the extra money, Käthe bought a property, called Zuhlsdorf, that had formerly belonged to her family. As a result of this purchase, Luther would address her in his letters as "Her Majesty, Lady Katharina von Bora and

Zuhlsdorf, My Sweetheart." Or in another letter, "To the Domina, brewer, gardener, and whatever else she can do." It was obvious to Luther that he had gained a valuable wife: "I am not passionately in love, but I love my wife and appreciate her tremendously."[64] This appreciation was noticeable in the salutations of Luther's letters. He would begin with all kinds of epithets: "my Käthe," "my chain," "my rib," "my Eve," "my boss," "my Moses," "my hog dealer," "my minister," "my brewer," "my sweetheart," "my morning star."

His appreciation for the woman who had become lord of his house was not entirely consistent with Luther's view of women in general, a view that is indicated in Luther's own words: "Weeds grow quickly; that's why girls grow more quickly than boys."[65] Luther tended to think poorly of the female frame:

> Women lack strength and stamina, and intelligence. Men have broad chests and narrow hips, and therefore, they have more intelligence than women who have a narrow chest, wide hips, and a wide rear end. That is why they have to stay home, sit quietly in the house, keep house, bear children, and nurture them.[66]

Luther's own physique was not quite like this description, and his wife certainly was not passive. Nonetheless, these facts did not prevent him from making these senseless and insensitive remarks.

Full House

It did not take long before Katharina's Aunt Lena moved into the Luther monastery. The family grew. Within eight years, six children were born. When both of Luther's sisters died, he and Katharina took the children in. Luther's one sister had five children, and the other had six, so Katharina had the care of seventeen children. It was no wonder that her days began each morning at four o'clock, earning her the title "morning star of Wittenberg." With all this busyness, she hardly had time to read the Bible, which displeased Luther. One year, he promised her fifty guilders if she would read the Bible cover to cover in the period from early October to Easter. Apparently, Käthe accepted this arrangement because on October 28, Luther mentioned to a friend, "She is taking this seriously, because she has already reached Deuteronomy."[67]

At this time a common practice for professors was to board a group of students, buffering a professor's meager salary by offering a uniquely educational home for the students. Luther opened up the family's home, telling the students they didn't have to pay him anything. Katharina thought differently, however, and she thus earned a less than favorable name with a number of students. Every refugee was welcome in the Luther family. Consequently, Luther once wrote, "Dear Käthe, if we do not have any more money, you will have to sell the silver mugs. After all, before you get something, you first have to give something away. God will take care that something else will come in its place."[68] Luther's hospitality led to the problem that after only two years of marriage, they had already accrued a debt of one hundred guilders. In the following years, not much would change. A surviving piece of paper provides a glance at their bookkeeping: "Note: 'balance sheet' between doctor Martin and Käthe, anno 1535/36." Everything was counted, and their property amounted to eight pigs, five cows, nine calves, and one goat. Even the parsley and the slaughtered ox were listed. Then the expenses were added up, resulting in a negative balance. Underneath, Luther wrote, "I am never going to make an accounting again because you only end up being sad."[69]

Especially for Käthe, life was made that much more difficult by marrying one of the most famous men in the world, albeit one who was often sick. Fortunately, Käthe had also been busy making homemade medicines from herbs and dung. The so-called dung-apothecary (a primitive form of naturopathy) was popular in those days. Luther wondered why God had put so many medicines in stools (probably because they didn't help him). When Katharina sent one of her medicines to Luther when he was traveling, he wrote, "Pig dung stops bleeding, horse dung mixed with wine is a remedy for colds, human dung closes a wound, but your dung doesn't help me."[70]

On July 6, 1527, he had such heart problems that he fainted. He had felt it coming and wanted to do confession that morning. He was afraid that he would die and have to appear before God. That was also the reason he wanted to have the Lord's Supper the next day. Spiritually and physically, he was in poor shape and asked for Käthe and their little son, Hans, so that he could say goodbye. He still had so much he wanted to do, such as write against the Anabaptists, but that was not to be. Luther also knew his enemies would mock him when he died. In those spiritual struggles he tried to meditate on God's grace, but he had to admit that it didn't work. He felt that he had lost Christ and that doubt had overmastered him:[71] "I love my Käthe, and I know that I love her more than myself. That means that I think I would rather die than that she and the children should die."[72]

Peasants' Revolt

The Peasants' Revolt would have significant consequences for Luther's image then and afterward. This was not a war but an armed insurrection. Furthermore, it involved not only peasant farmers but also the poor plebian classes in the cities. Though these revolts took place initially in Germany, they also happened in Switzerland and Austria. Nevertheless, the event is called the German Peasants' Revolt, and it began in the summer of 1524 with a revolt south of the Black Forest. A year later, in May 1525, this revolt came to its peak and was ultimately put down. What could cause such an event?

For many decades the country folk and the poorer people in the cities had been growing discontent as a result of rising prices and decreasing incomes. Added to these grievances were unreasonable taxation and unjust laws. Payments to the church were particularly hated, especially as the people noted that church leaders were often busier with their own affairs than with God and his congregation. When Luther appeared with his criticism of Rome and his message of freedom, many people understood this as support for their position.

Thomas Müntzer had assumed leadership of this movement. Quickly, Luther warned the people against him. Müntzer was born in Stolberg (Harz) in 1489, studied in Frankfurt and Leipzig, and in 1513 was ordained as priest. Between 1517 and 1519, he was often in Wittenberg, but after May 1520, he had preached in Zwickau, to much praise. Eventually, however, the city council suspected him of inciting a riot and ran him out of the city. From there he went to Prague, Jena, Erfurt, and Weimar. Finally, in 1523, he became a pastor in Allstedt, where he married, had a son, reformed the liturgy, and created enormous unrest with his "Sermon before the Princes." In this sermon, delivered in the presence of Electoral Duke John and his son, Müntzer challenged them to support the Reformation and immediately address the social inequities. By the end of April 1524, the trouble escalated. Müntzer left Allstedt and became minister in Mühlhausen. There he assumed the leadership of a self-organized army of peasant farmers, servants, and all kinds of people, and he directed a field campaign against the rulers.

Because Müntzer appealed to the gospel to justify his revolt as the fruit of the Reformation, Luther felt compelled to respond. According to Luther, Müntzer was responsible for the Peasants' Revolt but was mistaken in his views. The revolt that Müntzer wanted would not result in a more just society; his was an eschatological revolution, meant to bring about an entirely new world. The revolt was only valuable to the degree that it ushered in the eschaton (or eternal state). Luther did associate Müntzer with the end of times but as part of demonic forces. For Luther they were all the same: Carlstadt, Müntzer, the Zwickau prophets—each of them a pawn of evil: "Müntzer and Carlstadt both represent the Devil in person."[73] Something desperately needed to be done against the activities of Müntzer, who caused increasing unrest among the people with his preaching and writing. He was convinced that he was a new Daniel and began advising the princes how people should be physically forced to accept the gospel. In one of his treatises, he stated that Luther was too weak (*sanftlebend*) and irresolute, even going so far as to claim that his conduct spoke more of unbelief than dedication. To contrast the two, Luther believed in the power of the Word; Müntzer believed that there should be no words without deeds.

Violence

During Luther's inspection travels through Thuringia, he was confronted with these problems, and he was given two documents that voiced a plea for addressing the issues confronting the peasant farmers: the *Twelve Articles* and the *Christian Unification*. Both were drafted by a gathering of leading farmers in Memmingen, who appealed to him for his help, hoping that Luther would judge the righteousness of their cause. Luther initially showed understanding for their trouble. In his *Incentive to Peace concerning the "Twelve Articles" of the Farmers of*

Swabia, he encouraged the rebels to seek peace but in such a way that peace would also have to come from the side of the princes. Several of the demands in the *Twelve Articles*, according to him, were entirely justified and could be defended from God's Word. Clearly, the princes and bishops had countenanced injustice. Luther wrote,

> I praised the farmers that they want to be instructed by the Bible but warned them at the same time not to force their demands with violence because they do not have that right. After all, Christians do not fight with sword and harquebus for themselves but with the cross and with suffering, just as their duke, Christ, does not use the sword but hangs from the cross.[74]

When Luther visited Eisleben between April 16 and May 6 to initiate reform in the school, he also visited several other cities such as Stolberg and Nordhausen to engage the insurgents in dialogue and to address their demands in sermons. This met with no success. He noticed that not everyone appreciated his appeal for peace and his warnings against false prophets. Some people even attempted to disrupt his sermons during the church service by making noise. To Luther, these were not oppressed peoples seeking justice but wicked revolutionaries, thirsting for pillage and murder. As soon as he got back to Wittenberg, he wrote a booklet, *Against the Storming Peasants*. Part of that work was published separately in several printings using the title *Against the Murderous, Thieving Hordes of Peasants*.[75] The tone was sharp. Luther directed his writing against the insurgents who had rebelled against the ruling authorities. He saw these people as violent criminals who must be opposed with force:

> Therefore, whosoever can, should smite, strangle, and stab, secretly or publicly, and should remember that there is nothing more poisonous, pernicious, and devilish than a rebellious man. Just as one must slay a mad dog, so, if you do not fight the rebels, they will fight you, and the whole country with you.[76]

Some people saw Luther as a traitor who had chosen the side of the rulers out of fear. He was unhappy with this perception but decided to live with it. Luther felt that the order established by God was threatened and that a satanic chaos was developing under the guise of the gospel. Something had to happen; the authorities did not bear the sword in vain. The rulers hesitated, but bold and hardhanded action was now their God-given duty. There had also been heavenly signs that pointed in this direction: "So here in Wittenberg a child was born without a head and one with reversed feet."[77] As Luther explained, "To motivate the princes I wrote a pamphlet today in which I challenge them to bloodshed. Now is the time for the sword, and of wrath, and not a time for mercy."[78] Luther reasoned, somewhat strangely, that the best way to serve the peasants was to strike them down: "If someone thinks this is harsh, realize that rebellion is unacceptable and that at every moment it can destroy the world."[79]

The authorities followed Luther's recommended course of action, and the revolt ended with a horrible defeat for the "peasants." On May 23, 1525, Luther received reports of the battle that had been waged a week earlier (May 14–15) near Frankenhausen. The troops of various rulers had completely defeated Müntzer's army. About five thousand peasants were dead, and six hundred had been captured, including Thomas Müntzer. Within a few days he was condemned to die and was beheaded. Luther maintained that this terrible event was an example of what Jesus had said in Matthew 26:52: "For all who take the sword will perish by the sword." The peasants had only themselves to blame because they chose to mix politics with the gospel. Nevertheless, he regretted what had happened and his role in it. He was aware of the consequences: "I killed Müntzer. His death is on my account. And I did that because he wanted to kill my Christ."[80] Also, after this bloodbath, Luther stuck to his conviction:

> I am of the opinion that it would be better that all the peasants would have been killed than if that would have happened to the princes, and that is because the peasants took to the sword without having been authorized by God. This comes from Satan, and thus it can only lead to the devilish destruction of God's kingdom and of the world. Though rulers sin as well, they bear the sword empowered by God's authority, and that is also the way in which both kingdoms can exist. Therefore, it is not appropriate to be merciful and patient toward the peasants. They earned the wrath of God and

> the condemnation of God and people, namely, those who did not stop when they were encouraged to do so, those who also failed to accept the most favorable terms but continued on through the raging of Satan and brought everything into confusion.[81]

Erasmus

Like an ominous thunderstorm, the confrontation between Luther and Erasmus hung in the air during these years as well. Initially, it appeared as if these two giants would stand together for the same cause. Both wanted a return to the original sources, both recognized the authority of the Scriptures, both expressed their unvarnished criticism concerning the wrongs in the church, and both were fed up with theologians who busied themselves with issues that were inconsequential for ordinary people. Early on, however, Luther noticed a difference between himself and Erasmus. According to Luther, the Dutchman had insufficient appreciation for the sinfulness of people: "Every day I lose more joy in Erasmus. . . . Humanity appears to weigh more with him than the divine. Whenever you expect more from our human capacity, you judge differently than when you only want to know about grace."[82] Nevertheless, Luther defended Erasmus when he was targeted for much censure because he had rightly criticized the church:

> I always support him and give him highest praise as long as I can. And I try my utmost not to express myself on points on which I differ in opinion with him, to avoid strengthening the negative attitude with my comments. But if I have to judge him, regardless of all the appreciation I have as a theologian, and not as a philologist, then we will find with Erasmus much that, according to me, is inappropriate for the knowledge of Christ.[83]

On March 28, 1519, he also wrote Erasmus a letter, in flattering language unique to the style of the humanists, congratulating him with the many gifts he had but also commiserating with him on receiving so much criticism. "As far as that is concerned we are being tarred with the same brush," Luther wrote.[84] Luther believed that such a letter was wise, since Luther's name was being associated frequently with Erasmus.[85] From his side, Erasmus was unhappy with Luther because he himself was being blamed more and more for instigating the Reformation. He distanced himself from the Wittenberger and did not want to be involved in any way in the ecclesiastical conflict. It was said that Luther was the chicken that had been hatched from the egg that Erasmus had brooded. Erasmus wanted peace, but especially he wanted rest, and his income depended heavily on people being favorably predisposed to Rome. Gradually, but also quite deliberately and publicly, he distanced himself from all of it. Of course, Luther noticed that too:

> What Erasmus's opinion is, or what he says his opinion is, you can read very clearly in his books, in both his first as well as his most recent ones. Though I notice his ruses everywhere, I act as if I don't get his stratagems. He puts on an act as if publicly he is not my enemy, though I have figured him out better than he thinks himself. He has done what he was meant to do: he introduced knowledge of the source languages to call people back from blasphemous studies. Perhaps he will die with Moses in the fields of Moab (Deut. 34:5), because concerning godliness, he has not come to a better understanding. I would love to see that he would cease to engage himself with commentaries on Scripture and that he would stop with his paraphrases, because he lacks all knowledge to do this. Thus he engages his readers in vain and prevents them from developing understanding of Scripture. He's done enough to show what was bad, but he cannot both let us see the good and bring us into the Promised Land.[86]

For Erasmus, the time had come in 1524 to make a definitive break with Luther, as King Henry VIII had advised. He did this by initiating a discussion to clarify that in the heart of the matter, he had nothing to do with Luther. In Latin he published a treatise concerning free will, because this issue was to be discussed at a scholarly level. Erasmus's treatise was not a collection of theses like Luther's, as Erasmus had never dared to take a definitive point of view. Instead, for safety's sake, he approached issues with questions. For several years already, Luther had argued that humans did not possess a free will after the fall. Erasmus stated that free will enables people to take hold of the salvation that God had prepared. When Luther was in the monastery, he had become completely confused with the issue of free will. Erasmus, however, expected that free will would enable people to live more Christianly. He thought Luther's view was dangerous and would demotivate people from living godly lives. But Luther thought that Erasmus's view was dangerous because of the uncertainty it would create in people's hearts. These views had to crash head-on, but for the time being, nothing happened.

Luther's first reaction came in a sermon that he delivered on October 9, 1525. In this sermon he described the powerlessness of a person's will, using the well-known words "You are a stallion, and the Devil is your rider," a message that was meant not only for Erasmus but for every person.[87] By November 1, he had still read only part of Erasmus's booklet,[88] but that had been enough. Luther typically was not in the habit of reading his opponents' works completely; he read until he knew enough to react and used the rest as toilet paper.[89] Nevertheless, Erasmus's booklet did not end up hanging beside Luther's toilet; he read it all, though he disliked it and realized that a reaction would require a special effort: "It is indescribable how much I detest this little book [by Erasmus] concerning free will, even after reading a few pages. It will be a difficult task to respond to such a learned book from such a learned man."[90] Furthermore, he had no desire to get into a discussion with Erasmus; he had other pressing matters to attend to. In 1525, Luther had to deal with the Peasants' Revolt, the conflict concerning the Lord's Supper, and his own marriage. Nevertheless, after some time, he recognized that this was an important debate and finally responded. More importantly, he realized that it concerned the heart of the Reformation, as he stated at the conclusion of his book, where he thanked Erasmus:

> I want to praise you highly in this, and I am telling you openly that in contrast to everyone else, you are the only one who has focused on the matter itself, on the main issue, and that you have not bothered me with other issues such as the papacy, purgatory, indulgences, and more of those silly things concerning which almost everyone has dogged me. You are the only one who has seen the heart of the issue and truly tried to zero in on that vital spot—for that I want to thank you with all my heart.[91]

Not until December 31, 1525, a year after Erasmus's booklet had been published, did Luther begin his reaction. The size of his book, *On the Bondage of the Will*, indicates the careful thought Luther put into this response. In this work, Luther worked out the distinction between the hidden God and the revealed God, of which he had spoken already in 1518 in Heidelberg. At the outset, he stated that we do not have a free will, and concerning grace and eternal life, we have absolutely no power. God elects, God determines, and God gives—and why he chooses to give faith to one person and not to another remains hidden to us. It is none of our business. We must only concern ourselves with the revealed God, the God who comes to us and says, "Believe the gospel, and you shall live in eternity." Predestination is a given in the Bible, but how that works, only God knows. Whatever is beyond our understanding is none of our concern. We may hold fast to God's promises, and that is sufficient for a person. The importance of this work to Luther is indicated by Luther's comment that everything he had published could be thrown into the fire as long as the Large Catechism and *Bondage* would be spared.[92]

The breach was definitive. Luther was disgusted with Erasmus's attitude and opinions: "I hate Erasmus. I hate him with all my strength." To engage this man in a discussion was impossible: "Erasmus is an eel." Luther thought this was obvious: "Erasmus is, such as his facial expressions show, a person full of scheming and evil who mocks God and religion."[93] Erasmus reacted dismissively and accused Luther of being impulsive and guilty of slanderous lies and ridiculous accusations. After that, little was said. Luther did not return to this topic, since as far as he was concerned, everything had been said, and this wasn't a debate for the pulpit. Luther considered Erasmus a man of smooth talk, a moralist who presented Christ as an example but not a Savior. In 1533, disagreement between the two once again flared up.[94] After Erasmus had defended himself one more time, however, he was quiet. Two years after Erasmus's death in 1536, Luther gave his final judgment about him:

> Erasmus of Rotterdam wrote many exceptional works. He had the intelligence for it, and the time. There was nothing to prevent him;

> he had no official duties, did not preach, did not give lectures, and did not have to be involved in business. He had a lifestyle without God, lived in complete self-assurance, and thus he died, without asking in his final agony for a servant of God's Word or for the service of the sacraments. God spare me that I, in my hour of death, do not ask for a believing servant, indeed, that I would especially call the first available one and praise God. Erasmus learned those things in Rome, but because of his distinction and his books, we must now be silent about it.[95]

Liturgy

After his return from the Wartburg, Luther had put all the liturgical changes on hold and even reversed several, but he did understand that something meaningful had to change. He felt that change was necessary because the established liturgy was not supported by the Bible. Luther began with reforming the prayer book. Books like this were available in various forms and were used in monasteries for the set times of prayer. Luther, very familiar with the prayer book, opted to reform it rather than abolish it. The Lord's Prayer, the prayer of the Ten Commandments, and the Apostles' Creed stayed as they were. But the Ave Maria needed to change. Luther altered it so that suppliants would be praying not to Mary but to God, praising him for what he did, including his work through Mary. Mary did not disappear but was set in a more proper place. Luther also added a few prayers. His new prayer book was successful; during his lifetime it went through thirty-five printings. He emphasized that this work was meant to support believers as they prayed in their own words:

> From a book you will never learn to pray well. You can read in it and receive instruction how and in what way you should pray. And you can let it motivate you to pray, but the prayer should come from the heart, without all the words that have already been written, and you should use words that your heart desires.[96]

After this *Little Book on Praying*,[97] he followed with the *Little Book on Baptism*.[98] Luther likewise left much of the accepted baptismal liturgical procedures as they were, such as the practice of making the sign of the cross on the child's forehead. But he also abolished several elements.

The most far-reaching reform was evident in the mass. From January 1523 onward, partakers celebrated mass with bread and chalice. According to him, the people had been instructed sufficiently well to receive both elements at that point. In another booklet, *On the Order of the Congregational Worship Service*,[99] he described what the church service should look like. Luther gave much freedom to each congregation, as long as the service emphasized the preaching of Scripture. He replaced the daily mass with daily preaching services, realizing that the whole congregation could not always be there, except on Sundays, when everyone was expected to attend. A more thorough reflection on liturgy brought forth the work *On the German Mass*.[100] The liturgy set out in this work was implemented on Christmas Day 1525 and appeared in print a week later. Luther wanted to distance himself from the liturgical compulsion that existed under Rome, but he did realize that a degree of uniformity and order was necessary. Luther also made a change of clothing. At home he had worn everyday clothing for some time, and on October 9, 1524, he appeared in public for the first time without his monk's habit. Luther was officially and publicly no longer a monk.

By year's end in 1523, Luther indicated that he wanted the congregation to sing: "Following the example of the prophets and the old church fathers, I plan to make German psalms for the people—that is to say, spiritual songs, so that the Word of God is also present via the singing of the people. Therefore, we are looking everywhere for poets." They had to

> avoid words that were used at the courts, so that words are sung that the people can understand, preferably simple and generally well-known words. Those words should be beautiful, of course, and phrased well. Additionally, the meaning of the Psalms must come out clearly. Therefore, it will be necessary to translate somewhat more freely.[101]

Luther needed poets for this task, and because there were none immediately available, he began composing some songs himself, many

Figure 7.4 *Luther Making Music in the Circle of His Family*. Painting by Gustav Spangenberg, ca. 1875. Museum der bildenden Künste, Leipzig.

published in 1523. The most familiar one was "Dear Christians, One and All, Rejoice." As a rule Luther wanted the music to serve the text of the song.[102] He continued making hymns and had several hymnals marketed. Between 1523 and 1543, he produced thirty-six songs, supported tremendously by Johann Walter (1496–1570), who was in service as chanter to the elector in his court chapel. Walter, who had also embraced the Reformation, developed his musical talents and in 1524 in Wittenberg published *Spiritual Songs*,[103] the first reformational songbook with music for polyphonic choral singing. The book included hymns as well as six psalms. Gradually, other songs were added, and thus congregational singing would be established as a permanent characteristic of Protestantism. In the foreword that Luther wrote in Walter's songbook, he explained why he valued song so much. "I believe that no Christian will be surprised that the singing of spiritual songs is good and pleasing to God."[104] Singing can be done most effectively, Luther said, by implementing the use of musical instruments, as the Bible itself declared (see fig. 7.4). Song and music have no other purpose than for the spreading of the Word of God and Christian doctrine. It must ensure "that the holy gospel, which through God's grace has arisen again, be circulated and proclaimed." For everyone it is clear "that Christ is the substance of our praise and our singing and that we do not want to sing and say anything else than Jesus Christ our Savior."[105] For Luther, music was tremendously important and valuable to the church:

> I love music. The Anabaptists don't appeal to me because they condemn music. But (1) music is a gift from God and not of people. (2) It cheers the heart. (3) It drives away the Devil. (4) It gives innocent joy. Through music anger, greed, and pride disappear. I give music the first place after theology. That is made evident from the example of David and all the prophets who expressed everything they had to say in verse and hymns. (5) It rules in times of peace. It will continue to exist, and therefore, it will fare better with this art after our times.[106]

In 1530, he considered writing about the value of music. This he finally did in 1538, via a preface for the publication of a symphony by composer George Rhau (1488–1548).[107]

Education

As Luther's theology spread, the need for a reformation in education also became clearer. Some had interpreted the message of the Reformation to imply that instruction and knowledge were unnecessary. Others believed that busyness with one's hands was better than work with one's mind. Theological instruction was also deemed unnecessary, because all believers were now considered theologians. Studying languages was seen as pointless. What mattered was the indwelling of the Spirit working in and through people. Some rulers eagerly embraced this attitude so they could redirect the money meant for the schools and universities.

But according to Luther, the Devil sowed ignorance to prevent young people from knowing Christ and to undermine the spread of the gospel and the building of the church. He wrote a letter to the councilmen of all cities in Germany, appealing to them to establish and maintain Christian schools. He noted that so much money was spent on "bridges, roads, laneways, dams, and the like, so that a city could have temporary rest," and then asked them, "shouldn't you put forth more effort to spend as much as is needed for the poor youths and employ one or two suitable men as schoolmasters?"[108] He believed that God had given them an opportunity to thoroughly organize education at every level:

> Buy, dear Germans, while the market is at your doors; gather in the harvest while there is sunshine and fair weather; use the grace and Word of God while they are here. For know this, God's Word and grace is as a passing rainstorm, which does not return where it has once been.[109]

Knowledge of the classical languages—Hebrew, Greek, and Latin—he considered essential to enable people to read, understand, and preach the Bible. But education was also important for nonministers. Politicians would be able to learn from history about economics and political issues; mothers in families would learn arithmetic and make music for their families. Luther pleaded for well-equipped libraries so that people could study and do research. As a result, in many cities and villages, new schools were established, often in vacant monasteries. Melanchthon especially looked after the reformation of the universities.

Problems

Carlstadt remained a problem for Luther for a long time, even after he had been banished from Wittenberg. He found accommodations in Orlamünde and continued proclaiming his views: a rejection of infant baptism, a view of the Lord's Supper as a mere memorial meal for the congregation instead of a sign and seal from God, a call to iconoclasm, and a rejection of education and scholarship. As Carlstadt preached on these views, Luther grew worried and decided to go to Orlamünde, but the visit bore no fruit. Subsequently, he wrote a treatise in which he took issue with Carlstadt's views and those who embraced similar ones. His language was so extreme, however, that colleagues like Melanchthon rejected his tone. In Orlamünde, Luther's treatise was treated as toilet paper.[110] Essentially, for the impact of the Reformation, Carlstadt viewed the Lord's Supper as an act of the congregation, while Luther saw this sacrament as a form of God dispensing the forgiveness of sins.

Carlstadt understood the elements of bread and wine simply as signs, as symbols of the body and blood of Christ. Luther felt that Christ's presence in the elements was indispensible, because it was in this that he believed salvation came to us from outside. When he heard that people associated with Zwingli in Zurich also held views on the Lord's Supper similar to those of Carlstadt, he began to identify anyone who articulated a more symbolic character of the elements with Carlstadt.

It was not long before the people in Orlamünde were also fed up with Carlstadt and forced him to leave. Tired and poor, and in danger from the Peasants' Revolt, he indicated that he wanted to return to Wittenberg. Luther actually spoke a word in his favor with the elector. Consequently, Carlstadt and his wife stayed, secretly, with Luther for eight weeks. Carlstadt distanced himself from Thomas Müntzer's views and also modified his views on the sacraments. In 1529, he departed again, stayed for some time with the Anabaptists in Ostfriesland, and then went to Strasbourg and subsequently to Zurich. The last years of his life, until 1541, he spent in Basel, where, in 1537, he became the rector of the university, an unusual position given his attitude and views toward education and scholarship.

The separation between Luther and Carlstadt, who first worked as collaborative colleagues, was a typical experience for Luther around 1525. In many ways he had come to stand alone. Many had been disappointed in his role during the Peasants' Revolt, and former supporters, like the humanists, cut off relations after his falling out with Erasmus. For some, his marriage meant a kind of breach with his vows and with his past, and they felt they could no longer count on him. It became rather quiet around Luther, and that silence would only increase after 1525.

8

Father (1525–1530)

The Luther Family

Not long after their wedding, Katharina became pregnant. The Luther family received the news with joy but also fear; it was commonly believed that the child of an ex-nun and ex-monk would be a monster. The family was greatly relieved when on June 7, 1526, a healthy child was born: "Christ has blessed my Käthe and has given her a son. He is healthy and without deformity [*sano et integro*]. Thanks and praise for his inexpressible goodness."[1] As was customary, the child was baptized on the day of his birth, just two hours later. He was named after Luther's father, Johannes. The name seemed strangely appropriate given how distressed Luther's father had been over his son's decision to enter the monastery, potentially depriving him of grandchildren; now that fear had disappeared.

Before the birth, Luther had made a number of arrangements. He had asked Caspar Müller, the chancellor of the earl of Mansfeld, to be the baby's godfather. The custom of godfathers and godmothers was rooted in the belief that biological parents were actually unsuitable to make the baptismal vows. They were, after all, responsible for the birth of a sinful child, and therefore, it was better that others, substitutes in a sense, would make that vow and become the spiritual parents. Luther made no change to this custom. In the letter to Müller, Luther had indicated that the chancellor would probably not be able to attend the baptism, and therefore, he should appoint a proxy. As expected, the chancellor was unable to attend the baptism, especially since the child was baptized so soon after his birth. Around four o'clock in the afternoon, the deacon George Rörer administered baptism in the City Church in Wittenberg. Katharina was not present either.

There was another group of godparents standing around the old baptismal font: Johann Pfister, a former monk and now student in Wittenberg; Johannes Bugenhagen, who presented the baby for baptism; Justus Jonas; Lucas Cranach, the court painter; Benedicta Hohndorf, the wife of the burgomaster; and the jurist Christian Beyer. This was a significant group that had been chosen with care, because godparents served as a kind of life insurance. The baptismal vows functioned as a form of potential guardianship for the child, if something were to happen to the biological parents. For that reason people considered it wise to have several godparents. Luther himself had so many godchildren that at a certain point he lost track of which children he was godfather to and had to have someone sort it out for him.

He lacked no clarity concerning his own children. Within eight years, six children were born. Luther was forty-three when he first became a father, which in his time was considered an old age, but it appears to have posed no problems for the family. Luther was happy with his children and compared them, when he had three of them, with kingdoms: "I have legitimate children, and there is no papist theologian who has that. Those three children are three kingdoms, and I have acquired them in an honest way, rather than how [Archduke] Ferdinand acquired Hungary, Bohemia, and the Roman Empire."[2] Like any other parent, Luther wanted to care for his children as well as he could. Luther's care for little Hans, for example, concerned his spiritual well-being and the influence that Satan could have on him. He wrote to his friend Spalatin,

> Pray that Christ will keep my little one from the Devil, because you know that he will not leave a stone unturned to bring evil on me, using my son if God allows. Because now already the child has problems with all kinds of little illnesses, or more so from the raw milk which he is not used to that the mother must feed baby first.[3]

A couple of weeks later, things were going better: "Little Johannes Luther is doing well, at least as well as one would possibly imagine for such a child."[4]

Jerome Weller went to live with the Luthers, who paid him to care for and tutor little Hans. Hans was unique in that most other children did not receive an education this early; most were expected to work in the family and, after that, help in the field or earn money in a workshop. While Luther was staying in the Coburg Castle in 1530, from where he observed the developments at the Diet of Augsburg (discussed below), Weller sent him a message that Hans was ambitious and had made good progress. In response, Luther wrote his son a letter on June 19, which would become one of the best-known letters that Luther wrote. In this letter he compared heaven to a playground, where children joyfully sing, dance, and play, and where the most delicious fruit is hanging on the trees. The message to little Hans was that he too was allowed to go to that playground "if he eagerly prays, learns, and is devout."[5] The entry into this playground is free, Luther told him, but people cannot simply enter.

On June 7, 1533, Hans turned seven, and a day later he was registered as a student at the University of Wittenberg, which was not unique at that time, because a student would spend many years in preparatory study before beginning the actual university studies. The studies were challenging for him, however. It's possible that Hans found it difficult to concentrate in the busy Luther home, though it is more likely that he wasn't a natural scholar. When he was sixteen, his parents decided to send him to another school, and so he left for Torgau to learn under the care of the rector, Markus Crodel. In this school, a Latin school, he received instruction in language and music. Luther informed Crodel that he would also send his other two boys if Hans made good progress. He trusted the competency of this teacher and knew that there were few teachers like him, though he hoped that more would come: "I produce theologians, but I would like to produce people who are competent in language and music."[6] Hans remained there for a year and then returned to Wittenberg. After Luther's death in 1546, Hans studied law in Köningsberg, and apparently, after much difficulty and effort, he received a position as lawyer. He died in 1575.

Elizabeth

In the summer of 1527, Wittenberg was stricken with the plague. As quickly as possible, students and teachers from the university were transferred to Jena. Elector John the Steadfast appealed to Luther to also come to Jena, but together with Bugenhagen, Luther decided to stay where he was. He downplayed the severity of the plague:

> The plague has indeed appeared here, but its progress is not as bad as expected. The fear of the people is amazing: they flee! I have never yet seen such an unimaginable work of Satan. He incites such terrible fear and is pleased to incite fear in the hearts of people. Of course, his purpose is to disperse and completely destroy this excellent university which he hates, and not without reason. During the whole period of the plague, there were only eighteen people who died, out of everyone living in the city, maids, children, and everyone else. Today we buried the spouse of the burgomaster, Tilo Denes. Yesterday, she almost died in my arms. . . . Justus Jonas with his family went back to where they used to live, but his little son died nevertheless. I am staying here, and that is necessary because the people are terribly afraid. Therefore, Bugenhagen and I are the only pastors here. But Christ is here too, and therefore, we are not alone.[7]

The deadly disease remained and spread, so that the Luther household also had to deal with it:

> My house has been changed into a hospital. Hanna, Augustin's wife, has contracted the plague but is recovering. Margretha von Mochau scared us with a suspicious swelling and other symptoms, though she seems to be doing better as well. I am afraid for my Käthe, who is almost ready to give birth, and my little son has been sick for three days already. He doesn't eat anything, and he is not doing well at all. They say it is because his teeth are coming through, but now they believe that both are in grave danger. After all, the wife of pastor George [Rörer], who is also about to deliver, has been taken by the plague, and now they are trying to save the child one way or another. May the Lord Jesus have mercy on her. And so there is a struggle on the outside and fear within, and great fear. Christ is exercising

> a period of testing on us. But there is comfort with which we will confront Satan: namely, we have the Word of God to keep the souls of the faithful, even if their bodies succumb.[8]

For Luther such comfort also came with fear and doubts:

> On Saturday, I was in great despair when the wife of George, the chaplain, bore a premature child. Shortly after the child died, she died—a double death, in the first place because of the birth pains, but after that she was also stricken with the poison of the plague. Christ did not see our tears tonight, nor did he hear our prayers to spare her life that night, but he did provide comfort that she came to her end in faith. Full of faith and filled with the Holy Spirit she went to him. Because everybody trembles with fear, I took the minister and his family in. Thus far my Käthe is strong in faith, and she is healthy. My little Hans has been sick in bed for the last eight days, and we do not know what is wrong with him. I almost think it is the sickness of this time, but they say it's because of his teeth, and we'll believe that for now.[9]

Later that month, Hans's health improved, as did the health of those in Luther's clinic. Katharina's pregnancy made it through the plague, so that on December 10, Hans received a little sister. A few days later, Luther announced, "Our little daughter Elizabeth has been born. To Christ be praise and honor."[10] Elizabeth, however, would live only eight months. On August 5, 1528, Luther reported, "My little daughter, Elizabeth, has passed away. I am so overwhelmed with sadness, that she has left me behind with a somewhat motherly heart. Before this, I would never have believed that the heart of a father could become so tender when it concerns his own child."[11]

Magdalena, Martin, Paul, Margaretha, and the Rest

The Bible's language of God as Father and his people as his children motivated Luther to apply the relationships within the family to his understanding of the gospel. In one of the accounts of his *Table Talk*, Luther said to his newborn son Martin, "How did you deserve it, and why is it that I love you so much that I have made you my heir? By pooping, peeing, crying, and screaming throughout the whole house, so that I have to be worried about you."[12] When he expressed his appreciation about the care that Katharina had for her children, and at the same time for mothers in general, he said, "The love of a mother is stronger than all filth and fevers of a child. In a similar way, God's love for us is stronger than our filth. Though we are sinners, we remain, despite our filth, children of God. Nor do we fall from his grace on account of all our sins."[13]

These words reveal a lot about how Luther viewed God but also about how he related to his family. "We are there as parents to nurture you and to instruct you, and you are here to obey us," he said. "If we do not discipline anymore, then because of that, the youth would become wild, and that would be the end of our country."[14] At the same time, he held that "as parents, we live for the sake of our young ones, and we must encourage them so that later on they will become ministers and administrators."[15] He regarded the responsibilities of parents highly: "With their children, a father and mother can earn heaven or hell; it depends whether they provide a good or a bad example."[16] As far as that was concerned, he believed that whoever influenced young people controlled the future of the church: "There is no greater harm for Christendom than the neglect of children. If people want to aid Christendom again, then they should begin with the children, like it used to be in the past."[17] This also meant that Luther could be strict. Once when little Hans had misbehaved, Luther was so angry with him that he did not want to see him for three days. Katharina attempted to change his mind, and Hans even wrote him a letter, but Luther stuck to his decision. Luther felt that parents and caregivers must be resolute, though not hardhearted: "It's a very sad situation when children and students lose their trust in their parents and teachers. In this respect, there are mean-spirited schoolmasters who have ruined many wholesome characters with their brusque conduct."[18] Luther's beliefs about children prompted him to hold them up as examples of faith for adults. According to him, as far as faith was concerned, children are much happier. They are artless, do not enter into discussions, and do not doubt: "In faith they are far more scholarly than we old fools."[19]

Though we know mostly about Hans from Luther's letters, he also frequently mentioned his other children. On May 4, 1529, Magdalena was born. According to Luther, this delivery was quick, and his wife was soon back on her feet. Luther enjoyed being a father and regretted having to travel. Even while he traveled, he continued to be involved in his children's upbringing, even with their nutrition. From the Coburg Castle, for example, where he stayed from April through October 1530, he provided Katharina with tips on how she could best express her breastmilk by pumping. Though he was away from home, he could still look at his daughter after Lucas Cranach made a small portrait of her that Luther had hung on the dining room wall in the Coburg. He missed his children, and therefore, Luther was very happy that Käthe sent him a portrait of their Lena. He hung it up over against the dining room table so that during meals he could constantly see her and then forget many of his worries.[20] Martin Jr. was born on November 9, 1531; Luther remarked that youngest children often get the best share of their parents' love:

> Because they need the help and care of the parents more, they appear more precious to their parents. In that way, my Martin is my biggest treasure because he needs the most care. Johannes and Magdalena can walk and talk, and they can tell us what they need, and therefore, they do not need all that extra care.[21]

During the night of January 29, 1533, Luther and Käthe received their fifth child, a son, whom they named Paul, after the apostle from whom Luther had learned so much. Margaretha Luther was born on December 17, 1534. She was named after her grandmother, and when she was baptized, she received a number of godparents, just like her siblings. One of them was the ruler Joachim von Anhalt. Shortly before this birth, Luther had frequently visited von Anhalt to give him comfort during his illness and temptations. Luther's letter to this nobleman illustrated what Luther meant by godparenthood. Luther saw this as "the Christian office of spiritual fatherhood," in which it was the task of the godfather "to assist the poor pagan child to become a new holy and saintly reborn child, and through the bath of baptism become a spiritual father."[22] Luther and Käthe received a seventh child on January 22, 1540, but it was stillborn—the birth nearly cost Katharina her life.

At the beginning of September 1542, Lena, who was thirteen at the time, became very sick. Her parents hoped that she would get better if her older brother, Hans, were near her, so they quickly brought him home from his studies in Torgau. Luther wrote Crodel,

> My daughter Magdalena is almost at the point of death, and shortly she will go to her true Father in heaven, if God hasn't decided differently. She dearly yearns to see her brother one more time, so that I had to order a cart [to get him]. They have always been very fond of each other. Perhaps she may improve a bit if he comes. I am doing everything I can, so that my conscience does not torment me later for being neglectful.[23]

When Hans arrived on September 7, his sister's death was inevitable. Luther could do nothing else but pray: "I dearly love her, but dear God, if it is your will to take her to yourself, then I dearly want her to be with you." He talked to God about her, but he also talked to her about God. When he asked her, "Magdalena, my daughter, you would love to stay here with your father, but do you also want to go to your other Father?" she answered, "Yes, dear father, whatever God wills." She languished for two weeks. An eyewitness said,

> When Magdalena lay close to death, and wanted to die, her father fell on his knees by her bed. He wept bitterly and prayed that God would release her. Then she died and rested in the hands of her father. Her mother was also in the room, but because of her grief, stood a little further away from the bed.[24]

Luther tried to comfort her:

> Dear Käthe, remember where she has gone! It will be good for her. . . . Children do not get involved in discussion: they believe whatever you tell them. With children everything is simple; they die without grief or fear, without discussion, without being beleaguered by the fear of death, without physical pain, regardless of how they pass away.[25]

He wrote to Justus Jonas,

> Our dear daughter Magdalena has been reborn to eternal life in Christ. Though my wife and I should be thankful for the wonderful

> passing and a blessed end, in which she has escaped the power of the flesh, the world, the Turk, and the Devil, the power of natural love is so great that we cannot go without tears and without pain in our hearts, indeed, without part of ourselves dying. Deep in our heart, after all, we remember how this very obedient and exemplary daughter appeared in life and death, how she did things, how she talked, so that even the death of Christ (and what is the dying of any person compared to his dying) cannot take that away as it actually should.[26]

At Home

Katharina exercised tight control over home matters, and from time to time this clashed with Luther's fairly unorganized manner of doing things: "If I should ever marry again, I will carve a wife out of stone who will obey me."[27] At one time, Käthe wanted to buy an extra vegetable garden, but Luther was opposed. Nevertheless, she managed to get what she wanted through her pleading and tears. Because he did not have enough money for the purchase, he borrowed 17.5 guilders from the treasury of the church.[28] It was as if Luther spoke from experience when he said, "O, dear Lord God, marriage is not something natural or physical, but it is a gift of God; it is the most wonderful and the most pure of living and rates higher than celibacy. But if things go sideways in a marriage, it immediately becomes hell."[29] In the same *Table Talk* discussion, Luther also mentioned, "Through God's grace I have received an extremely happy marriage. I have a faithful wife totally the way Solomon describes it (Prov. 31:11): *The heart of the husband trusts in her*. She does not disappoint me."[30] This was rather meager praise for the woman whose efforts enabled Luther to continue his famous work.

The large household could not function without servants, but how many were in the Luther household is not known. We do know the name of Luther's personal assistant, Wolf Seberger, who was responsible for the cellar, the garden, and all the business interests. Luther said he was faithful but lazy. He had no use for that, seeing he himself was so terribly busy:

> Every day I am inundated with so many letters that the table, the benches, the stool, the lecterns, the window ledges, planks, in short,

> everything, is full of letters with questions, quarrels, complaints, requests, etc. The burden of ecclesiastical and political life is caving in on me; this is how poorly the spiritual and secular officials understand what their office really is.[31]

Some days Luther wrote up to forty letters, in addition to preparing sermons, lectures, and treatises. Fortunately, he had some secretarial help from George Rörer, who with his son, Paul, lived with them in the monastery after the passing of his wife.

On top of all that, he bore the responsibility of caring for the six children of his sister Margarethe, who came to live with them after she had died. One of them, Lene, married professor Ambrosius Berndt in 1538. Festivities with hired musicians took place in the Luther house. Luther used the opportunity to extol the virtues of marriage once again but felt compelled to critique the ornate bridal gown. Berndt died in 1542, and so Lene returned to live at home again. In May 1545, she wanted to marry Ernst Reuchlin, a medical student, but Luther opposed the marriage, questioning Reuchlin's intentions. His opposition was in vain, however, because Lene insisted, and they married anyway.[32]

There was also the dog, Tölpel.[33] This animal chewed at least one of Luther's letters[34] that we know of and was probably responsible for the loss of more correspondence.

The house in which Luther lived was almost permanently under construction. It required constant renovation: new windows, a proper bathroom, expansion of the stalls, a spring in the garden, and extra rooms. All this building had to happen in the midst of all the other regular activities. During one in-house renovation, a section of wall caved in and nearly crushed Luther and Käthe.[35] The house was decorated by a gift that Käthe gave her husband for his birthday in 1540, a new and special entryway into their home (see fig. 8.1). Käthe had designed this entry herself. It represented the gospel of the cross, so that everyone who entered would see it. On each side of the wide doors, a kind of seat was built into the recesses of the entryway, and above it appeared the Luther rose (see fig. 8.2).

After meals, Luther usually led a devotion from the Psalms. Afterward, there was some time for games or exercise. One of his medical doctors reported,

Figure 8.1 The entry that Käthe gave Luther for his birthday in 1540. Photo courtesy of Touristoffice Wittenberg.

Figure 8.2 A detail from the entry depicting the Luther rose. Photo by onnola, Lutherhaus, Lutherstadt Wittenberg, 2014 (CC BY-SA 2.0).

> After they had had some more or less serious discussions during meals, Luther really liked to see his boarders and table guests become involved in some games, in which he would also participate. He enjoyed watching the youth when they had sack races or jumping from hat to hat, and more of such games. He also had a bowling lane installed, and participated himself, and demonstrated all kinds of bowling tricks. With this, he sometimes compared the hitting or missing of the pins with life itself, how they would have a strike at one time and miss out on another. Therefore, he taught the young folks that they should never laugh at others when they missed the pins, because that could happen to them later in life as well.[36]

Property

In 1535, Luther and Käthe bought a small garden for twenty guilders, and for nine hundred guilders, they bought an orchard with a spring and a brook with fish. In the fall of that year, they purchased another field with an adjacent garden for another 180 guilders. All this property was needed to provide for the family and many guests and to allow the family some economic independence from the unpredictable and often scant marketplace, where they often couldn't get what they needed anyway.

Lean times were a thing of the past, though, when Luther began his building projects. They finally had enough money to renovate the monastery into something where they could live comfortably. Luther had already informed the elector that "if I would want to build a place to live, I would probably not do that in this pigsty."[37] But now that Käthe had planted an herbarium and installed a home brewery, and since, in the meantime, they had so many children, family, and students living in the monastery, they would try to make something nice out of it. They intended to build several cellars, including a wine cellar, as well as a spacious living room, stalls for the horses and cattle, and a number of heated rooms and extra living space to rent out to students. The work took quite some time. The renovation started in 1541, when Luther had a bathroom built (about fourteen feet by fourteen feet). In June 1541, he also bought a house for Käthe because he expected that after he died, the monastery would be too large for her.

On Easter 1542, he calculated what he had spent on renovations and new construction: a total of 1,805 guilders. This money was spent for the brewery, stalls for the animals, the bathroom, the cellar, additional rooms in the house, the chimney, stairs, a garden, a spring, the back of the house where they had work space, and the roof. Although the lean times were over, the financial situation for the Luther household was a constant problem. Luther's hospitality resulted in expenses that exceeded the income, and if Käthe had not grown a lot of the food herself and sold part of it to earn some extra cash, the situation would have been completely untenable. She was also the one who constantly reminded the student boarders to pay their board, which resulted in Käthe unfairly getting a bad name.

Discussions

With the burning of the books on canon law, Luther had inadvertently given himself another huge job. Without such books, people called on Luther to answer all kinds of questions. Regarding marriage, for example, he was inundated with requests for advice, and he did not hesitate to give it. In one situation he allowed a pastor, whose wife left him for another man, to enter again into marriage.[38] Elsa Moser's husband was kidnapped by the Turks, and when she thought that he had died, she married a preacher. But when her first husband unexpectedly returned, Luther was asked who should have the first claim? According to Luther, the first one had first claim, and therefore, the preacher had to leave.[39] Jobst Kern, a preacher in Allstedt, had married a nun who wanted to continue her celibacy even after their marriage. Jobst objected, and she left. Luther said that they should seek reconciliation but that Jobst could remarry if that discussion failed to produce any positive results.[40] Stephan Roth from Wittenberg got a job as the city secretary in Zwickau. He moved, but his wife did not want to accompany him. Luther failed to convince her, and then he blamed Roth for failing to assert his leadership in the marriage.[41] Johann Lang had married a wife who was much older than he. When she died, Luther did not know whether he should offer Johann condolences or congratulate him.[42]

On account of these types of questions, Luther decided that it would be better to write a booklet so that others could find answers.

Consequently, in January his *On Marital Issues* was published.[43] Luther departed from many of the traditional rules but also from the views of many reformed jurists, whom he thought too strict or unreasonable.

Luther's message of God's undeserved grace and the freedom of a Christian had been eagerly and joyfully accepted by many; unfortunately, many interpreted this message as downplaying the importance of obedience. During Luther and Melanchthon's visit to the churches in Kursachsen, they discovered preachers who proclaimed that good works were a threat to grace and that it was better to disparage them. Clearly, they had understood little about the workings of grace.

Melanchthon thought that something had to be done quickly. Erasmus and Rome had already predicted that Luther's message of grace would result in licentiousness. Luther believed that the result of a reformation of doctrine should be a reformation of lifestyle. Melanchthon thought that the solution would be to emphasize penitence as a prerequisite for grace. He felt that the law had to be preached first so that people would become conscious of guilt and repent; then, the gospel could be offered to them. Luther could agree only marginally with him; he was afraid that they would again end up with some stipulation that one has to follow a particular order of steps to receive grace: God would give grace only if the person would first feel guilty.

Johann Agricola (1492/1494–1566), principal of the school in Eisleben, who was annoyed already that his friends Luther and Melanchthon had not appointed him as professor in Wittenberg, did not agree with Melanchthon's view at all. His slogan was "Penance comes after the gospel." According to Agricola's views, the law and God's judgment could potentially disappear entirely from the sermon. Even though Luther believed this disagreement was only a war of words, the quarrel needed to be resolved officially. They sought to do this at a meeting in Torgau from November 26 to 29. Luther proposed a compromise and acceded to Melanchthon that preaching repentance was necessary but also agreed with Agricola that penitence is a product of faith. That sounded like a good solution, but because Melanchthon and Agricola would not budge from their views, the conflict boiled up again later on, only more acrimoniously.

Figure 8.3 *The Seven-Headed Martin Luther*. Print by Hans Brosamer. Cover page of Johannes Cochlaeus's *Sieben köpfen Martini Luthers*, 1520. From Otto Henne am Rhyn, *Kulturgeschichte des deutschen Volkes*, vol. 2 (Berlin, 1897).

The whole discussion underscored the necessity of visiting the churches, as Luther indicated in his preface[44] to Melanchthon's handbook for church visitors. This work, titled *Instruction for Church Inspectors*, was published in 1528, after Elector John the Steadfast had given orders to visit all the churches. In the introduction, Luther stated that it would be appropriate to reinstate the apostolic tradition of experienced, wise men visiting congregations and ministers. Catholic opponents mocked this idea; the treatise by Cochlaeus concerning the seven-headed Luther is most descriptive of this criticism (see fig. 8.3).

Education

To counter the lack of understanding of the Christian faith among young and old, Luther constantly promoted efforts for good catechesis and regular church services that would teach it. He knew that catechistic preaching may not be popular among ministers, but he believed that it was enormously important and useful, though few ministers could do this work well.[45] In 1518, he published a simple explanation of the Ten Commandments and a year later a similar work concerning the Lord's Prayer.

According to Luther, this work had made a positive impact, because in September 1528, he noticed that a boy or girl of fifteen years knew more about God's Word than all the scholars at the theological faculties had before then. The people were again learning

> the Lord's Prayer, the Apostles' Creed, the Ten Commandments, about penance, baptism, prayer, the cross, life, death, and the sacrament of the altar. And also [they were learning] what marriage, secular authority, what a father and mother, wife and child, husband and son, servant and maidservant are. In short, I have made sure that all classes have ended up where they are supposed to be, and that everyone knows how he must live and how he must serve God in his position. In those who have accepted this, it is visible how much fruit, peace, and virtue this has produced.[46]

He wanted to make something better available, a work that used questions and answers to clearly teach doctrine. In early 1529, Luther's Large and Small Catechisms came out. The Small Catechism was meant for children and young people, and the Large Catechism he wrote for ministers who wanted to address their ignorance. Luther considered the Large Catechism one of his best works.[47] He continued to use this catechism himself:

> I am still like a child who is being taught the catechism; every morning I read a section aloud, word for word, and if I have the time, the Lord's Prayer, the Ten Commandments, the confession, the Psalms, etc. And still I have to read and study these every day. Yet I am not as steadfast as I should be, and therefore, I must remain a child and pupil of the catechism, and I do that eagerly.[48]

The responsibility for the knowledge of the Christian faith was foremost a responsibility of the parents, and therefore, Luther believed that every father was compelled to listen to his children recite the catechism once a week.[49] The sequence that Luther used in his catechism was commandments, faith, prayer, sacraments, and then other topics. This order would become traditional for many Protestant catechisms, such as the Heidelberg Catechism. With each of the sections of commandments, faith, prayer, and baptism, Luther also made a hymn, so that people could remember the content even better.

Toward the end of February 1525, Luther had again resumed his task as professor, and he began by lecturing on Deuteronomy. At first he did this with a small group in the Augustinian monastery. In the summer of 1525, he again gave lectures publicly at the university. Beginning with Deuteronomy was strategic; Luther believed that he needed to counter the notions that the Old Testament was not worth much and that we could leave the law behind. Many thought that the gospel made the law of Moses redundant. He did not want to accede to that school of thought, and with these lectures he sought to clarify that Moses "is the source and the father of all prophets and of the Holy Scriptures, and that with this, he is heavenly wisdom and the heavenly voice itself."[50]

From the summer of 1525 to 1526, he lectured on the Minor Prophets. At the beginning of 1526, his lectures on Jonah appeared in book format. These became a great success, with thirteen German printings and three in Latin. From July 30 to November 7, 1526, he lectured on Ecclesiastes. He found that this work was so difficult for him that at a certain point, he didn't want to continue. On September 5, he quit, but he continued again on September 25, because he realized it had to be finished. Between November 1526 and August 1527, he was so busy with the conflicts around the Lord's Supper that he could not give lectures. When he resumed this work, he offered lectures on 1 John, Titus, Philemon, and 1 Timothy. Afterward, he began with the Song of Solomon, but because of several interruptions, he could not complete those lectures until 1531.

Rulers and Turks

After the Peasants' Revolt, Luther was faced with more questions about the proper role of government. A knight, Assa von Kram, who had participated in the bloody struggle against the rebels, asked him whether a man could be saved if he had been a soldier. Luther responded pointedly to this question in his booklet, published in 1526, *Whether Soldiers Can Be Saved*.[51] In this work he made a distinction between the office and the person. It was not one's office or role that determined one's salvation but one's individual stance before God. The government must use the sword and commit some injustice to prevent a much greater injustice. Again, Luther rejected rebellion against tyranny.

This consistent appeal to obey the government did not prevent Luther from solidly criticizing the rulers who had acted unjustly. For example, Elector Joachim von Brandenburg had initiated a relationship with Katharina Hornung and made her his mistress. Katharina, however, was married to Wolf Hornung, who, in a quarrel with his wife, struck her, thus giving the elector a good excuse to banish him from the country. In 1527, Katharina wanted to return to her husband, and when Elector von Brandenburg wouldn't let her go, she appealed to Luther, who immediately threatened the elector with God's judgment. Luther's eagerness to do this no doubt owed in part to the fact that Brandenburg was an opponent of the Reformation. Brandenburg did not react to Luther's threats, so Luther took issue with this matter in a public letter. Katharina should be given her freedom, Luther wrote, or at least be given the opportunity to talk to her husband about an eventual divorce. After this public letter to the elector, he also sent a pair of letters to other princes. Luther did not succeed, most likely because Katharina had changed her mind and had informed Luther that he must stop his nagging and that, indeed, she wanted to divorce her husband. Luther was not happy about this and published Katharina's letter, along with a foreword declaring that Katharina was a whore and that the elector should be castrated. How this sordid story ended is not known, but it is clear that Luther felt free to speak his mind to the rulers.

Luther did agree with the rulers on one issue: the problem of the Turks. The "Turkish danger" often spoken about in the sixteenth century referred to both religious and political threats. Luther had a problem with the peasants, but the emperor had a problem with the Turks. Since the accession of Sultan Suleiman the Magnificent (r. 1520–1566), the Ottoman Empire had made great gains, capturing the city of Budapest in 1526. Behind this threat against Western Europe, the emperor, the pope, and Luther was Islam. When the armies of the sultan attacked Hungary, Luther wrote a booklet, *Concerning the War against the Turks*,[52] though it wasn't published until 1529.

Luther saw the Turks as an instrument of the Devil and as an expression of God's wrath against the lack of repentance among Christians. Nevertheless, he stressed that the government is called to oppose this threat with force and thus to protect freedom and the Christian faith. Therefore, the emperor and the other rulers must train and equip a well-organized army but at the same time trust in God, not in weapons. He appealed to the church to pray both for deliverance from the approaching enemy and for remorse and repentance.

Though the Turks had withdrawn by the time the booklet appeared, they invaded Hungary again in early July 1529. Luther had not been in the Coburg Castle for long before he began to reflect on the themes of Islam again:

> From the bottom of my heart, I am beginning to burn against the Turks and against Mohammed, because in them I see the unbearable rage of Satan, who rampages against our bodies and our souls. Therefore, I want to pray against it and plead and will not cease until I know that my crying has been heard in heaven.[53]

Because of his fear of Islam, Luther translated a treatise against the Qur'an that had been written by the Dominican Richard. According to this work, people should realize that Islam is fundamentally different from the Christian faith, even if he had to concede that the Muslims treated their religion more seriously than many Christians.

Luther saw the whole conflict with the Turks in the context of the approaching end of the world as described in Revelation 20. By the fall of 1529, the Turkish armies had advanced to the gates of Vienna. Western Europe saw this as a sign of the approaching end of the world. Many demanded that the emperor intervene, but he would need the financial and military support of the rulers, both Catholic and Protestant. That would cost him money and concessions, and his campaign against Luther was therefore put on hold again.

Conflict concerning the Lord's Supper

Concerning the Lord's Supper, Luther was also searching; he was convinced that the conventional view in his day was not right. The Lord's Supper was not a sacrifice, and the bread and wine were not changed essentially into the flesh and blood of Christ. But what was it then? If it was not to be called the "mass" anymore, what should the name be? "We can observe the mass as sacrament, or as testament, or thanksgiving, in Greek that is Eucharist, or supper of the Lord, or remembrance of the Lord, or communion, or whatever pious term that appears to be appropriate."[54] Lack of clarity among other reformers did not help the situation. Collectively, the reformers agreed that the mass was not a good work, nor was it a sacrifice that the congregation offered to God via the priest. Furthermore, while they all agreed that the doctrine of transubstantiation was wrong, they still disagreed about what the Lord's Supper actually was. The diversity of opinions concerning the Lord's Supper (in German *Abendmahl*, or "evening meal," a term not found in Scripture but coined by Luther) were so divisive that this sacrament instituted by Jesus, meant as a meal to declare the unity of believers, became an issue that would separate Lutherans and Calvinists for many centuries.

In many ways the Lord's Supper was the fundamental issue of theological disagreement. One's views on the Lord's Supper determined other views about sin and grace, Christ and the Holy Spirit, the church and congregation, discipline, the relationship between the Word and sacrament, and more. It was not strange, therefore, that a major aspect of the conflict between Rome and Luther concerned the mass. This was also an issue that elicited a lot of discussion among the reformers. It is regrettable that concerning this sacrament of atonement the differences generated so much conflict that Protestants remained separated for centuries.

The conflict had begun with Carlstadt, the first one who denied any presence of Christ in the Lord's Supper and argued that it was a matter of the congregation. Another person who identified with this view was Caspar von Schwenckfeld (1489–1561), a nobleman who had been won for the Reformation in 1519 when he had read Luther's works. At an early stage in his thinking, however, he expressed concern that the message of justification might jeopardize sanctification. Schwenckfeld was

Figure 8.4 Huldrych Zwingli (1484–1531). Woodcut by Hans Asper, 1531.

somewhat mystically inclined, and that would certainly have pushed him in the direction of the Swiss reformer Huldrych Zwingli (1484–1531), because the latter emphasized inward reflection (see fig. 8.4). Zwingli's view was that the bread and wine were symbols of Christ's body and blood. When Jesus said, "This is my body," he meant, "This means my body." Zwingli had developed this idea after reading a letter from the Dutch lawyer Cornelis Henricxzoon Hoen (ca. 1440–ca. 1524) in which he proposed this view. Hinne Rode, the humanist rector of a school in Utrecht, shared this letter with Luther, Bucer, and Zwingli, among others. Luther thought that it was rather strange that Jesus would have meant something that he did not say, and therefore, he rejected the explanation. Bucer was more favorable to this explanation, and Zwingli thought it was an ideal solution. Schwenckfeld agreed with Zwingli but turned to Luther with his questions. When Luther failed to respond, he went to Wittenberg to speak to him face-to-face.[55] Though they spoke with each other, they failed to find common ground and parted for good.

Behind anyone who posed a question concerning the bodily presence of Christ, Luther immediately saw the three-headed monster Carlstadt, Müntzer, and Schwenckfeld arise. His attitude made it almost impossible to have a reasoned discussion with anyone on this matter. When Luther noticed that Zwingli's view shared many similarities with Carlstadt's, who had also been influenced by Hoen, Luther dismissed him. Zwingli and Luther continued to debate with each other by means of letters and books, not always helpfully. Luther maintained that this issue concerned Christ himself: "The fanatics strangle my Christ, my Lord, and God the Father and his words, and also my mother, Christendom. And consequently, they also strangle my brothers, and they would also like to have me dead."[56] Here again, Luther's tendency to personalize theological debates caused problems. What he had found after seeking so long, namely, that salvation lay outside himself in Christ, he did not want to relinquish again.

Marburg

In the spring of 1529, the imperial diet was held in Speyer. Once again the Edict of Worms against Luther was repeated and confirmed. The rulers who agreed with Luther submitted a protest, from which the term Protestant arose. Clearly, it was time that they should effectuate political and ecclesiastical unity to present a single reformational front to the emperor and the pope, who now truly wanted to do something about this German problem.

Philip of Hesse (1504–1567), one of the most important princes on the Protestant side, invited Luther and Zwingli, with their respective supporters, to come to his castle in the hope of achieving a compromise in the conflict over the Lord's Supper (see fig. 8.5). On September 30, Luther and Melanchthon arrived with their delegation. The Swiss, together with Bucer from Strasbourg, arrived a few days earlier. To prevent the two hotheads from attacking one another, on October 1, Luther and Oecolampadius met separately in a room, and in another room Melanchthon and Zwingli met.

The big discussion began the following morning at six o'clock. Elector Philip had placed a table in the middle of the room so the participants could stand around it to discuss the issues (see fig. 8.6). Early in the discussion, Luther turned back the tablecloth, and with a piece of chalk he wrote on the table, *Hoc est corpus meum*, Latin for "This is my body." That action did not bode well, because Luther had

Figure 8.5 Castle of Marburg. Photo courtesy of Daniela Frank (CC BY-SA 3.0).

Figure 8.6 An image depicting Zwingli and Luther discussing the Lord's Supper issue in Marburg. From the Zwingli door in the Grossmünster in Zurich.

constantly held that if Jesus says, "This is my body," then the bread is his body. He covered the words again with the tablecloth, but in the afternoon, in the heat of the discussion, Luther turned back the tablecloth and declared, "See, here it is."[57]

The debate continued on Sunday morning, October 3, but again, they made no progress. During the afternoon, it was determined that the discussion had come to an impasse, which both sides regretted. Because an outbreak of the plague continued to rage near Marburg, they felt compelled to cut the discussions short. Luther could not sacrifice the physical presence of Christ, and Zwingli refused to adopt this view. Luther suggested that they would have to leave it up to God's judgment, which both agreed to. Luther asked Zwingli for forgiveness for the times that he had been too sharp. He was, after all, only a man of flesh and blood. Zwingli said more or less the same and emotionally stated his desire for friendship. Luther felt it was appropriate at that moment to express the wish that he hoped that God would soon permit the folks in Zurich to come to better insight. The tears were soon dried, and the Swiss wished the same to Luther.

To avoid going home empty-handed, the elector asked Luther to make a list of all the points of agreement. Luther later wrote to Katharina,

> We agree on almost all points, except that our opponents stick to the view that it is only bread in the Lord's Supper, and they maintain that Christ is only spiritually present. Today the landgrave wants to negotiate with the intention that we will come to agreement, and if we continue to disagree, we will still accept each other as brothers and as members of Christ. The landgrave really wants to put some effort into this. But we don't want that "brother" and "member" [of Christ]. We want peace, and we also want the best for everyone.[58]

There appeared to be many points on which they all agreed, fourteen in all, which everyone seemed eager to affirm. Actually, the only point that they disagreed on was point fifteen. Unfortunately, that was the very point that had prompted this meeting in the first place. The importance of this point for Luther was evident from his concluding remark to the Swiss that he could accept them neither as brothers in Christ nor as members of the body of Christ. Indeed, they had agreed concerning point fifteen that they all rejected transubstantiation. Zwingli had even moved toward Luther's position by declaring that the Lord's Supper was more than just a symbol and that it provided comfort. But whether Christ was really present in the bread and wine or not left them divided.

As often happens after this kind of meeting, both sides declared themselves the winner. However, in actual fact there were only losers. Luther revealed his feelings about all this in his response to Zwingli's death in 1531: he died on a battlefield, clearly of God's judgment. He should not have embraced such a bizarre view of the Lord's Supper, according to Luther. More and more, Luther reinforced his claim that Christ was physically present in the bread and wine, even though he agreed that these elements remained plain bread and wine. He pushed his point so far that when questioned how the body of Christ could be in more than one place at a time, he concluded that the exalted human nature of Christ is so closely connected to his divine nature that it is omnipresent. Those who rebuked this contorted argument were accused of prioritizing logic over faith. Thus the discussion about the Lord's Supper ended in Marburg. Luther reported on October 12,

> Present were Oecolampadius, Zwingli, Bucer, Hedio, together with three high councillors: Jacob Sturm from Strasbourg, Ulrich Funk from Zurich, and N. N. from Basel. With extreme humility they appealed for peace. We negotiated for two days. I answered both Zwingli and Oecolampadius and held up this text to them: "This is my body." I countered every objection. The day before, we spoke heart-to-heart and amicably: I spoke with Oecolampadius, Philipp with Zwingli. In the meantime, Osiander, Johannes Brenz, and Stefan [Agricola] arrived from Augsburg. Those people are stupid and inexperienced when it comes to debating. Even though they themselves may have felt that their conclusions didn't prove anything, nevertheless, concerning the presence of the body of Christ, they did not want to budge. And according to us, that was rooted more in fear and shame than in unwillingness. In every other topic, they conceded. . . . In conclusion, they asked if at least we would

> recognize them as brothers. The landgrave really pressured us to accept that. But I cannot allow that. Nevertheless, we did shake their hands as a sign of peace and love, so that those angry writings and words could come to rest. Everyone will defend his opinion, without railing against the other but not without defense and rebuttal. And that is the way we parted.[59]

Afterward, Bucer did not leave the matter alone, and Luther viewed him with a mixture of skepticism and appreciation:

> Bucer has begun to embrace the same opinion about the Lord's Supper as we have, if the letters that he wrote to me and Philipp do not deceive us, which I actually do not believe. Whether the others wanted this too is not apparent thus far. Bucer truly does his best to convince the others and has already achieved that much, that everyone concedes that the body of the Lord truly and physically is present and is handed out. But the others say that in this way he is only handed out and is presented as food to the devout and believing souls. Bucer, however, agrees that the minister presents him to unbelievers, and they take him in their mouth.[60]

Coburg

After the imperial Diet of Worms in 1521, Emperor Charles V had scant time to concern himself with the developments in the German Empire. The hostility of King Francis I of France had especially demanded so much of his attention that he had been unable to determine whether the decisions taken against Luther and his supporters had ever been carried out. Around 1525, Luther's movement had spread broadly but had not developed anywhere into a concrete reformation. In many churches a few things had been changed, including the preaching. But one could hardly speak of a "reformed" church. Only when political leaders had declared themselves for the Reformation could something actually happen, leading to a genuinely new church.

Not until 1530, when the Reformation had been embraced by many rulers and cities, did the emperor arrive at Augsburg to convene a diet to resolve the Luther problem. He extended a friendly invitation to the rulers and theologians, but it was already clear that he wanted to proceed in the spirit of Worms. Charles needed unity in the empire, not least because of the constant Turkish threat. But as a faithful Catholic, he wanted unity in the church and active opposition to every possible heresy. Therefore, he wanted to hear the beliefs of the reformers from their own mouths. Luther could not come because he was still a declared fugitive; in Augsburg he would have been immediately imprisoned. He tried to be as close as possible to the action in Augsburg, though, and stayed almost half a year in the imposing castle fortress of Coburg, situated at the southern tip of his elector's territory.

On April 3, 1530, the delegation left Wittenberg to meet up with the elector and his retinue at Torgau. Together they would travel to the Diet of Augsburg. On Good Friday, April 15, they arrived at the little city of Coburg. Luther preached a number of times, and after a week, he was lodged in the impressive castle. The others traveled to Augsburg, about 150 miles from Coburg. Luther stayed behind, together with his attendant, Veit Dietrich (1506–1549), one of Luther's students, who had become his personal secretary. Luther was assigned two regal rooms with views of the forests of Thuringia. Almost immediately he wrote out a number of texts from the Psalms on the walls, such as Psalm 118:17 and Psalm 74:21, to encourage himself. Outside his rooms he observed the tremendous cawing of innumerable crows. In his imagination, he had already "arrived in the midst of a diet," namely,

> [the imperial Diet of] the Crows, the proud-hearted kings and the great ones of the empire who meticulously look after the needs of their subjects and attend to their concerns, and with tireless voices cry out their decisions and doctrinal proclamations through the air. . . . They despise the silly fuss with gold and silk. . . . They are all black, they all have dark eyes, they are unanimous in their music, nevertheless, with a pleasing distinction between the voices of the older ones and the younger ones. I am sitting in this diet, and I rejoice about the unanimity of all these fathers of the fatherland and the sustainers of society.[61]

Once, Luther went into the forest with Veit Dietrich to shoot at those birds with arrows. In their flight, he also saw a clear parallel: "You only have to clap your hands, and they fly away in fright. That is the way it will also be with the papists the moment God sounds his Word."[62]

Luther was well guarded and looked after in the castle, and though the site was meant to be secret, he received visitors regularly, so much so that he feared that the Coburg would become a new pilgrimage site. He appreciated the mail they brought with them that kept him up to date with events at home and abroad. Life was good in the Coburg, as was evident from the fact that during the 165 days that Luther stayed there, he and his guests consumed about three hundred gallons of wine. Käthe admonished him that he should be more constrained.[63]

Less pleasant were the many physical ailments that afflicted Luther. He complained that a poor set of glasses someone had given him was the least of his problems. The wound in his leg from years earlier had opened up again, and the medicines that were sent did not help. Most problematic were the ringing noises in his head that caused so many headaches. Sometimes it was an annoyingly soft sound, but often it was a banging like the sound of thunder. He knew where it came from: "The Devil is visiting me with a whole delegation." But he realized that there were other causes, such as the hard wind that blew around the castle and the heat of summer. Also, he admitted that the large quantities of wine that he drank caused headaches.[64] When the noises in his head finally ceased, he suffered from toothaches and a sore neck. These ailments bothered him all the more because there was little for him to do: "I do not have any other choice than to be a lazy, worthless donkey."[65] He could not read or write due to illness but kept himself occupied with praying and singing and with sleeping, games, and sports.

Despite these depreciatory words, and despite his ailments, Luther, as he had intended, still managed to accomplish a lot during his stay in the Coburg. When he arrived, he had developed a plan and had informed Linck that he would "make a Zion from this Sinai" and would "build three tabernacles: one for the Psalms, one for the Prophets, and one for Aesop."[66] The Coburg fortress was his Sinai. Did he entertain the notion that he was Moses, busy with God's law, while down below in Augsburg, Melanchthon together with the people served the golden calf and would end up joining the Romish idolatry? Luther did not expand on these thoughts; Melanchthon understood the warning in Luther's voice. Therefore, Luther preferred to transform his Sinai into Mount Zion, where Peter proposed to raise three tents, for the Lord, Moses, and Elijah, as in Matthew 17:1–13.

As far as the Psalms were concerned, Luther dictated short commentaries to Veit Dietrich on Psalms 1–25. His extensive commentary on Psalm 118, *The Beautiful Confitemini*,[67] was more important. For two weeks, between June 13 and June 26, he interrupted his translation work on the Prophets. Concerning Psalm 118, he said, "I love this Psalm tremendously . . . because it has already been very useful to me and has helped me out of great distress in a way that no emperor, kings, or sages of the saints could have helped me."[68]

The animal fables of Aesop (ca. 550 BC), according to Luther, contained a great number of practical gems of wisdom that could benefit everyone, and therefore, he began a new German translation, a task he never completed. In addition to these "tabernacles," he wrote a treatise about church discipline, a famous little treatise on Bible translation, and another treatise in which he appealed to parents to send their children to school.

On June 5, 1530, Luther received a message that his father had passed away. He had become ill in February, and Luther had sent him a letter of encouragement. He strongly desired to go to Mansfeld, but his health would not allow it. Years earlier he had attempted to convince his parents to move to Wittenberg, unsuccessfully. Even more strongly, he hoped that his father's faith in Christ would break through, and according to Luther this had happened, because he was sure that

> in a short while we will again see each other in Christ's presence, also because departure from this life means much less for God than when I travel back from your place in Mansfeld or if you were to travel from Wittenberg to Mansfeld. It [dying] is only a small hour of sleep, and then everything is already different.[69]

Nevertheless, his father's passing grieved him greatly. When he received the notice, he withdrew with his book of Psalms and wept long and passionately.[70]

Augsburg

Luther was far from the diet and had to depend on information from letters that had been underway for a long time. He could not do much more than write an *Exhortation to the Clerics Who Have Come Together at the Diet of Augsburg.*[71] This was an appeal to the bishops to finally carry out reform. In the meantime, they could see for themselves what that had produced, namely, that faith again provided comfort and did not only require exertion. At the same time, he repeated that he was no innovator but that he wanted to bring the church back to the original path that it had forsaken.

Melanchthon was the appointed person to speak on behalf of the reformed group. This concerned Luther, who thought Melanchthon was so amicable and peace loving that he might compromise for the sake of peace. He did express his satisfaction, however, with the draft declaration, called an "apology"; in fact, it was the first version of a work that would become the confession of the Lutheran Church, the Augsburg Confession. When Luther saw the draft, he said, "Your apology, which I read completely and carefully yesterday, pleases me."[72] In the letter to the elector, he said a bit more: "I have read the *apologia* written by M[aster] Philipp, and it pleases me well. I would not know what has to be improved or changed. That would not be good either, because I cannot walk so guardedly and softly."[73] Luther knew himself well enough to know that he was not suited to write such formulations. This was no criticism of Melanchthon. On the contrary, Luther praised him for his prudence.

But the praise would soon end. Luther sat in the Coburg Castle, waiting for whatever would transpire in Augsburg. They kept him up to date, but sometimes that took too long for him. He became annoyed and wrote to Melanchthon that if he didn't say anything, then Luther wouldn't say anything anymore either, a promise Luther kept for three weeks. There was a good reason for Melanchthon's silence: he and the others did not want Luther to discover that they were trying to strike an agreement with the emperor and the pope.

Apparently, Luther had a suspicion that something like this was happening. He informed them that he thought their approach in some matters was too soft. "You are better off falling with Christ than to remain standing with the emperor," Luther had advised Melanchthon.[74] Luther became very concerned about the diet. He felt that Melanchthon went much too far in his rapprochement with the emperor and the pope. He should be more steadfast in his defense of the reformational doctrine and be far less concerned about the breach in the church and the power of the emperor and pope. Luther informed him, "With fervor I hate your miserable concerns," saying that it was time for Melanchthon to begin a fight with himself against his lack of faith and trust.[75]

The latter statement sounded combative, but it was a cry of someone who had come to stand outside reality. That was the contrast between the Wartburg and the Coburg. In the first castle, Luther was the man of the future; in the second, he was a man of a bygone time. To a degree they kept him up to date with the developments, but it was no longer that important whether Luther was in favor or not, because among his supporters there were constantly more voices to pursue discussion and even strike a compromise.

On June 25, 1530, Melanchthon read the confession to the emperor that (mostly) he had written, a document that carefully explained the reformers' doctrine. Luther opined that it could have been sharper and that Melanchthon had given in a little too much to Rome. He thought Melanchthon was afraid of the emperor and was mistaken in his apparent mildness. Charles listens to us first, Luther warned his colleagues, and then he will strike. Despite his criticism, he was able to agree with the contents of the document. He also understood the difficulty Melanchthon had, and according to the letters that he sent, he was sensitive to the depressive circumstances in which he lived. Luther's comfort was louder and more emphatic than his criticism. Luther, too, was extremely concerned about the continuing developments and therefore spent much time in intensive prayer. At least three hours per day Luther prayed out loud and beseeched God for mercy.[76] Those prayers kept him going, from the conviction that "the Christian must be just as convinced that God hears his prayer as he is in embracing and believing that God is real."[77]

Six weeks after Melanchthon had read out the Lutheran confession of faith, a reaction came from the Catholic side. Because they had not agreed among themselves, it had taken a long time. One group wanted tough and hard-nosed action, but another group was sympathetic to the issues that Luther and his supporters had presented. Melanchthon drew up a defense document responding to the Catholic reaction to the Lutheran confession. This document, which became known as the Apology, was a different document than the draft of the Augsburg Confession, which was also called an apology. Of this document Luther was very critical: "I received the apology and asked what you want to accomplish with this request, and wherein and how much you want to give in to the papists."[78] Luther wrote that he

> walked around with this day and night. I consider it from all sides, look at it this way and then that way, go through the whole Bible, and constantly the surety grows within me about our doctrine, and I am confirmed in it. If God wills, I will not allow anything to be taken from me, whatever happens.[79]

Additionally, Luther had been annoyed that the Wittenberg delegation had said that in this approach they had followed the authority of Luther: "In this question I do not want to be your leader, or be named as such. . . . If it is my issue, I will provide that leadership myself."[80]

But it was not Luther's issue, not at all. The distance between Melanchthon and Luther in this matter had grown painfully evident. The quantity and the broad scope of the letters that Luther wrote and sent from the Coburg Castle made it very clear that he did not want theological stratagems and ecclesiastical politics. He was very worried that the gospel that he had once more discovered would again disappear into darkness. This was tied closely to his conviction that "a small heresy in theology would topple the complete doctrine. . . . The doctrine is not ours but belongs to God, and therefore, we may not allow a single dot on the 'i' to be missing."[81] Renewed discussions between the pope's delegation and the Lutherans followed, but Luther did not see any sense in this: "I hear that you, though not eagerly, have begun a peculiar task, namely, an agreement between the pope and Luther. But the pope doesn't want it, and Luther is opposed."[82] Luther was dismayed: "I am almost bursting with anger and worry. I want you to stop those negotiations and come home. . . . And if that leads to war, then so be it. We have prayed and done enough."[83] On August 30, the Lutheran delegation did stop. They were not making any progress, and the emperor conceded that the issue should be resolved by a council.

Prince Johann Friedrich, the oldest son of the elector, returned to Wittenberg, and along the way he visited Luther at the Coburg. When he arrived, he did not recognize Luther on account of the latter's new beard (like he had in the Wartburg). On behalf of his father, the prince presented to Luther an expensive signet ring with the so-called Luther rose as the insignia, a token of his father's gratitude. The elector had requisitioned this ring from a goldsmith in Augsburg. It was a beautiful ring, but for Luther it was far too large. The prince asked Luther to accompany him back to Wittenberg, but despite his urgent longing for his wife and children, he wanted to stay a little while longer. Luther worried that the Devil had the potential to incite the theologians who had remained behind in Augsburg to make unacceptable concessions.[84] Luther stuck to his position and appealed to others to do the same. The elector, Melanchthon, and the other participants of the delegation from Wittenberg left Augsburg at the end of September and arrived at the Coburg on October 1 to pick up Luther. The whole group departed on October 4, and around seven o'clock on October 13, Luther was finally home again. It had taken him eight days to travel from the Coburg to Wittenberg because he stopped along the way to preach in several places.

The big question now was, what would the emperor do after this diet? Many feared that he would use force to push back the Reformation. Therefore, the Protestants asked Luther whether they should obey or resist. The question had kept him occupied for some time, though he had changed his thinking somewhat since the Peasants' Revolt. His newest view on the issue was articulated in his treatise *Warning to His Beloved Germans*.[85]

Luther was still of the opinion that revolts were unlawful, but this did not mean that the people had to follow the government blindly. Luther stuck to the view that he articulated in 1523 in his treatise about the secular government: "If a ruler is wrong, are his people duty bound to follow him? Answer: No. Because it is unacceptable for anyone to act against the (established) right. People must obey God, who has the right on his side, more than man."[86] Luther made a distinction between the people and the princes. As far as it concerned the people, they could oppose but not revolt. But he yielded more to the thought that the ruling princes not only had the right but also the duty to disobey the emperor if the gospel was threatened and that they had the right to engage in armed opposition. If it came to a war, he himself had to remain silent and leave the decision making to the politicians:

> As a preacher in a spiritual office, it is not appropriate for me to wage war, or call to arms, but I should be the one who should counsel you not to wage war and appeal for peace. . . . But for the rest, I will let my pen rest, remain silent, and not become as involved as I did in that recent revolt.[87]

Luther's lessons from the Peasants' Revolt had been a costly learning experience, and now he tried to stick to his own conviction that ministers should not get involved in politics but instead leave that to other Christians.

Luther had, surprisingly, become a father to biological children, as well as a father figure to many reform-minded people throughout Germany. But as the Reformation saw new developments in the late 1520s, the limits of his fatherly role were becoming painfully apparent.

9

Professor (1530–1537)

Reorientation

Luther arrived home from the Coburg in rough shape. The ringing in his ears just didn't stop, and he said it sometimes sounded as if he heard all the church bells in the area all at once.[1] He was often bedridden and developed heart ailments. He was forty-nine and tired of everything: "No food or drink appeals to me. I am already dead, and they only have to bury me."[2] "I eat, drink, and sleep, but I can't read anything, write, or preach."[3]

Nevertheless, he continued his lectures on the Song of Solomon, which he completed on June 22, 1531. Two weeks later, July 2, he began a series of lectures on Galatians and completed these on December 12, the second time he had taught through Galatians.[4] In preparing for the new lecture series, he had reviewed his first lectures, given in 1516–1517, and had come to the conclusion that they were inferior and were too affected by his quest for an understanding of justification and his struggle against works righteousness.[5] Now that he had progressed in his thinking through much Bible study and conversation, he could make these lectures more reflective. He enjoyed this work so much that he could say, "The letter to the Galatians is my little letter, and I am married to it. It is my Käthe von Bora."[6] The lecture notes recorded by several students were published in 1535, accompanied with a foreword by Luther. This series would become an important manifesto for his theology. Luther opined that people who do not have a proper view of righteousness would collapse under the attacks of doubt, crushed by the erroneous idea that a person must do everything himself.

After his work on Galatians, he had to rest for three months, but then he continued his work on the Psalms, that is, on two of them: Psalm 2 and Psalm 51. Psalm 2, Luther said, is full of Christ. Those who see him in this psalm look into God's heart. Psalm 51 brought him to the heart of theology:

> The knowledge of God and man is divine wisdom and true theology. She is in this sense knowledge of God and mankind, so that she is ultimately related to the God who justifies and to man, who is the sinner, so that in essence, the subject of theology is really man, who is guilty and lost, and God, who justifies and who is the Savior.[7]

What Luther meant by this is best revealed in a woodcut that Lucas Cranach published in 1530. (Cranach had also painted a portrait of Luther in 1528; see fig. 9.1.) According to Luther it was also portrayed in the insignia he developed and used from 1530 for all his letters, the insignia that would become known as the Luther rose. In a letter to Spengler, Luther explained what his ring meant and what it stood for:

> First should be a black cross in a heart, which retains its natural color, so that I myself would be reminded that faith in the Crucified saves us. "For one who believes from the heart will be justified" (Rom. 10:10). Even though it is a black cross, which mortifies and which also should hurt us, yet it leaves the heart in its natural color and does not ruin nature. . . . That is, the cross does not kill but keeps man alive. For the just shall live by faith, by faith in the Savior. Such a heart should stand in the middle of a white rose, to show that faith gives joy, comfort, and peace. In other words, it places the believer into a white, joyous rose, for this faith does not give peace and joy like the world gives (John 14:27). That is why the rose should be white and not red, for white is the color of the spirits and the angels (Matt. 28:3). Such a rose should stand in a sky-blue field, symbolizing that such joy in spirit and faith is the beginning of the heavenly future joy, which begins already but is

Figure 9.1 *Portrait of Martin Luther*. Painting by Lucas Cranach the Elder, 1528. Lutherhaus Wittenberg, Wittenberg.

> grasped in hope though not yet revealed. And around this field is a golden ring, to signify that such bliss in heaven is endless and more precious than all joys and goods, just as gold is the most valuable and precious of metals.[8]

Education

Despite the fact that Luther preached about forty times a year in Wittenberg, his main task was giving lectures on the Bible. His students eagerly anticipated these lectures. Spalatin reported early in December 1520 that about four hundred students attended his lectures, an enormous number in those days. One student mentioned that all the class was impressed with Luther's deep knowledge of Scripture and his application of its truths to the Christian life. He gave students the opportunity to respond, took them along on his journeys of discovery in the Scriptures, and knew how to impart to them his joy in studying the Bible.[9] A student from Lübeck reported a fairly detailed description:

> He was a man of medium height, with a voice that was both sharp and soft—soft in its sound, sharp in the expression of the syllables, words, and sentences. He didn't speak too quickly or too slowly, but somewhere in the middle, without hesitations and very clearly. His speaking was well thought out as if the one thing flows forth into the next. He did not explain things by a confusing labyrinth of words, but first the words, then the sentences, so that you could see quite clearly that the contents of his explanation came directly from the text.[10]

In March 1532, Luther again lectured on the Psalms. Time and again he would return to this book in the Bible that he had become so familiar with and had learned to pray in the monastery. In November, he began lecturing on the so-called psalms of ascent, or pilgrim psalms (Psalms 120–34). These kept him busy for almost a year. There were no new developments in his theology, but he dedicated himself to teaching and passing on to the students what he had learned himself. The Psalms for him were the key to a life with God. Those who want to obey the first commandment can do that best, Luther believed, by reading through the Psalms, to learn them and to pray them. He concluded this series with Psalm 90.

Immediately after these lectures, in June 1535, he began a study of Genesis. Luther was in poor health, but he hoped that he could finish this lecture series before his death. He worked on this project for ten years, and it would indeed be his last project. Luther used the genealogies of Genesis to calculate how old the world was and how old it would become. As a result, since he began calculating in 1540, he concluded that the world was 5,500 years old. Because he assumed that the world would not reach the age of 6,000 years, he expected that the end would come soon.

With many other tasks, Luther found it difficult to continue his work on Genesis. When he had only reached chapter 24 in 1540, he wanted to stop. Urged by others, he continued anyway and was able to complete it. In 1535, Luther had also become dean of the theological faculty, a role he retained to the end of his life. He dedicated himself in time and energy to the university as a "foundation of the true religion." He wanted the university to appoint a music instructor, believing that future ministers and teachers should be able to sing and have working knowledge of music.[11] Luther was also busy writing reference letters for students who needed scholarships. Frequently, he would approach the elector for money, arguing that the church and the world needed good theologians; he also besieged burgomasters and rulers of other states or regions with requests for money. Students were preparing themselves for service in the kingdom of Christ and to the honor of God. Therefore, Luther told these rulers, it would be unfortunate if the students would have to terminate their studies due to a lack of funds.

Luther also looked after the needs of the students in other ways, warning them, for example, not to waste their money in a pub. He had no objection to students enjoying themselves with song and drink but urged them to know their limit and stay within it. Very specifically, he warned them of several notorious pubs that he believed should be nailed shut. He also railed against students who were regularly involved in fights with the citizens of Wittenberg. They should remember that they had come to Wittenberg to study, and therefore, they should behave properly.[12] He also implored the city officers to charge the prostitutes who had a number of students as customers; those students who could not control themselves were advised to go and study somewhere else.[13]

Collected Works

Because Luther's works were popular with the public, more and more collections of his writings were published. Luther himself felt that there was no need to save his works, although with the second printing of his collected works, he admitted that these publications showed "how things with me, or better, how developments have gone with the good Word of God, how much and from how many great enemies it has had to suffer these last fifteen years, and how powerful it has become, how it has grown, and how also I have come farther from day to day and from year to year."[14] In 1537, when plans were made to prepare another edition of collected works, he even said that as far as he was concerned, they could burn everything he had written and that only *On the Bondage of the Will* and the Large Catechism should be saved. His fear was that his works would stand in the way of the study of the Scriptures. But he realized that he could not prevent such publication, and he again pointed out that especially the Bible should be studied.

To make it clear how that should be done, he used three concepts that he drew from Psalm 119, namely, prayer (*oratio*), meditation (*meditatio*), and trial (*tentatio*). Knowledge of Scripture comes to a person only by way of prayer for the Holy Spirit's aid. Meditation is calm reflection—reading the Bible, comparing Scripture with Scripture, and allowing the Word to take root in the heart. In trials one learns how powerful and rich the Word of God is. Those trials come not only externally but also internally, such as to those who attend church but do not understand what it's about. In a church service, Luther made a strong effort to shape the liturgy in such a way that whatever came from the Word (whether Scripture reading or preaching) would be answered by the congregation with song and prayer.

Irreverence in the church service annoyed Luther terribly. People who came into the church service only to grumble and bleat would do better, Luther said, to leave the church in peace and join the animals: "If they want to grumble and natter, they should do that with the cows and pigs. They will probably react."[15] On a Sunday in June 1545, he was so distressed at the poor singing of the congregation that he walked out of church. Bugenhagen, who was leading the service, also became angry: "You have chased our father doctor Martinus out of church, and you will do that to me too so that I cannot preach to you any longer."[16]

According to Luther, the liturgy of the worship service is simple. It simply means that "our dear Lord himself speaks with us through his holy Word, and we speak with him in prayer and praise."[17] He described how that was done in his *German Mass* (1526), a reformed format of the existing Latin mass. With this, he proposed that churches should hold different kinds of services. A revised version of the Latin mass such as Luther had provided in the *Formula of the Mass* (1523) could be retained for students. If they learned that one, they could also participate in the services outside Germany. Because Luther realized that many people came to church out of curiosity or custom and that therefore many church attendees lacked a living faith, he wanted church services suitable for these people as well. Besides these services, he commended gatherings for people "who wanted to be serious Christians and confessed the gospel in word and deed."[18] Such meetings did not have to take place in church but could be held in people's homes.

Though that was what Luther wanted, in practice things often went differently. Very little of what Luther wrote of this time in Wittenberg speaks of a blossoming church or congregation. He complained that people who should have been living out the gospel more (grace) actually put more effort into living according to the law. On the flip side, those people who desperately needed to live more worthily of Christ appealed to the freedom of the gospel.[19] It appeared as if the people were already tired of the Word and would rather stay home to read a portion of Scripture than go to church to hear a sermon.[20] The work tired Luther as well: "I have preached here for twenty-four years, and I have walked the route to the church so often that it would be a miracle if not only my shoes but also my feet had not been worn out. I have done my part, and I feel good about that."[21] Luther also complained about the unwillingness of people to sacrifice. When the cost of living became more expensive in Wittenberg, the people skimped on the offertory in church, angering Luther. If people did not donate but thought first of themselves, the financing of the theological training would be jeopardized.[22] If they did not watch out, Luther warned, God would punish the Wittenbergers for their greediness.[23]

Baptism

Similar to the other reformers, Luther had searched what the Bible actually taught about baptism. He wanted to put an end to the easy manner in which children were baptized but did not espouse believer's baptism. Faith cannot be made into a condition for baptism, Luther thought, because then God's promises would depend on what a person does. In his *Concerning Baptism—to Two Ministers*,[24] published in 1528, Luther had already emphatically stated that baptism is an act of God.

Luther also kept himself occupied with practical aspects around this sacrament. He had become the consultant of choice for every city and every ruler in the German Empire that had embraced the Reformation. From Nuremburg he received the question whether the emergency baptism administered by midwives was valid. Catholic canon law had stipulated that such baptism was valid, since it also embraced the belief that unbaptized children were lost forever. Sometimes baptism was administered when the child was only partly born, and then parents were not even sure whether the midwife, at the height of the delivery, had administered it properly. In case of doubt, Luther advised to baptize the baby again. The child and the parents must be absolutely sure that the sacrament had been legally administered and received. Luther consistently chose certainty.

Schmalkalden

Since the emperor had rejected the Lutheran confession, it was important for the Protestant princes and rulers to unite their strength. As a son of the Roman church, the emperor could not accept the division of the church. More so, as son of the Habsburgers, he would be even less willing to accept a division of his empire. The obvious option was to use force to compel the rebellious rulers back into the Catholic fold. In November 1530, the Diet of Augsburg decided that the Edict of Worms had to be enforced and that all the ecclesiastical changes had to be undone everywhere. Luther reacted extensively with his *Warning to My Beloved Germans*,[25] stating that what had been achieved should not be surrendered. Wrongs had been abolished, false doctrine had been combatted, and biblical preaching had taken its place. That could not nor should be surrendered,

> because our gospel has—God be praised—provided us with great and good things. Before that, no one knew what the gospel was, what Christ, baptism, confession, sacrament, faith, spirit, flesh, good works, what the Ten Commandments were, what the Lord's Prayer was, what praying, suffering were, about comfort, about the secular government, about marriage, parents, children, servants, about woman, maid, Devil, angels, the world, death, right, forgiveness of sins, bishop, pastor, church, and what a Christian is, what

the cross is. In short: we knew absolutely nothing about what a Christian had to know.[26]

In December 1530, representatives of all the cities and territories that had declared themselves for the Reformation met in Schmalkalden, about twenty-five miles south of Eisenach. After two months of discussions, they formed the Schmalkaldic League, with Elector Johann of Saxony and Landgrave Philip of Hesse as the most notable leaders. Though many rulers and the cities of Bremen, Lübeck, and Magdeburg participated, it was impossible to get all the Protestant rulers to join. Regardless, this military league was formidable, even though in reality it could not hold its own against the armies of the emperor. For the time being, nothing happened; Charles had more pressing matters to deal with.

In the meantime, Luther had greater opportunity to reflect on the question whether opposition against the government was allowed. In the early days of the Reformation, he strongly opposed civil disobedience, and the Peasants' Revolt had confirmed his belief that obedience to the government is biblically commanded and that opposition would be in conflict with Romans 13. Legal experts explained to him, however, that the emperor was the governing authority for the people but not for the princes and rulers. He then abandoned his opposition against a political league, though he continued to warn against trusting in weapons instead of trusting in God.

Between 1531 and 1532, negotiations were held to establish a religious peace between Catholic and reformational territories. Luther supported such a peace, appealing to Romans 13 and resisting the idea that the Reformation could be spread by means of war. The Word would find its way without weapons. But he also believed that peace should not be embraced at the cost of the truth or at the price of reintroducing the mass where it had been abolished. On July 23, 1532, the religious peace was reached. A few weeks later, Elector John the Steadfast died, and as with Frederick III, Luther preached at the funeral service and at the grave. Luther notably spoke of his relationship with Elector John as being more personal than with his predecessor: "When the bells sound for someone whom you have loved, they sound quite different."[27]

Minorities

Problematic situations arose for people who chose to embrace the Reformation while their city or ruler remained faithful to Rome. How did these people cope with their status as religious minorities? A number of inhabitants from Leipzig went to neighboring villages to listen to Lutheran sermons and to celebrate the Lord's Supper. Duke George of Saxony immediately arrested these people, banishing fourteen of them who were unwilling to return to the Catholic faith. Since they did not receive letters of good behavior, they faced a most difficult prospect of being allowed to live somewhere else. Luther heard about the banishments and sent a public letter of comfort to the people.[28] As a result, the priest in Leipzig, Johann Koss, railed against Luther during a sermon on December 29, 1532, but he suffered a heart attack and died shortly after, which Luther saw as a clear judgment from God.[29]

In the spring of 1533, there was another shocking incident in Leipzig. On his deathbed, Dr. Augustin Specht had rejected Communion since he requested it in both kinds but was offered only the bread, and therefore, the authorities refused to bury him in consecrated ground. As a consequence, many people attended his funeral, using the event as a public demonstration. The authorities sought as many of the participants as possible, and eighty of them were banished from the city. Luther again wrote a letter and appealed to the people to remain steadfast and thus "hit the Devil in his face with the cross."[30] That remark was interpreted by the duke as a cry to incite rebellion, and therefore, he charged his colleague Elector John to deal appropriately with "this runaway and perjuring monk." John said, however, that Luther himself could decide whether he wanted to write letters to persecuted Christians. John added that George himself would be wise to finally make his change from Saul to Paul. Luther defended himself emphatically; he did not want to call people to rebel. It was even true

> that since the time of the apostles there hasn't been a doctor or author, no theologian or legal expert who has confirmed and provided instruction concerning the position of the secular authorities so clearly, as well as I have done, and I know that I have done this through the grace of God.[31]

This long polemic demonstrated that Luther had taken particular offense at being called a "runaway and perjurer." Perhaps, Luther admitted, he had perjured himself when he failed to keep his monastic vows, but at least he was a "redeemed perjurer" who had freed many people from the thought that by means of their life in a monastery they could earn their righteousness. With his perjury, Luther had brought the certainty of salvation. Every person in authority should be happy with this, Luther argued, because now ex-monastics had the freedom to live not for themselves but for others.

Less

The combination of poor health and too much work over the years forced Luther to make a change at the close of 1531. He departed for the castle Pretsch, where the owner, marshal Hans Löser, had invited him to come and rest for a few days. He hoped that "some physical activity would drive out the sounds in his head and that weak feeling."[32] Löser thought that Luther would go hunting with him, but instead, Luther wanted to withdraw into nature to meditate.

From the end of March 1532, due to health concerns, Luther was unable to preach as often in the City Church; he sometimes preached at home in the monastery in the midst of family and those who lived there. He realized that some people criticized this practice, accusing Luther of supporting those who despised church attendance.[33] There was little basis for this criticism, because preaching less in the church was a relative concept for Luther. He did so much more. He preached, for example, in the City Church every Sunday afternoon between August 1532 and April 1533, or he preached in the Castle Church, usually on 1 Corinthians 15. In addition, he wrote sermon outlines for colleagues, who had a reputation for poor preaching. Luther criticized preachers who preached too long or too vehemently.

Luther was also involved in the reformation of other cities. Sometimes he would go there himself, but more often he would provide written advice. He would often be asked, for example, whether the government or the church had the right to abolish the mass. Other questions concerned who had the right to building and property if a monastery was vacated by monks or nuns and left empty. Governments were rather eager and greedy in acquiring such properties, but Luther believed that the buildings and the proceeds had to be used for their original purpose, namely, service to God and the church.

Luther also attempted to cool down overenthusiastic efforts at reform. In a number of places, people wanted to introduce and strictly maintain church discipline, but Luther warned them that a radical reformation would drive people away. Moreover, the people should be calmly taught by means of sermons and catechesis. Ministers should first reach the inner person before addressing externals. Despite his reservations about strict discipline, Luther was nonetheless a proponent of maintaining some church discipline. Members of the congregation who quarreled were allowed access to the Lord's Supper only if they had been reconciled. He realized the inevitability of some attending the Lord's Supper who shouldn't, but he said, "We will have to bear this."[34] Excommunication was a form of discipline, one that Luther used when a certain Heinrich Rieder demanded 30 percent interest on loans.[35]

There were also questions about how many papist rituals should be tolerated. On this matter Luther wrote a letter to Georgius Buchholzen, a minister in Berlin, who complained that his ruler had embraced a reformed church order but that in the liturgy he had still wanted to retain many papist elements. Luther responded that if his ruler allowed him

> to preach the gospel of Jesus Christ, purely, clearly, and in its entirety, without human additions, administer both sacraments, baptism and the body and blood of Jesus Christ, in accordance with the institution of the Lord, and would allow the discontinuation of the calling upon the saints who are no help in emergencies, nor mediators or intercessors, and that he no long permitted the sacrament to be carried around in a procession, that he would abolish the daily masses, and also abolish wakes and masses for the souls of the dead, and no longer permit the consecration of water, salt, and spices, but would allow the singing of the responsive verses and hymns in Latin and German, then it would be permitted that he would walk along in the name of God, bearing a silver or golden cross, as well as a beret or garment of felt, silk, or a robe.[36]

Luther wanted to clarify to Buchholzen and others that these things were not essentials. As far as he was concerned, the minister, just like Moses's brother Aaron, could wear three garments over each other. And if rulers were unsatisfied with one procession, they could "do it seven times, just like Joshua and the children of Israel when they marched around Jericho." If a ruler also wanted music and dance, then he should do this "just like David did when he led the procession that bore the ark into Jerusalem." He believed all of this was fine as long as none of it was misused and people did not think these things offered them salvation. "If I could make those arrangements with the pope and the papists," he said, "I would thank God and be extremely joyful. If the pope gave me freedom in these matters and allowed me to simply preach, then just to please him, I would put on a pair of pants if he were to ask me to do that."[37]

Pastor

In the midst of all his work, Luther remained a pastor, as he had been from the very beginning. A touching example of this was the care he provided to the Wittenberg burgomaster Benedict Pauli. In 1533, during bird hunting, Pauli's son was accidentally killed. Luther comforted the father and admonished him that he should not see this death as a punishment from God. He understood the father's great grief but also pointed out that he had to accept that this too came from God's good hand. He directed him to the Bible's stories of believers who bore the suffering that came on them and assured Pauli that this grief would not separate him from the grace of God.[38] Luther also dissuaded Jonas von Stockhausen, the head of the city government in Nordhausen, from considering suicide: "You should lay your ears to our mouth, and then take our words to heart, because then God will comfort and strengthen you through our word. . . . We received life from God and may not simply throw it aside."[39]

In July 1535, plague again struck Wittenberg (see fig. 9.2). Luther thought that the people were far too quick in their panic and that they exaggerated the dangers enormously. According to him, the students were especially guilty of this, seeing an opportunity to interrupt their studies and return home to their overly concerned mothers.[40]

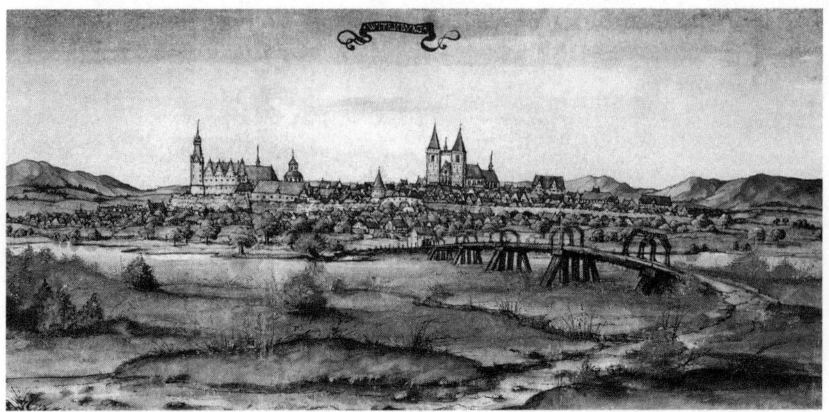

Figure 9.2 The city of Wittenberg as seen from the Elbe River. Drawing from the travel book of the count of Paltz, Ottoheinrich, 1536. Universiteitsbibliotheek, Würzburg.

Michael Stifel, the preacher at Lochau, raised a completely different concern. This minister had come up with a remarkable calculation regarding Jesus's return. Luther also embraced the conviction that Christ's return would happen during his lifetime, but he had no use for speculations concerning the exact timing. Stifel had calculated that Christ's return would happen on October 19, 1533, at eight o'clock in the morning. Luther knew this man well, having solemnized his marriage and been instrumental in getting this minister his position. But when he asked Luther to write a preface to his booklet about Christ's return, he refused. Luther admonished him to stop publishing fanatic speculations, advice that angered Stifel. "In all my life," Luther noted, "no opponent has ever railed against me as he has done. He abused me with the accusation that I was a Pilate and Herod."[41] Early in September, the elector forbade Stifel to preach because he would not listen to any admonitions. On October 18, large crowds of people came to Lochau. Stifel again preached and cried out three times, "He will come," but when nothing had happened by nine o'clock the next morning, the people went home again. Stifel was deposed, and because he had no income, Luther provided shelter for him in his monastery. In 1535, he again became a preacher; Luther took it calmly: "He has retained some spiritual anxieties, but that will certainly not hurt him."[42]

Luther also produced a popular booklet on prayer, based on his relationship with a unique individual. Peter Beskendorp was a barber and miracle doctor. The combination of those two professions was quite normal in those days; shaving, of course, had obvious potential for medical mishaps. On March 27, 1535, Beskendorp actually stabbed his son-in-law to death. The two did not get along well, and a dinner table quarrel had spiraled out of control. Because Luther intervened on his behalf, the charge was reduced from murder to manslaughter. Beskendorp was banned from the city but escaped the death penalty. Almost prophetically, a few weeks before he attacked his son-in-law, he had asked Luther how one should pray. Therefore, in 1535, Luther had begun the treatise *A Simple Way to Pray, for a Good Friend*.[43] The little booklet became a great success and is still read and used by many people worldwide. Luther's simplicity in prayer is evident from one of the evening prayers that he had written for himself: "Dear God, I am now going to sleep and lay your matters down with you: you will no doubt do it better than I. And if you don't do it better than I, then you will mess it up. But when I get up again, I'll try to work at it some more."[44]

Conflicts

Having conquered their common enemy, some of Luther's followers began to debate internal matters. Luther did not always conduct himself in a friendly and forgiving fashion in these conflicts; he was prone to seeing anyone who disagreed with him as a threat to "his" gospel. The greatest conflict concerned the convictions of Johann Agricola, whom he had first encountered in 1527 when Agricola had protested Melanchthon's appeal to uphold the importance of the law now that the gospel received so much attention. Ten years later the controversy flared again.

Agricola and his family had moved from Eisleben to Wittenberg, and they were living temporarily with the Luthers. Initially, everything went well, but the friendship became strained when Luther traveled to Schmalkalden for several weeks and asked Agricola to preach for him several times. When Luther returned, he heard that Agricola had proclaimed that the wrath of God is apparent not in the law but rather in Christ's death on the cross. Clearly, Agricola wanted to distance himself from everything that had to do with the law, whereas Luther had argued that there was no grace without remorse and that the sense of remorse would only come if one, through the law, had come to recognize one's guilt and sin.

The discussion between Luther and Agricola, whom he labeled an antinomian (someone opposed to the law), grew into a public conflict when Luther deemed it necessary to publish Agricola's antinomian theses and his own reaction.[45] Luther also organized a public disputation that would be held on December 18, 1539, which he hoped would lead to reconciliation with his friend. But Agricola did not appear, and Luther gave only his view on the topic. Later, Katharina spoke to Luther on behalf of Agricola. That led to a second disputation and Agricola's moving toward Luther's views. The latter was satisfied and announced that the quarrel was over, though he understood that the problem had not been entirely resolved. This became apparent at Easter when Agricola again expounded his views from the pulpit. A new disputation changed nothing, and Luther called him a hypocrite, relegated him to the followers of the Devil, and with his *Contra the Antinomians*,[46] brutally wrote him off.

Luther's colleagues thought he had again overreacted. Agricola went to Berlin, and from there he submitted a complaint against Luther to both the rector of the university and Bugenhagen in Wittenberg. He demanded that Luther retract his accusations, but his complaint was ignored. Moreover, Luther was not at all inclined to retract his views. Melanchthon attempted to mediate and managed to get Agricola, with whom he did not agree at all, to withdraw his complaint, telling him that Luther had not meant any personal offense. Agricola was willing, but for Luther it was too late, and as a result, the bond with his former friend was permanently broken.

As for other conflicts of this period, one of the most notorious was the occupation of Münster by a group of Anabaptists in 1534–1535. Led by a few Dutchman, this group sought to establish the New Jerusalem, but it ended in a bloodbath. Notably, Luther never said much about these events. He believed that what happened there was so clearly un-Christian that he didn't need to comment on it. Luther did, however, use Münster as an example of how quickly preachers could mislead a large group of people. He also believed that in such situations, the death penalty could be exercised.[47]

Trent

Luther had continually called for a church council, and such a council, according to him, should be free, universal, Christian, and German. By "free" Luther meant that it would be led not by the pope or curia but by the Holy Scriptures and that there would be an open discussion with an open Bible. By "German" Luther believed that the ecclesiastical and political conflict was especially relevant to the German Empire and that therefore such a council should be held in Germany.

Matters did not transpire the way Luther had wanted, because the council took place in Trent (in northern Italy) and only after years of preparation. The representative of the pope was Pietro Paolo Vergerio (ca. 1498–1565), who traveled around the German Empire in the early 1530s to conduct discussions and promote a future council. Vergerio, who would join the Reformation in 1549, arrived in Wittenberg on Saturday, November 6, 1534, where he was officially received.

The following day, he met Luther, who had prepared so thoroughly for the occasion that he went early for a shave and put on his best suit. A heavy golden chain and several rings gave him an impressive and refreshed appearance, and no illness of any kind was noticeable—precisely Luther's intention. According to Luther, the barber asked him why he needed to be served so early on a Sunday morning. Luther told him that he wanted to hide his true age and appear young and refreshed to make it very clear that the pope wouldn't be rid of him for a long time. The message to Rome via Vergerio had to be clear: "If Luther, who has not nearly reached the age of graybeards, has already caused so much division among us, what will happen before he has actually become old?"[48] Luther went to the meeting together with Bugenhagen, who was born in Pomerania, and joked on the way: "There they go, the German pope and his cardinal Pomeranus, God's implements."[49] Luther was referring to himself as the German pope.

At the meeting, out of respect, Luther doffed his beret, but he did not show any other kind of respect. Vergerio wrote later of how he had perceived Luther:

> He's a little over fifty, but he is so robust and strong that he appears younger than forty. He is rather fat, but he tries to look as slim as possible. He speaks at a moderate pace, not particularly harshly, and German, not too uncouth. . . . He has those restless, moving eyes that—believe me, sir—the longer I looked at them, the more I thought that they looked like the eyes of a demon-possessed man who I once saw. That's how sunken, restless, angry, indeed, raging his look was.[50]

Apparently, the visit to the barber had helped, but those eyes did not change and were obvious to others. The attitude that Vergerio described was strikingly portrayed in a fresco in the Palazzo Farnese in Rome, where one can see a papal cleric, possibly Cajetan in Augsburg, explaining something to Luther (see fig. 9.3). But the reformer looks at him unmoved, implacable, and dark. That's how they saw him, and that is how he was.

Together Vergerio and Luther spoke about the council. Luther honestly admitted that he expected little of it but said that he would certainly be willing to come, even if it was in Bologne. But Rome should realize that he would not budge from his convictions. With that message and the assurance that Luther would come to the council, Vergerio again left Wittenberg but not before he had attended a service. He was quite unhappy with it. The organ playing was chaotic, the singing of psalms by the congregation, according to Vergerio, sounded like the braying of drunkards in a bawdy house, and the sermon was only a tirade against everything that was wrong with Rome. Vergerio left quickly, but three years after Luther's death, he joined the Protestants.

Due to the preparations for the council, the elector instructed Luther to draw up a document that could serve as a confession of faith. It was the elector's wish that in this document, Luther would focus especially on the position of the pope.

Subsequently, Luther drew up a confession of faith that would be known as the *Smalkald Articles*. He especially emphasized the doctrine of justification, the central issue for Luther. Luther held that

Figure 9.3 Luther with a Romanist cleric (possibly Cardinal Cajetan). Fragment of a painting by Francesco Salviati, 1560. Palazzo Farnese, Rome.

we are justified only by means of the atoning work of Christ, which we obtain by faith. "This article of faith cannot be compromised," he wrote. "Nothing can be taken away from it, even if the earth or heaven or whatever should fall."[51] Not long before, he had already clarified that this was the decisive article for him, "because if this article remains standing, the church remains standing, but if this article falls, the church also falls."[52]

Luther's bringing justification to the forefront, contrary to what was requested of him, was also his reaction to the action of Melanchthon and others at the Diet of Augsburg. From the Coburg, Luther had informed them that on this issue, they had moved too far in Rome's direction. As far as the position of the pope was concerned, the issue that the elector especially wanted this document to highlight, Luther was quickly finished: he is the Antichrist. Concerning the church, he said that "even a child seven years old knows what the church is, namely, the holy believers and the lambs who hear the voice of the Shepherd."

Luther's litany of issues gave the document the style of a theological testament, and that was almost literally what it became because Luther suffered several heart attacks while working on them.[53] He recovered and finished the document.

In Schmalkalden, thirty-eight Protestant theologians met and discussed the articles. Some of them wanted a more open attitude toward Rome, and others rejected that. Within the group it didn't appear as if unanimity over against a council was paramount, because that would take place in their absence anyway. The rulers had decided that they would not be permitted to participate and adopted the articles (without signing them) in 1580 as the confession of faith for the Lutheran church.

When it was announced in June 1536 that the council would meet in Mantua in Italy on May 23, 1537, the reformers thought that they had failed to ensure that the council would be free and German. Under those circumstances, could they expect anything at all from the council? Luther and Melanchthon advised them to participate anyway. Melanchthon even saw this council much like the Council of Constance in 1414–1418, and therefore, in 1536, he again published three of John Hus's letters. Luther feared that the council would single-mindedly confirm the Roman course and strengthen the power of the pope.

Just once more, Luther wanted to clarify his view of the church and the papacy, which he did thoroughly in 1539 in his *About Councils and Churches*.[54] He named seven characteristics by which one can recognize the church of Christ: sermon, baptism, Lord's Supper, absolution, offices, liturgy, and bearing the cross. Of the last characteristic, Luther wrote,

> In the seventh place, one recognizes Christian people on the outside by the holy cross, that is to say that they experience all kinds of misfortune and persecution, all the temptations and evil (as it says in the Lord's Prayer) of the Devil, the world, and our flesh, and that they grieve internally, are vulnerable, are shocked, outwardly poor, despised, sick, are weak, suffer, so that in everything they are like their Head, Christ. And then the cause can only be this, that the church holds on to Christ and God's Word, and thus suffers for

> Christ's sake, Matthew 5: Blessed are you when others persecute you on my account. . . . Where you now see and hear this, you know that the holy Christian church is there.[55]

The church, according to Luther, is the church that suffers, because it is the body of Christ. The church is truly in danger if there is no suffering, no persecution, and no pressure from the Devil: "Nowadays, the Devil brings the church into peril with the greatest imaginable persecution, namely, that the church without persecution can live relaxed and in surety. Woe to us, who would become so blinded by satisfaction and prosperity so that the Devil leads us into a trap."[56] The church is visible, according to Luther, where the Word is brought, the sacraments are celebrated, and suffering is sustained. Luther wrote in his *About Councils and Churches* that if the pope stood above the council, it would not be a Christian gathering but a tyranny, and in doing so, the Protestant image of Trent had been largely formed *a priori*. Luther's warning won out over Melanchthon's expectations, and the Schmalkaldic League in 1537 therefore rejected participation in the council.

In April 1538, Luther and Melanchthon stayed at the court in Torgau with the Protestant rulers and princes to discuss what they should do if the emperor initiated war against them. The council date had been moved up constantly, and there was fear that the council was to serve as a kind of pacifier to give the emperor an opportunity to prepare for war. Some asked whether it was permitted to oppose the emperor with armed force. Luther, who had always dismissed this form of opposition in the past, now reasoned differently. In this situation, he no longer saw the emperor as a lawful government, as Romans 13 required one to obey such a government, but instead saw the emperor as an agent of the pope, the Antichrist. Thus the opposition now looked remarkably different. Here, the issue no longer concerned money and property but eternal salvation. Unlike the rulers and several of his colleagues, Luther did not want or endorse a preemptive attack, but he did feel that opposition was acceptable. Luther, however, would not experience that anymore; by the time the emperor attacked, Luther had already passed away.

Wittenberg Concord

The divisions caused by the debates over the Lord's Supper weakened the reformational movement. The strife came at the cost of energy that could have been better used for the theological and political fight against the pope and emperor, who were busy planning their counter-offensive. After the death of Zwingli in 1531, his follower Heinrich Bullinger demonstrated more openness and allowed more discussion about the Lord's Supper. This attitude also dovetailed with attempts of the Strasbourg reformer Martin Bucer, who tried everything to maintain (or restore) unity among the Protestants. Bucer was also the man who approached Luther to come to an agreement concerning his views about the Lord's Supper. This struggle required a tremendous amount of effort, because even while Bucer worked day and night for unity, he was constantly confronted by Luther's volatile temperament, made so unstable because Luther suspected anyone who differed in opinion on this issue of sacrificing the message of the Reformation to the Devil. Regardless of how blunt and implacable Luther could be, Bucer kept trying and did so from a deep appreciation for Luther, whom Bucer saw as a prophet of God.

The schism between the Swiss and Wittenberg appeared insoluble. From Switzerland came the charge that if Christ is physically present in the bread and wine, it won't make any difference whether someone believes or not, because he will receive Christ anyway. Luther's side responded that grace is no longer grace if faith must be the condition to receive the benefit of the Lord's Supper. In the meantime, Bucer struggled to find a formulation with which everyone would be satisfied. After innumerable trips, discussions, and letters, it finally appeared that they had found an agreement between Strasbourg and Wittenberg (that is, between the German states in the southwest and those around Luther), and unity with the Swiss appeared possible.

A discussion was organized in Wittenberg. Luther took the stage first with an opening tirade against the Swiss, who weren't even there, and then suggested that the conference had to effectuate an imaginary unity. With a few sentences, Luther almost destroyed a small piece of ecclesiastical unity that had been in preparation for several years. Fortunately, that did not happen, and after some solid discussions, the

Wittenberg Concord was finally established, with tears and thanksgiving. Luther changed as well. In his sermon on Ascension Day, he avoided his invective.[57] As additional evidence of his change of mood, Luther organized a communal meal at his house and hired singers and musicians. After the theologians had finished the concord, the cities accepted it but only after a number of intense visits. This achievement remained, however, a first step. Unity with the Swiss didn't happen. When the Lutherans finally wanted to continue the discussion, the Swiss stopped. When Calvin convinced the other Swiss theologians to reconvene, Luther had died, and his successors did not participate. Thus, the separation between the Lutheran and Reformed churches continued to exist for centuries.

10

Prophet (1537–1546)

Red

Until 1524, Luther had looked quite a bit like a monk. He had worn the monk's habit and had kept the tonsure, the unique hairstyle of monks, though his tonsure was often covered by the doctor's beret that he had received when he earned his doctorate in 1512. On Sunday morning, October 9, 1524, Luther preached in his normal monk's habit as usual, but for the afternoon service he made a drastic change: he appeared in the pulpit wearing black clothes. This attire resembled the clothing normally worn by scholars and prosperous burgers. Outwardly, he had permanently parted with his monk's attire, though inwardly, Luther would forever remain a monk.

In 1526, the city of Wittenberg provided Luther with a striking purple garment. From that time onward, Luther would more often wear red, the color that the old Christian tradition associated with a prophetic calling. It suited him, not least because people saw him as a prophet (as he did himself). At the conclusion of his booklet concerning the parental responsibility to send one's children to school, he said, "Now, dear Germans, I have told you sufficiently, and you have heard what your prophet said. I am the German prophet . . . who must warn you for possible injury and danger and who must teach you in a Christian fashion."[1] Indeed, he was a prophet, but he would end up being one who proclaimed impending calamity rather than a time of joy and blessing.

Increasingly, Luther expressed his prophetic self-assuredness, saying, for example, that "they wrongly call me a Hussite, because there is a difference between him and me. If he were a heretic, then I am ten times more a heretic than he, because he said much, much less important things than I have said. With him, the light of the truth had only just begun to dawn."[2] Luther thought of himself as "a great doctor who stands above all bishops, priests, and monks."[3] It's not difficult to see how Luther's idea of himself made him defensive of his beliefs, sometimes to the point of discarding all criticism. Luther may have occasionally realized this himself, as some of his remarks indicated a desire to be more agreeable to others.

Officially, Luther was not a prophet but a professor. He remained a preacher his entire life, a role he loved and performed with great dedication and great exhaustion. Nevertheless, he was rather a preacher than a prophet (see fig. 10.1). "I am not a prophet," Luther said, "because God did not give me the gifts of prophecy. I am actually a preacher."[4] This statement reveals the importance he ascribed to preaching: "Every preacher must be so sure and should be so convinced that he has and that he preaches the Word of God that he would be willing to die for it, specifically because preaching concerns life."[5] The reevaluation of the office of preacher did not mean, however, an increased appreciation for the preacher himself: "A pastor or preacher doesn't make the gospel. And through his sermons or through his office his word does not become gospel, because then everything he says would be gospel. In his sermons, he only passes on the gospel."[6] Preaching it is a fairly simple process: "Preaching the gospel is none other than that Christ comes to us, and we are brought to him."[7]

Today we have remarkable knowledge of Luther's preaching in Wittenberg because many of his sermons were transcribed and saved by a deacon named George Rörer. There are quite a few of these sermons, indicating that Luther frequently led services. In 1529, Luther preached 121 times, since Bugenhagen, the local preacher in the City Church, was absent for a large part of the year. Albert Burner, a student in Wittenberg, described Luther in the pulpit:

Figure 10.1 Altarpiece in the Castle Church in Wittenberg. Painting by Lucas Cranach the Elder, 1547. Middle panel: the Last Supper; left panel: Philipp Melanchthon administering baptism; right panel: Johannes Bugenhagen as father confessor; lower panel: Luther as preacher, with Katharina von Bora in the audience.

> He appears open, mild, and happy. His voice is pleasing and sounds good, so much so that I am amazed at his eloquence. What he says, teaches, and does is very devout, even though his godless enemies maintain the opposite. If you are not made of stone, after you've heard him once, you will want to hear him again, because that is how powerfully his words affect the heart and soul of the audience. In short, he lacks nothing that belongs with perfect Christian devotion.[8]

That is a beautiful testimony, but Luther himself embraced the conviction that he depended on God for all these things, as we see in one of his prayers: "Lord, God, you have established me as bishop and preacher in your church. You see how unsuitable I am to carry out such an extensive and heavy office, and if I did not constantly receive your guidance, I would have ruined it long ago. Therefore, I cry out to you."[9] This prayer that Luther had given to preachers as an example reveals his view of the office of preacher. The preacher is dependent on prayer, and preaching is both a burden and a joy: "I have been considered worthy by God that he gave me the charge to serve in the office of preacher."[10] This privilege must be treated carefully. A preacher should not want to make an impression, but he must speak normally and simply, not unlike a mother speaking to her child as she is feeding it. "In their speaking, preachers must be plain, clear, and straightforward," Luther insisted, "so that people with an elementary understanding can understand and remember it."[11] He must understand that he is not standing there as an ordinary man but as one relaying the very words of God.[12] Luther was critical of the ministers who quickly made a sermon using an outline from a book, seeing them as too lazy to study the Scriptures carefully themselves: "Therefore, dear gentlemen and brothers, pastors and preachers, pray, read, study, be zealous. In these terrible and awful times we may not be lazy, snore, or sleep. Use the gifts that have been entrusted to you, and reveal the mystery of Christ."[13]

Ministers and Congregants

Luther felt it unfair that people did not want to pay for ministers. He was not interested in money for himself, but his colleagues were in need. "What a bunch of thankless animals," he declared. "If you do not do penance, you are unworthy of the gospel, and I will stop preaching to you."[14] Luther, like his colleagues, was also frequently frustrated that his listeners did nothing with the sermons. He understood that preachers should not crave praise from their audience; rather, they should simply bring the Word of God. But Luther was frustrated that so few appeared to properly engage the sermon.

At one point, Luther was so agitated that he quit. He had preached so much already, but the only result was "that no one acts accordingly; instead, the people become so rude, cold, and lazy that it is shameful, and they do even less now than before."[15] Now that it had become clear to people that church attendance was not a work of merit and thus that they received no credit for this with God, they stopped going altogether. On February 28, 1529, an exasperated Luther informed the Wittenbergers, "I do not want to be a shepherd of such swine."[16] The sermon did make an impact, so after some urging, he resumed his work. It did not last long, however, and he had to say, "It makes me sad to preach anymore to you."[17] On January 1, 1530, he had had enough and informed them that he was quitting since the people didn't want to listen anyway. On January 23 and 30, he still preached because Bugenhagen was unavailable, but afterward, Luther went on a preaching strike and avoided the pulpit for ten months.

Luther could also become very annoyed at people's behavior in church, such as their excessive coughing. Luther felt that his people should learn from the example of Muslims, who were notably reverent in their mosques.[18] He also criticized the many people who left the church after the sermon and skipped the long prayer. Luther had his hands full with all the requests he received from the members of the congregation and the ministers. He made a special effort to get better stipends for the ministers, better rights for their widows, and provisions for the sick and the aged. Though he often complained about the behavior of ministers who were lazy, drank too much, or had a poor knowledge of theology, he directed most of his criticism at the congregations who failed to look after their ministers properly or who slighted their ministers for pointing out their sins. In one case, the farmers in the village Lissen had sought to replace their minister because they thought his voice was too soft. Luther's judgment was clear:

> If those farmers had to choose a minister themselves, and then one who is learned, devout, handsome, young, eloquent, one who doesn't scream, who likes eating and drinking, tells them what they would like to hear, plays dice with them, and plays, etc., etc., . . . then in that manner they will never get one.[19]

By contrast, Luther defended the farmers when they became victims of money and politics. On April 9, 1538, Luther wrote a protest to the elector. He urged him to do something about the attitude of the nobles. Luther complained after many people suffered from a mouse plague in the autumn of the previous year, so that Wittenberg was left without flour, and the drought of the spring resulted in a real famine. If something were not done quickly, many people would die of starvation. Luther had heard that the nobles kept back their supplies of grain, waiting until the situation had caused even more inflation in prices.

He felt he could do nothing but ask the elector to take action. Yet he felt called to do something against people who "scandalously practice usury, plunging the country and the people into destruction."[20] So in a sermon he highlighted these serious sins, and he wrote a pamphlet to appeal to other Protestants to protest the practice of usury. They were urged to clearly explain what a terrible judgment awaited those who desired to make money from the suffering of others.

Sicknesses

Luther's ailments could easily fill a medical textbook. Between his trip to Augsburg in 1518, when he first mentioned serious stomach problems, and his death in 1546, Luther endlessly remarked about all his health issues. He had problems with his stomach and his intestines. He suffered heart problems, kidney stones, a leg wound that did not heal properly, dizzy spells, rheumatic issues, endless ringing in his ears together with deafness (Ménière's disease), hemorrhoids, headaches, vertigo, chronic stress, insomnia, and constant fatigue. During those three decades, he was almost always ill, and after he had married, his wife worried. In 1527, when Luther was close to death, Katharina sat by his bed and said,

> My dear doctor, if it is God's will, then I would rather that you would be with our Lord God than with me. But it's not only about me and my child but about the many Christian people who still need you. You don't have to be concerned about me. I commit you to God's will—God will save you.[21]

Luther reported in detail about his ailments, even his stomach problems. A little remark such as "I had to go to the toilet fifteen times in two days" says enough.[22] In addition to these problems, he suffered the nasty effects of the then unknown Ménière's disease:

> It starts when my head is filled with the sounds of a clock, indeed, like thunder, and if I had not immediately stopped working, I would have fainted. I could not see a single letter anymore. . . . That is why I am lying here, shaking with cold. With the help of medicines and other appropriate aids, gradually the tumult in my head abates.[23]

Several times Luther reported these attacks, as well as other physical complaints that had an increasingly negative impact on his mood. Luther's physical suffering made him even more headstrong, implacable, and sharper in speaking and writing than he normally was. Melanchthon was often the victim, mentioning even after Luther's death that he had suffered much because of him. Both Martin Bucer and John Calvin first sent their letters to Melanchthon, so the latter could judge whether Luther was in the mood to read such a letter.

Despite the constant medical issues, Luther was able to accomplish much work. In 1521, he was sick for seven months but still published thirty treatises, wrote a hundred letters, and preached seventy times. In 1530, he was sick for ten months but produced thirty treatises, one hundred seventy letters, and sixty sermons. In 1536, he was ill for eight months and produced ten treatises, ninety letters, and fifty sermons. In 1545, again sick for ten months, he nevertheless produced thirteen treatises, eighty letters, and thirty-five sermons.

His fits of depression and insomnia led him to bouts of drinking. Luther was confident that God, having forgiven him many greater sins, would also have compassion for this problem: "Since the Lord God tortured and crucified me for twenty years with the celebration of the mass, he will also give me credit that in honor of him I occasionally have a stiff drink."[24] Luther's beer consumption, however, was not excessive for a time in which beer and wine were often purer than the water supply. Emperor Charles V, for example, who was known for his sparse drinking, drank three bottles of wine at his midday meals. Katharina, who had her own brewery, had to provide fifteen to twenty gallons of beer for a household of thirty to forty people. That is approximately a half gallon of beer per person per day, which included the children. Luther warned expressly against excessive drinking and opined that young people used too much alcohol, damaging their youth and health,[25] adding that parents often provided a poor example.[26] He called Germany a country "that was plagued by the devil of boozing."[27] That Luther himself sometimes drank excessively was well known and, according to him, necessary. When he was in Torgau in 1532, he credited his seven-hour sleep to the local beer. The fact that in a letter to Käthe he remarked that he was just as sober as he would be in Wittenberg is telling.[28]

The combination of beer and prayer—also a form of *ora et labora*—was salubrious: "For days I felt sick, and since Sunday until last night I haven't been able to pee a drop. I could not rest, not sleep, and everything I ate or drank came out again." He thought he would die and would never see his wife again. "Here, the people prayed to God so earnestly on my behalf that many people had to cry. And now God opened my bladder and within two hours I've peed at least three liters [about three-quarters of a gallon]. I feel like I have been reborn."[29]

In early February 1537, Luther was in Schmalkalden, where the Protestant rulers and their theologians consulted on what they should do if the emperor made an armed attack on the reformers. Luther, who already had problems with his kidneys when he arrived, became extremely ill. His vomiting, kidney stones, and diarrhea worsened since there was no apothecary in Schmalkalden; it was decided that he had to return immediately to Wittenberg. The elector provided two wagons for the trip; in the first wagon, Luther lay in a bed, and in the second were his five travel companions, including his doctor from Erfurt, George Sturz. In the second wagon they also kept a coal fire burning, on which they cooked their meal and heated cloths for Luther. After the first night, the kidney stones were dislodged, and Luther finally had some relief.

It was short lived, however, because after a few days his kidney stones returned. A few weeks later, while he participated in a church service, he fainted and was unable to resume his work until early July. The following November, he had to celebrate the Lord's Supper at home, because he had so many problems with kidney stones. He also complained about bladder stones, which he blamed on bad wine. His doctors, however, maintained that it would be good for him to go on a diet. But such advice fell on deaf ears; he was not going to let himself die of hunger: "I eat whatever I think tastes good and will die when God wills." Luther was known as a bothersome patient who often blamed his problems on the Devil's attacks rather than on his own unhealthy lifestyle. Luther would not leave his wine alone.[30] At one point at the dinner table, Luther remarked, "Tomorrow I have to lecture about Noah's drunkenness, and therefore, tonight I will indulge in a good drinking session so that I can speak from experience about this event." One of his colleagues reacted, "But no! You should be doing the opposite." In response, Luther said, "You should simply acknowledge that every country has its unique shortcoming. The Bohemians devour food, Slavs steal, and Germans booze a lot."[31]

In July 1538, he was again so sick that he expected to die. He recovered but suffered such a bad case of gout that he had to walk with a stick. He admitted that it was difficult in such times to patiently await the will of God.[32] Work wasn't easy for him: his letters became shorter, reading was becoming difficult, and responding to requests to write about particular topics was challenging. At the same time, Luther complained that what he could do in an hour, someone else would do in three hours. In January 1541, he discovered an abscess in his neck, and in February he had an attack of fatigue because of heart issues. In March he suffered a nose and ear infection. He longed to go to God.[33]

Subsequently, he had a time of respite, so that he believed that the Devil had taken a few days off: "I get my normal hours of sleep, and I am eating as I am used to doing. Perhaps Satan has taken a few days' vacation."[34] But in March 1542, Satan was apparently back, because Luther wrote that he was tired of living.[35] In January and February 1543, he could not work because of terrible headaches and kidney stone attacks. Many solutions were attempted, including keeping the wound in his thigh open to (it was supposed) reduce his headaches. From all over, people sent him medicinal-like stones, potions, and advice. Dorothea, the countess of Mansfeld thought that increased exercise would be more beneficial than these remedies, though it was she who had sent him sneeze powder to help against headaches. In early 1544, Luther was able to preach again and give lectures, but the headaches soon returned so that until Easter he was unable to work: "I have lived long enough. Let God send me a nice hour of dying; then this lazy, useless bag of maggots can be interred along with the other people, and it can be given to the worms."[36] Travel was no longer possible either, regardless of how important some of those visits would have been:

> Coming or going is no longer possible for me, and even sitting is difficult. From this I notice how old I am and that my body is

> gradually sinking away in the direction of the earth. Let God be swift to help me with his grace. Therefore, I need to be at peace and rest until matters change, be it to live, or to die, whatever God wills.[37]

Just about the time that things were going better (1545), Luther received an Italian pamphlet that reported his death. It alleged that he had given orders for his body to be venerated but that people refused. Around his grave there was so much noise that they wanted to exhume him, but when they did that, it appeared that his grave was empty because the Devil had stolen his corpse. Luther reacted with a pamphlet in which he clarified that if a living Luther had already been a plague for the pope, a dead Luther would mean his death.[38]

In June 1545, he was again stricken with a kidney stone attack. In January 1546, he described himself as a "graybeard, decrepit, slow, exhausted, bald, and one-eyed.[39] A month later he would die.

Bigamy

Philip of Hesse, one of the most important political leaders of the Reformation, became the source of the unique problem of bigamy (see fig. 10.2). His marriage with Christina, the daughter of George of Saxony had been miserable for years, though they had seven children. Part of this marriage problem was Philip's venereal disease, which he had contracted through his frequent extramarital escapades. According to him, this issue caused him great struggles with his conscience so that he did not feel entitled to celebrate the Lord's Supper. The solution to his problem appeared to be seventeen-year-old Margarete von der Saale, whom he had met in 1539. Philip wanted to be married to Margarete, but he was married already. Divorce was forbidden, and thus Philip found himself with a wife he did not want, a woman he could not have, and a case of syphilis he could not cure. Margarete's mother refused to allow her daughter to become a concubine or mistress and demanded a proper marriage—even if it were a double marriage. Needless to say, this matter was highly inconvenient for the reformers, because Philip of Hesse was the most important of the Protestant rulers, and without him, the currently shaky situation of the Reformation would be made

Figure 10.2 *Portrait of the Hessian Landgrave Philip I* (1504–1567). Painting by Hans Krell, unknown date (possibly 1534). Wartburg-Stiftung, Wartburg.

worse. The punishment for bigamy was the death penalty, but if they did not allow his bigamy, Philip would get the death penalty anyway as his promiscuous life would keep him to his syphillis and kill him.

In his distress, Philip approached Luther, Melanchthon, and the elector of Saxony through Martin Bucer. He attributed the whole situation to his poor marriage and blamed his wife, saying nothing of his adultery. He claimed that he had found supporting arguments for bigamy in the Old Testament and also that he knew stories of other rulers who had more than one wife. Additionally, he warned the reformers that in the absence of an acceptable solution, he would have to go to the emperor, implying that he would join the Roman Catholic side if he had to. On December 9–10, 1539, Bucer consulted Luther and Melanchthon. They agreed that they would give Philip "confessional advice." In special situations of spiritual distress, such advice was given to people who lived in sin but were also stuck without any apparent recourse. This advice could deviate from usual norms because the pertinent individual could only be helped in that unique way. For Philip this meant that they would allow him to engage in a second marriage but that he had to remain silent about it. He also had to stop his adulterous affairs. From the outset, the reformers did not like this situation, but they saw no other solution in order to hold onto Philip, both for eternity and for the matter of the Reformation.

On March 4, 1540, the marriage was solemnized in Melanchthon's and Bucer's presence. Philip wrote Luther that he was very happy and that his conscience was also enormously relieved. The extent of his joy was evident in that he sent Luther about 250 gallons of wine as a gift. In this case, it was not only the wine that gave Luther headaches, because soon word had spread of Philip's double marriage. Philip's mother-in-law had excitedly told people how happy Philip was with her Margarete. Soon his Catholic colleagues began to ask difficult questions. Philip was hunted; according to law he had actually deserved capital punishment. Luther, for his part, eventually discovered that Philip had often continued his affairs and that his struggling conscience had been a bit of a sham. If he had known everything beforehand, "not even an angel could have convinced me to give such advice." Now that this issue had been made public, Luther knew very well that Melanchthon and he would be the objects of controversy: "All the dung will be dumped on us."[40]

Melanchthon could not stand this kind of thing at all; on the way to Hagenau to participate in a religious discussion, he became so ill in Weimar that they feared for his life. Luther wrote him a letter of comfort and said that continuing to think about the matter was pointless since the foulness had happened already. Christ would deal with it, and moreover, such mishaps were probably inevitable in the future. Additionally, the situation wasn't as bad as the sin of David, and that matter eventually turned out for good as well.[41] The letter did not have its intended effect, and when Luther heard that Melanchthon had continued to deteriorate, he went to him to comfort him personally. When he arrived in Weimar on June 23, 1540, he found Melanchthon deathly ill. He was unable to speak or hear. Luther was shocked. He ran to the window and began to pray: "Now our Lord God had to come into action. I threw the matter before his feet and assailed his ears with all his promises about hearing our prayers that I could find in the Bible. If he didn't hear me now, how could I believe in his promises?" Then he took Melanchthon's hand and said, "You are not going to die." He urged Melanchthon not to give in to the temptation to die and thus become his own murderer. But Melanchthon refused to eat. Then Luther said, "If you don't eat now, I will censure you!"[42] Whether it was because of this threat or because of prayer, Melanchthon revived. Luther was ecstatic and wrote to Käthe:

> I eat like a Bohemian, and I booze like a German, and God be praised for this. Amen. That is because Master Philipp was truly dead and—like Lazarus—has risen from the dead. God the dear Father heard our prayer. We see that, we embrace it, and yet we can hardly believe it. Let no one say amen to our scandalous unbelief.[43]

In the meantime, the matter that had caused Melanchthon's illness was creating more unrest. Luther was now being accused of unclear teaching on polygamy in his lectures on Genesis. Luther felt this charge was unfair, because "if I have to defend whatever I said or did years ago, especially in the early years, then I would have to venerate the pope."[44] Philip of Hesse wanted to publicly acknowledge the confessional advice, but Luther opposed this on the grounds that since it was confessional advice, it was a private matter that was covered by the confidentiality of confession. The matter did not settle until a few years later, but by that time, the damage had become so great that Philip's support was scarcely useful for the Reformation. Luther's concern had been the landgrave's conscience, but when it appeared that that conscience functioned rather selfishly, he realized that he had taken the wrong approach. It was also abundantly clear that the secret advice they gave Philip of Hesse and his equally secret marriage were no longer secret at all. His bigamy was widely known and widely criticized. From all sides people asked Luther how he and the others could ever have permitted this and even defended it with biblical arguments. He expected that gradually the issue would come to rest: "At worst, this will last a quarter of a year, and then this song will have run its course."[45] Luther wanted to remain quiet while the issue passed. It did pass, but the destruction in its wake was enormous.

Jews

Luther also caused terrible destruction with his treatises about the Jews. His language was strongly anti-Semitic and could easily be used in the national socialistic propaganda against Jews. His advice to force Jews to live in separate districts and burn down their synagogues was followed with dedication years later by the Nazis. Unfortunately, Luther was no exception in this respect. Erasmus, usually praised as a supporter of tolerance, made no secret of his deeply rooted disgust of Jews. Luther's aversion, however, is more commonly known than that of the humanist.

In the beginning of Luther's career, he had appeared to be more tolerant concerning Jews. In 1523, he published his treatise *That Jesus Christ Was Born a Jew*,[46] which was first published in Latin and shortly afterward in German. The German version was dedicated to "a baptized Jew, Bernhard," who taught Hebrew in Wittenberg. The assumption was that this treatise would strengthen Bernhard's faith in Christ and that he would become an example to other Jews, "so that those who were predestined for this, are called to their King David who will lead and save them."[47] That was not only Luther's hope but also his expectation. But that was not to be. Even though in 1523 he had tried and hoped to win the Jews for the gospel, by the end of his life he had lost all hope of achieving this. That hope transformed into hatred, so that many have accused him of being anti-Semitic. Regardless, those who read about his appeal to burn synagogues and his claim that Jewish people are liars by nature will have little motivation to defend Luther. Poor treatment of the Jews was, according to Luther, punishment for their unbelief. Jews who requested baptism were not to be trusted because they probably didn't mean it anyway.[48]

Though it had been forbidden for Jews to live in Kursachsen since 1432, this mandate was repeated and expanded in 1536 with a prohibition to trade in this area or even travel through it. Josel von Rosheim, essentially the spokesperson for German Jews, requested that the elector repeal this mandate. He had asked Luther if he could make arrangements for a discussion at court. Luther refused. In a public letter he wrote that Jews continued to harden their hearts and oppose the rediscovered gospel. It had always been his objective to treat the Jews amicably, Luther claimed, but they "misuse this in a scandalous fashion and participate in activities that as Christians we cannot tolerate." And thus it appeared that they "cursed and blasphemed their own flesh and blood, namely Jesus Christ of Nazareth." He informed Josel that, despite Luther's own wishes, they couldn't be friendly any longer, since the Jews "misuse my favor through their hardening of heart."[49]

This letter shows that Luther's view of Jews progressively worsened. The next step in that development was his treatise *Against the Sabbatarians*,[50] in which he argued that with the coming of the Messiah, God's covenant with Israel had ended. The fact that the Jews had to wander all over the world for the past 1,500 years was punishment for rejecting Jesus as Messiah. By virtue of this, Luther gave the advice to drive the Jews out of the German territories, reasoning that they were a threat to the Christian faith, an indignity to Christ and to the Virgin Mary.

Toward the end of 1542, Luther wrote his *Concerning the Jews and Their Lies*.[51] This work was intended to strengthen Christians in their faith and enable them to refute Jewish arguments. Luther did not direct this book to the Jews, declaring that their stubbornness rendered any attempt at reasoning pointless. In the first part, Luther rejected trust in the law and circumcision. In the second part, the core of his work, he defended the argument that Jesus was the promised Messiah from the perspective of the Old Testament.

The third section became most famous and notorious. Here Luther spoke vengefully about the criticism he perceived concerning himself. Luther's inability to separate a theological argument from his own sense of identity had thwarted him for years, but nowhere did it have such disastrous consequences as in this treatise. Luther additionally believed many legends about what the Jews had done to Christians, such as the poisoning of springs and the ritual murder of Christian children. He also believed the rumors claiming that Jews said among themselves that Mary was a whore and that Jesus was a miscarriage that lived. For Luther it was clear: Jews are a sickness, a boil, and they must be eliminated. To that end, he listed a number of specific measures. First of all, synagogues should be burned because that is where the blasphemy takes place. For the same reason, Jews' homes should be destroyed. Their prayer books and their Talmuds should be confiscated. Since their money had been stolen from Christians, Luther thought, their money and jewelry should be seized. That money must be used for the support of Jews who had become Christians. Jews who did not qualify would have to earn their money by means of forced labor. It would probably be better, Luther reasoned, to drive them away, because a society in which both the Christian religion and Judaism were practiced was, according to Luther, impossible.

Luther based these calls on the idea that Jews were heretics who had to be treated just like other heretics. His appeal had success. In several territories, the rulers decided to banish the Jews and confiscate their possessions. Regardless of whether Luther's proposals were motivated from his concern for the Christian faith and his disgust at the rejection of Jesus as the Christ, his proposals explicitly contradicted the Christian faith. Luther could not know that centuries later, these words would be eagerly cited by other Germans who enacted them. Luther could have prevented this murderous association by holding to the basic principle of *sola scriptura*. He eagerly slapped the ears of others with this principle, but his failure to hold himself to this standard resulted in horrific consequences.

Nature

Luther had an eye for the riches of nature and how God reveals himself in creation, but he also realized that there is a knowledge that far transcends that of nature:

> Everyone knows something about biology. I know, for example, that a dog's tongue is good for a wound, and that a cat catches mice, and that a hawk catches partridges, etc. The one knows a lot about nature, another less, through one's experience or through instruction. But God has not revealed everything about nature, and therefore, our mind is curious and wants to know still more. From this comes the study and research of nature. . . . It is not a bad thing that you don't know everything. If you know that fire is hot and

> water is cold and wet, that in the summer different work needs to be done than in winter, that is sufficient. As long as you know how you must look after your field, your cows, your house, and your child, then you have enough knowledge of nature. But with this, realize that in fact it only concerns the knowledge of Christ.[52]

For Luther, the month of May represented "an image of the resurrection of the dead. Look at how lovely the trees are, how beautifully everything becomes green. How beautiful is the month of May!"[53] While in his garden, he noticed the growth of creation and could only say, "How amazing are God's works!"[54] When he observed extraordinary natural phenomena, he interpreted them as special signs of God. On January 18, 1538, Luther, Melanchthon, and others saw an impressive comet. This led to a discussion about the meaning of this event. Luther was worried and saw the comet as a sign from God that soon he would intervene in another way. When there came an unusual amount of fish in the Elbe River in the spring of 1538, Luther thought that that was a bad omen. And indeed, the season was so dry that it threatened the harvest. Luther prayed fervently for rain: "Lord God, give our children and our families our daily bread. Look upon us in fatherly love."[55] That rain came on May 26: "Oh, let us thank our loving God, because what he has given us is worth thousands of guilders, because now it will rain grain, wheat, oats, barley, wine, spices, onions, grass, and milk. And we act as if it is nothing."[56] On April 18, 1539, he witnessed a solar eclipse, which happened again almost a year later on April 7, 1540.

Despite the fact that Luther had been responsible for the introduction of far-reaching changes and had many supporters, new discoveries in natural science had difficulty attracting support from Luther's side. In the summer of 1539, the views of Copernicus were discussed at Luther's dinner table. Copernicus's new view that the earth revolved around the sun instead of the other way around did not appeal to Luther. He thought it was scientific nonsense, arguing that the Bible clearly stated that the sun moves.[57] A geocentric view of the universe appeared to fit better with his faith, that not only God but also the Devil and his cohorts influence nature, the weather, and people. Similar to many contemporaries, Luther also believed that witchcraft and black magic were real. According to him, women who tried to steal milk, butter, and eggs by means of magic had to be burned.[58] He was convinced that witches could generate bad weather and that devilish beings could have sexual intercourse with men and women, superstitions that pushed Luther to contribute to the terrible persecution of women accused of witchcraft. He was critical of astrology and maintained that there was no evidence that our future could be read in the stars. Astronomy, however, concerned the work of God, such as stars, and was a worthy study.

Nevertheless, Luther preferred to be busy with the earth, through activities such as gardening. On New Year's Day 1527, Luther ordered a threshing machine and seed for the spring from his friend Wenzeslaus Linck in Nuremburg:

> I am very happy that you've promised me seed before spring. Send as much as you can, because I'm eager to have it. On the other hand, if I can do something for you, let me know, and I will certainly do it. Even if Satan and his cronies rage, in the meantime I will laugh at them because I rejoice about my garden, that is to say, about the blessings from the Creator and the enjoyment I have in his honor. Send more seed for my garden, preferably different kinds. If I live, I want to be a gardener.[59]

He continued to live, but he did not become a gardener. He continually thought of his garden, but his other work was too pressing. He regretted it because

> as an old and worn-out man, I would rather enjoy these days in the garden and calmly look at the things an old man can enjoy, namely, all the wonderful things that God has made: young trees, flowers, bushes, and birds. I would have such pleasure in them, if it wasn't for the fact that because of all my earlier sins I deserve to be deprived of them by all those objectionable and often useless matters.[60]

This love of nature also explained his admiration of paintings, particularly Italian art, "because in their paintings they could truly imitate nature so masterfully and truly imitate to reproduce not only the color and the shape in every respect but also the actions, as if the shapes live and really move."[61]

Animals too appeared frequently in Luther's writings, and not only the donkeys and swine to which Luther would compare his opponents. Luther wrote fondly of dogs, keeping one in his house, and considered it a unique creature of God:

> When he looked at his dog, Tölpel, he said, "Look at that dog. There is nothing wrong with his whole body. He has fine, sparkly eyes, strong legs, nice white teeth, a good stomach, etc. Are they not the most beautiful natural gifts? And God gives them, of all things, to such an animal devoid of reason."[62]

Luther was convinced that on the new earth there would again be dogs: "Of course! God shall make a new heaven and earth, and then he will also make new dogs ('Tölpline') with a skin like gold and hair like pearls."[63] People, according to him, could learn from a dog: "Oh, if I could pray the way a dog looks at meat! All his thoughts are single-mindedly directed at that meat; he does not think, wish, or hope for anything else."[64]

The Turks Are Coming

"The one says that the Turks are coming, and another says that they're staying away. What is certain is that neither emperor nor king nor rulers are arming themselves. The emperor is preparing himself to fiercely persecute the gospel in the Netherlands. May God prevent it. Amen."[65] In this letter Luther casually mentioned the anticipated persecution in the Netherlands and again raised the problem of the Turks. He saw the rise of the Turkish (Ottoman) Empire and their threatened conquest of the German Empire as a punishment from God for the blasphemy of the Catholics and their scorning of God's Word, as well as for the moral carelessness among the Protestants.[66] In 1540, Sultan Suleiman the Magnificent conquered large parts of Hungary, and in 1541, the Turks again had Vienna in their sights.

Elector Johann Frederick urged Luther and Bugenhagen to ask the ministers to raise their prayers against the Turks. Luther favored an appeal to penance; he saw the Turks as a well-deserved scourge from

God. Germany was ripe for judgment, Luther said, and God would bring that about by means of the Turks. Repentance was the appropriate remedy, and that could begin right away if the soldiers would put a stop to all their cursing.

Nevertheless, Luther did believe that they should take up arms against the Turks, seeing them as a danger for the freedom of the Christian faith. He spoke of the danger of the Turks in his criticism of Islam. In February 1542, Luther received his first copy of the Qur'an in Latin, and for the first time, he could read what the Muslims believed directly from their most authoritative source. Luther concluded that Islam was like a plague that God sent to confront spiritually lazy Christians. A lack of conviction among Christians provided Islam with the opportunity to advance. In 1542, when Theodor Bibliander, a theologian in Zurich, finished a German translation of the Qur'an, Luther supported its publication so that Christians would know about its lies, fables, and atrocities. Whoever wants to fight against the enemy, Luther argued, must be acquainted with their weapons. Therefore, Christians would do well to know what is in the Qur'an:[67]

> I would love to live to see the gospel brought to the Turks, which, according to me, could be done. I believe, however, that I will not experience this, but you will experience it because you will have to deal with them a lot more. Those personal things that are told about Mohammed do not interest me, but we should address the doctrine of the Turks. We should take a close look at it . . . because we can discuss it more effectively with them than with Jews because Muslims recognize many things that are found in the New Testament.[68]

Colloquies

Because he believed that the church of Rome had done too little to restore the breach in the church, the emperor took the initiative to organize several religious discussions between Catholic and Protestant theologians. From the reformed side, people like Melanchthon and Calvin were present. Luther was not. Physically, he was not well. Temperamentally, he was not very well suited for this kind of interaction, in part because he had become increasingly pessimistic about whether the situation in Rome would ever be right again. Ecumenical meetings with murky solutions did not appeal to Luther at all.

For a while a sense of optimistic expectation surrounded the Diet of Regensburg. The emperor convened a committee of three Catholic and three Protestant theologians and commissioned them to draft formulations that both parties could accept. The basis of this discussion was the document that Bucer and the Catholic theologian Johannes Gropper had formulated in January 1541, the *Regensburg Book*, in which they had articulated an agreement concerning justification. The Protestant side was represented by Bucer, Melanchthon, and Johann Pistorius, a preacher from Hesse. From the outset, Luther doubted the potential good of this committee and expected that Melanchthon would be too peace minded, mild, and accommodating. In the end, this effort would still not provide the desired result. The council's formulation of justification included, albeit in covered terms, the words "by faith alone," and the committee was briefly happy. But Rome immediately rejected this solution. Luther likewise thought the agreement was a rather flimsy construction that would probably collapse in subsequent discussions. He suggested that Melanchthon might as well come home because it was better to be clear, as Scripture is: "We simply stick to the view that one is justified by faith, without works of the law. Then the Devil, Eck, Mainz, and Hein, and whoever else may rail against me. Then we'll see how much progress they make."[69]

Indeed, the negotiations came to an impasse several weeks later. Luther was again consulted concerning the results as far as they had come, but he rejected everything. Luther demanded that the pope would have to confess that he had misled the souls of believers and would have to condemn everything Rome had achieved with lies, errors, and slander. The emperor too should first confess his guilt for the way he had persecuted the Protestants. Unity with Rome, according to Luther, was not a possibility.

Future Expectations

Luther's reaction to the Regensburg results was closely connected to his views concerning the times in which they were living. In the winter of 1529–1530, Luther had already stated that the return of Christ was imminent. When he translated the book of Daniel, it was clear to him that the Ottoman Empire was the last ungodly empire named in Daniel 7. The anti-Christian empire of the pope had preceded it. To make the vision of Daniel clearer, he included a small map in the publication. According to him, Christ would return even before Luther had completed the translation of the Bible.

In May 1541, he expanded the introduction to the book of Daniel and included commentary on Daniel 11:36 in which he portrayed the pope as the ruler who exalts himself above God and speaks against him. His kingdom is gradually but certainly defeated. That began with John Hus and would now be completed: "The holy John Hus prophesied about me in prison in Bohemia when he wrote: 'They will now roast a goose (because Hus means "goose"), but in a hundred years they will hear a swan singing. Under it they will suffer.'"[70] Luther was the swan (which is a symbol visible on many Lutheran churches in Europe), who heralded the last era of history.

Luther had preached about this from Matthew 24 in 1539 and 1540 and had pointed out the similarities between his time and the one Jesus had foretold. The fact that the pope projected himself as ruler but appeared to be unconcerned about the unbelief of the Jews and the Turks, not to mention the seductions of the Anabaptists, made it abundantly clear that he was the Antichrist. In Germany there were hardly any people at all who paid any attention to the Word of God, a situation that would not improve:

> By the time that I die, every schoolmaster, every teacher, and every verger will want to make his own Bible translation. Our translation won't be counted anymore. All our books will be discarded, the Bible, the postil, because the world constantly wants something new. When the church fathers came, the writings of the apostles did not count anymore; when the scholastics came, the church fathers did not count anymore. Subsequently, the scholastics couldn't agree with each other, and the one wanted to outdo the other. See, people are like that, because the world is arrogant. Therefore, Paul says (2 Tim. 4:4), "They will wander off into myths."[71]

But many did profess true faith in Christ, and that was a sign of the approaching end.[72] There was no more hope for this world, according to Luther:

> I could wish that I, and all my children, had died, because this world is going to experience some remarkable times. Those still living will see that it will become increasingly worse. Therefore, the Lord God will take his own away, and that proves what John says (Matt. 3:12). . . . Now he gathers the wheat into barns, but the chaff he will treat quite differently: "He will burn it with unquenchable fire," the text says. That is what he did to Rome. First, the devout people had to die by the sword, but after that, he came and overthrew the government so that people could work at the reconstruction of the city. And people are still doing that today. The pope is doing that too, but he will not be able to complete it. That is what he will do to Germany too. Also there, he will take the pious away and after that terminate Germany, because it has thoroughly deserved the punishment, and doesn't stop there.[73]

> I don't know any other solution than that it'll go the way as I dreamed, namely, that the last day comes. It is, after all, impossible that the papist church or the Roman curia will reform itself. That is just as unlikely as a Muslim or a Jew allowing himself to be converted and changed. And in the empire it's not getting better either. For thirty years now they convened as diets, and thus far they have not accomplished anything. In fact, it is even becoming worse. . . . I see no other solution than the coming of the last day. All help is in vain; it is simply hopeless. That is probably why God allows the gospel to be spread now so that before that time he can gather his Christians together as he has always done. When he wanted to destroy a kingdom, beforehand he would send preachers to them to call them: "Come here, come here. Come, come!" Good people, learn that.[74]

Luther divided history into four periods. The first was the period of the apostles, and the Jews were the foes. After that was the time of martyrs, and against them stood the tyrants of the time. The third period was that of the ecclesiastical teachers, such as the church fathers, and they were opposed by heretics. Now it was the time of the Christian church, which had to contend with lukewarm, arrogant Christians.[75] Each of these four thriving periods was opposed by clear adversaries. Very quickly, the papacy was the exemplar of that lukewarm, arrogant Christendom. The pope was the Antichrist, and Luther was therefore God's last prophet. He was the last trumpet, who announced the coming of the Christ. Even if the world would not want to hear this trumpet, the angels in heaven did, and they would help bring about the end.[76]

To illustrate his message, Luther developed ten woodcuts, made by Cranach, that mocked the pope (e.g., see fig. 10.3).[77] Luther wrote the captions. The illustrations and descriptions were equally vehement and crude, with some exceptions. In one case, Luther wrote more positively, "What I leave behind, is not a church that appears sad, because she flourishes through the pure and true doctrine, and she grows everyday by means of the best and most upright preachers."[78] He believed in the power of the Word, but his life had been defined by a tension between believing and seeing, between confessing and experience, a tension that Luther was unable to escape. Thus, on the whole, Luther offered an increasingly depressing evaluation of the church toward the end of his life.

Luther expressed this sentiment again in 1542 in the foreword to a booklet about the Old Testament prophecies concerning Christ. This booklet was assembled by Urbanus Rhegius, the superintendent of Lüneburg, who passed away shortly before its publication.[79] In his sermon on June 14, 1545, Luther articulated his great embarrassment: "Why do we actually continue to preach? We might as well quit. . . . Everything seems to be lost."[80] His frustration came through criticism of usury and extortion, artificially high pricing, the great luxuries of the rich, and the lazy idlers who expected to be supported by the community but were too miserable to work themselves.

Bishopric

Luther observed with sorrow how much influence the rulers and the city governments had acquired over church life. His plan had been to set up Protestant bishoprics, as the church had for many centuries, with bishops as spiritual leaders. He achieved that only partially; the politi-

Figure 10.3 *Passions of Christ and Antichrist.* Woodcut by Lucas Cranach the Elder, 1521. British Library, London.

cians had seen a clear opportunity to take over the leadership. So there are examples where the political authorities used the Reformation to strengthen their own power, but there are also situations where things were done Luther's way.

In 1541, for example, when the bishop of Nuremburg died, Elector Johann Frederick wanted a pro-Reformation successor. Nicholas von Amsdorf, the court chaplain in Magdeburg, received this position and thus became the first Lutheran bishop. Luther conducted this ordination but with a transformed ritual that reflected Luther's views of the bishop as a normal minister.[81] Everything else remained the same, as if the bishop carried out his work of supervision, pastorate, and preaching.

When Joachim III, Elector of the Margraviate of Brandenburg, introduced the Reformation into his region, he asked for Luther's verdict about the newly proposed order. Luther first related how happy he was with this reform. In principle, he had no objection to maintaining the last unction, but he did not see this as a sacrament and considered the reforming of this ritual a bit troublesome. He did object to the procession on the Feast of the Holy Host (*Fronleichnam*), but aside from that, some processions could be acceptable if the gospel was preached purely and both baptism and the Lord's Supper were celebrated in accordance with biblical principles. Luther repeated what he had said in another context: if the elector wanted the preacher to wear three mass vestments or walk around seven times in a procession instead of one, that was no problem. If he wanted the minister to sing out in front of the procession and dance and jump, that was fine, as long as these things were not seen as a necessity for salvation.[82] Luther could imagine that others had problems with these "Romish" elements, but they were no problem for him.

Trent

In December 1544, the University of Leuven published a document of theses to clarify a number of Catholic positions against the Protestant heretics. Melanchthon did not want to react to these, fearing even more fragmentation. As usual, Luther disagreed and published his *Contra the 32 Articles of the Theological Sharpshooters in Leuven.*[83] It bothered him that biblical doctrine and the message of grace were constantly opposed. Those "donkeys" in Leuven had made him angrier than was fitting for a person of his age.[84]

In December 1545, the Council of Trent reconvened, and Luther responded with a prayer: "Lord, arise and scatter your enemies. Amen, Amen, Amen."[85] He had no illusions about the Council of Trent. According to him, it would go just like the Council of Constance (1414–1418), with many promises and few results—and that's not to mention that there they also condemned and burned John Hus. When the council was in the midst of preparations, Luther was already clear about the outcome: "I don't believe anything about it, I don't hope anything, and don't think anything. It is all for nothing."[86]

Luther immediately set the tone with his *Against the Papacy at Rome Established by the Devil*,[87] making himself very clear what he thought of the pope and council. It had become obvious what the pope was, "a desperate mischief-maker, an enemy of God and people, a destroyer of Christendom, and the top dwelling place of the Devil himself."[88] Based on church history, Luther argued that the idea that the pope was head of the church or a council was a complete innovation.

The primacy of the pope was a human invention without any basis in the Bible. What was necessary was a bishop in Rome who was not the head over other bishops and did not meddle in politics but simply preached and looked after the needs of the church. In a letter dated July 1545, Luther said,

> The pope screams that we are heretics, and therefore, we may not participate in the council, but the emperor wants us to agree with the decisions of the council and with his decisions. Perhaps it is God who has made them so foolish, in view of the fact that they curse us and then at the same time ask us to agree. But that must be their raging wisdom.[89]

According to Luther, they were doing their best to present the Protestants

> as shameful people who refuse to listen to the pope or to the church, and to the emperor, the empire, and even to the council, even though we frequently requested a council. . . . But it is the Lord who will mock these scoffers. . . . Let the pope first admit that he must listen to the council even if it disagrees with him. Only then will we debate the whole question. They are crazy and foolish.[90]

Death

Luther's death was approaching, and he knew it: "I am so slow, tired, cold, that is to say, an old, useless man. I have completed my race (2 Tim. 4:7). The waiting is only until the Lord gathers me to my fathers (1 Kings 19:4) and commits me to decomposition so that also the worms will receive their portion."[91] At his daughter Margaretha's sickbed, he spoke of his own desire to die:

> Together with her brothers she was ill, but though the others have long recovered, a stubborn and terrible fever has gripped her for ten weeks, and she fights for her life and health. I will not take it ill of the Lord if he takes her out of this demonic time and world, and together with my family I would also like to be taken, because I yearn for that day and for the end of the raging of Satan and his cohorts.[92]

The event that had terrified him since childhood was close now—in fact, death had been close all his life. He had written much on death, because he knew that death was the greatest problem for humans—not necessarily dying but facing what comes after. How can a sinful person appear before the holy God? In May 1519, he published a sermon on how someone could prepare for death.[93] The sermon belonged to what in the Middle Ages was called *ars moriendi*, literally, "the art of dying well." Sermons of this genre focused on how a person could appear before God as best as possible and give in as little as possible to the Devil, who tried to rob humans of faith at the last moment. In such medieval works, the deathbed became the last meritorious effort. In Luther's sermon, however, the deathbed became a place of trust and surrender. Dying was a matter not of putting your best foot forward but of trusting in Christ.

The peace that comes from knowing one is righteous before God had been preached to others, but Luther himself had struggled to grasp it. Death remained very ominous. From his perspective, Luther said, "Our God is the greatest adulterer in existence."[94] The reason for this accusation was that through death, God breaks up every marriage. Even so, Luther believed that there would be a reunion of married couples after they died.[95] When he was asked whether humans would recognize each other in heaven and on the new earth, Luther responded that those who are in Christ will recognize each other better than Adam and Eve did in Paradise.[96]

Death did not have a place in the church, Luther believed, and the dead didn't belong there either. He wanted to end the tradition of burying the deceased in or around the church. According to him, a cemetery should be located outside the city, not to keep death out of the picture altogether but to keep the smell of death away and to give the dead rest. This rest should also be extended to the living, since a graveyard should be a place for rest, peaceful prayer, and silent memory. This is why Luther decided to bury his beloved Elizabeth just outside the city. Such was the practice in the time of Scripture, and Luther felt they should now reclaim that practice. Many cities followed Luther's example and moved the cemetery outside the city gates.

Grief and Comfort

Luther did not do any pastoral work in the congregation, but through his letters he was actively involved in pastoral care. Frequently he had comforted people in grief, often parents who had lost a child. Luther knew from his own experience what such a loss meant: "Then part of my own body dies, as well as that of the mother."[97] Such pain and grief are also integral to being a Christian: "Such emotions and feelings are the result of divine creation, which God has planted in us by nature and which are not wrong in themselves."[98]

When Luther was staying in the Coburg, he sent Justus Jonas, then at the Diet of Augsburg, a congratulatory letter on the occasion of his son's birth. A few days later, however, Luther had to inform him that the child had already died. Luther did not write directly to Jonas but informed Melanchthon so that the latter could personally inform the father and provide support. Shortly afterward, Luther wrote a letter of comfort, telling Jonas that he should not see this death as a sign of being forsaken by God. Occasionally, he would also have to send a similar letter to parents of students who had died during their stay in Wittenberg.[99]

Luther also offered comfort and encouragement to those who doubted their election. Jerome Weller, for example, lived with the Luthers and provided care for little Hans. When Luther resided at the Coburg Castle, he heard that Weller suffered from severe depression, apparently a family affliction. In 1531, Luther also had to write a letter to comfort Jerome's sister, and provide her with assurance because she also worried whether or not she was among the elect.[100] Luther did his best to help Jerome and provided support from Scripture, trying to convince him that his difficulty came not from God but from the Devil. He should not succumb to these assaults but combat them by socializing more, participating in games, and seeking out opportunities to enjoy life—such as eating, having the occasional stiff drink, and not being overly concerned with sinning occasionally. If the Devil would confront him with these sins, then he should quickly tell him that Christ had died for his sins. In all respects, Luther supported him and continued to work closely with him after Luther returned to Wittenberg. Nevertheless, he had to acknowledge that it was unimaginably difficult to break through such depression.[101]

Conflict

During the summer of 1545, Luther set out to visit Leipzig, Merseburg, Halle, Zeitz, and Eisleben. There were several reasons for this trip, but the main reason was that he was tired of Wittenberg. The people seemed to ignore his messages, and he could no longer tolerate the messy and irreverent way the congregation conducted the liturgy. Therefore, he went on a trip to find a new place to live for himself and his family: "I would rather wander around and beg for bread than that I would allow myself to be tortured by and have worries about the mayhem here in Wittenberg and be forced to observe the loss of so much of what I worked hard to build up in the first place."[102] Since immorality had become so prevalent, he wanted to get away—and fast.

This was not a random or quick decision. Only a few days after his departure, on July 28, he wrote Käthe: "I would really like it if I did not have to return to Wittenberg. My heart has grown cold, so that I don't like being there anymore." He told her that she should "sell the garden and homestead, the house, and everything that belongs with it. . . . Let's get out of Sodom as quickly as possible."[103] The message was taken so seriously in Wittenberg that the elector immediately took action. The university feared that if Luther would not return, Melanchthon would leave as well. A delegation consisting of Melanchthon, Bugenhagen, George Major, burgomaster Matthei, and the judge Hans Lufft departed after Luther on August 1 in the hope of changing his mind and to inform him of concessions that the politicians of Wittenberg were willing to make. The delegation appeared to achieve its goal; on August 18, Luther returned home. There may have been a financial reason for this speedy return as well, because Luther had written in early August that he did not expect to sell the monastery quickly. There were people in Wittenberg "who do not have such an expensive house as we do" and were not able to sell theirs either.[104] Though he wanted to move away, what was he to do if he could not get rid of his house?

There were, of course, other, more ecclesiastical reasons for his trip. In Merseburg, Luther had two unique tasks. On August 2, in the cathedral church he consecrated prince George von Anhalt as bishop. It became an elaborate ceremony, carried out completely in the ancient ecclesiastical style: Luther laid his hands on the bishop after Antonius

Musa preached a sermon. The church was overfull with representatives from both ecclesiastical and political arenas and many interested participants. Immediately after the consecration of the bishop, there was an announcement: the marriage of Sigismund von Lindenau (one of the higher clerics in the cathedral organization who had been married in secret for the preceding seven years, though few were actually aware of it) was declared official. The ecclesiastical ceremony followed two days later in a service in which Luther preached, and the new bishop, Anhalt, officiated at the solemnization of the marriage itself. On August 6, Luther preached for the last time in the cathedral church and then traveled on to Zeitz.

In Zeitz he was received by Dr. Matthäus Ratzeberger, the personal physician of Elector Johann Frederick. Ratzeberger also treated Luther's many medical issues, including, among others, kidney stones, headaches, and dizzy spells. He gave him urgent advice to return to Wittenberg, which he refused. Instead, he traveled on to Leipzig to consecrate the new university church.

Not until August 18 did Luther and his travel companions return to Wittenberg. The events showed once again that Luther was searching. What must he do, and where must he go? Did he realize that his time had passed—not only his time on earth but also his time as reformer? It had become clear that the Reformation had taken root in other places, with other leaders. Wittenberg became the place where it began, and Luther became the man who started it all, but now the significant events were taking place elsewhere, led by other people. It is notable that Luther did not die while he was involved in Europe's intense political or ecclesiastical issues. Rather, he died after he had been busy for many days in a little city trying to resolve an ordinary quarrel between two brothers.

Eisleben

In early October 1545, Luther set out for Eisleben with Melanchthon. The purpose of the trip to his birthplace was to reconcile the relationship between the counts of Mansfeld, the brothers Gebhard and Albrecht. They had quarreled about how to resolve their financial problems. Developments in mining required new techniques, and because the cost of the investments were higher than the returns, Gebhard ended up in debt. The brothers disagreed on how to handle it, especially after Albrecht had taken advantage of his brother's indebtedness by gradually taking over his property and his rights. Luther's desire to restore this relationship had much to do with his family in Mansfeld, as they suffered under the strain caused by these debt problems. The trip ended up being a waste of time because when they arrived, they found that both counts were away, engaged in a military campaign with the Duke of Braunschweig-Wolfenbüttel. Luther and Melanchthon returned home to Wittenberg to celebrate Luther's sixty-second birthday. It would be his last.

On December 6, Luther and Melanchthon again traveled to Eisleben. The counts were home but uninterested in reconciliation. The negotiations did not progress well, and Melanchthon became ill. Luther was already unwell, and after Christmas they returned home. At the beginning of the New Year, Luther was home. In Wittenberg the New Year was a major celebrated event. University students used so many fireworks that the university and the city council asked the elector to forbid the fireworks.

As for Luther, he was approaching the end. On January 17, he sent a letter to his friend Jacob Praepositus in Bremen informing him that he was "old, spent, tired, cold, and now was also partially blind."[105] That same day, he preached for the last time in Wittenberg. On January 23, he again set out, for the third time, toward Eisleben to, as he said himself, clean up that "sad business."[106] His sons Johannes (age nineteen), Martin (age fifteen), and Paul (age thirteen) accompanied him so that they could visit the family in Mansfeld again. Melanchthon was still sick and stayed in Wittenberg. Additionally, Ambrosius Rudtfeld, the boys' tutor, and Luther's assistant, Johannes Aurifaber, joined them on the trip.

The winter weather was poor, so that initially they could get no farther than Halle. The Saale River had flooded, and ice prevented them from crossing. Returning to Wittenberg was not an option either because the Mulde River, which they would have to cross, was also flooding its banks. In a letter to Käthe, Luther compared the Saale River to an Anabaptist. As far as he was concerned, he preferred to quench his thirst with beer from the Torgau or wine from the Rhine.[107] Luther wrote that they were still stuck in Halle and that he had used the time to preach in the City Church, appealing once again to the people to remain faithful to the Word and not to occupy themselves with the veneration of saints and relics.

On January 27, the travelers were able to cross, but the weather was so poor that it took them almost two days to cover the twenty-five miles between Halle and Eisleben. The counts even sent an escort of sixty horsemen, who met them on the opposite side of the Saale, which did nothing to speed up their travels. In keeping with his former monk's custom, Luther did not ride on horseback. He became more and more ill and even had a heart attack, as he reported to Melanchthon after his arrival:

> Along the way, I fainted and had heart issues. I was walking, but it was heavy going for me so that I began to sweat. Afterward, when I was sitting in the wagon, and my shirt was soaked with sweat, I was chilled to the bone and had problems with a muscle in my left arm. Therefore, I felt such a constriction in my heart that I could hardly breathe. I blame my foolishness for going afoot. Now it's going somewhat better, but how long that will last is hard to say, because you really can't trust the situation when you are older; even when you are younger, matters are not sure.[108]

It was already late when the travelers reached Eisleben on January 28. His three sons, who had been terribly bored while waiting in Halle, were immediately sent to family in Mansfeld. Luther stayed with the city secretary, Johann Albrecht, who lived by the market square, not far from the counts' castle. Though he did not feel well, he wanted to get to work to reconcile the two quarreling brothers. Life was good, "eating and boozing," and the Naumburger beer was a relief for Luther's digestive system: "This morning, within three hours, I've already been to the toilet three times."[109] On January 31 and February 2, 7, and 14, he preached in the St. Andreas Church in Eisleben, and he participated two times in the celebration of the Lord's Supper. His last sermon was shorter because Luther was physically unable to carry on, but he did appeal to the people one more time "to remain faithful to

Christ's words and to come to him."[110] In previous *Table Talk* discussions, Luther constantly expressed his conviction that the Word of God would not be lost due to persecution. He was equally convinced that he would soon die: "When I have returned to Wittenberg, I will lie down in the grave, and I will give the maggots a nice fat doctor to eat."[111]

The negotiations with the counts did not flourish, and according to Luther, hell must have been empty and all the devils assembled in Eisleben.[112] Nevertheless, after two weeks of discussion, they finally had a breakthrough. Luther was relieved and wanted to go home:

> We hope—if God wills—to come home this week. God showed his great grace here, because both gentlemen, with the help of their counselors, have come to agreement, with the exception of two or three points. That also counts for the fact that Count Gebhard and Count Albrecht have again become brothers in the Lord. Today I have to confirm that. I want to invite them to my table so that they also speak with each other again, because thus far they have said nothing to each other but only embittered each other by means of letters. In the meantime the young counts are quite jolly among themselves, and in sleighs with little bells they make trips through the snow. They have dress-up parties and are in good spirits with each other, as is also the son of Count Gebhard. And therefore, we should seize with both hands that God hears prayers.[113]

The brothers were prepared to reconcile, and on February 16, the agreements were established. Luther's last preserved writing, found on a table after he had died, also dates from that day. It is only a little scrap of paper with a few sentences:

> You cannot understand Virgil's *Bucolics* [*The Eclogues*] or his *Georgics* if you have not first been a shepherd or a farmer for five years. I believe no one can understand the letters of Cicero unless he has worked for forty years in a well-run state government. Do not let anyone think they have tasted the Holy Scriptures sufficiently, if they have not, together with the prophets, led the congregation for a hundred years.
>
> Therefore, it is such a miracle in the first place with John the Baptist, in the second place with Christ, and in the third place with

the apostles. You should not attempt to understand this divine Aeneas, but you should simply venerate the track they left behind.

We are beggars. That is the truth.[114]

In conclusion, their discussions concerned the Bible, the Word that opened the gates of paradise for him but that people do not understand completely. Listen, therefore, Luther said; knock until you hear it, again and again. "We are beggars. That is the truth." When we approach God, we can only hold up empty hands; he provides, but nevertheless, we never get it in hand.[115]

The End

Justus Jonas and Michael Coelius (1492–1559), court chaplain to the counts, wrote a detailed account of Luther's end on February 17. They were both in attendance during the night.[116] On February 17, the negotiations were to be concluded. Luther did not feel well and was not involved. Around ten o'clock at night he went to bed and prayed Psalm 31:6, a familiar deathbed scripture: "I hate those who pay regard to worthless idols, but I trust in the Lord." In that prayer he did not forget to include a brief petition against the pope and the Council of Trent.

That night at one o'clock he was awakened by another heart attack. Though his room had been heated during the night, he still asked his servant to stoke up the fire in his room, suffering from chills related to the heart attack. Massages with warm cloths and heated pillows did not help. Luther suddenly began to sweat, and the people around him (among others, the two counts and their wives and Luther's sons Martin and Paul) thought that this was a sign of improvement. Luther knew better and saw this as an omen that he would die: "It is the cold sweat of death. I will give up the spirit because my illness is getting worse." With the words of Simeon (Luke 2:29) he spoke to the people standing around his bed: "I will go in peace and joy. Amen." Three more times he repeated the words of Psalm 31:6, and then he was silent. Countess Anna anointed him with healing oils, but Luther did not recover. When he was asked if he could die in faith in Jesus Christ and whether he remained in the doctrine that he had professed in his name, he whispered his affirmation. A little later, around quarter to three, he breathed his last and died, only a few hundred feet from the place where he had been born.

In the morning, Justus Jonas immediately sent a messenger to Elector Johann Frederick, and the latter informed Melanchthon, Bugenhagen, and Cruciger. Melanchthon was lecturing on the letter to the Romans when the messenger entered the lecture hall and gave him the message of Luther's death. Melanchthon replied with the words of 2 Kings 2:12: "He who sits on Israel's chariot, he who has led the church in the world in these last days, has died." Afterward, together with Bugenhagen and Cruciger, they went to inform Katharina that Luther had passed away. She was virtually the very last one to hear that her husband had died.

Buried

In Eisleben, Luther was laid in a coffin made of tinplate, and a death mask of his face was created. The painter Lucas Furtenagel, a friend of Luther from Halle, quickly traveled to the city to make a portrait of the reformer. The next day, Justus Jonas led a memorial service in the Andreas Church. Out of respect, all the children in Eisleben were dressed in white. From February 19 to 20, ten citizens kept a wake in the church, followed by another sermon.

The people of Eisleben wanted Luther to be buried there, but the elector wanted Luther to rest in Wittenberg. Consequently, Luther set out on his last trip on February 20. Outside the city, the children of Eisleben sang on their knees as the cortege of forty-five riders accompanied the reformer to Wittenberg. On the coffin they had draped a black silken cloth with a large white cross, which would be saved by his posterity until the eighteenth century. On February 21, the cortege was met in Bitterfeld by a delegation of representatives from the city council and from the elector. In every village that the cortege passed, the bells pealed. Reports of the trip are silent about the continued bitter cold, but they do mention the multitude of tears shed by everyone as Luther passed. When they finally arrived at the Elster Gate on the morning of February 22, an honor guard of professors, students, administrators, and citizens awaited, along with Katharina and her daughter Margaretha's wagon. In procession, the cortege passed by Luther's house and across the Collegienstrasse to the Castle Church. The tinplate coffin was placed in a wooden coffin, and during the memorial sermons led by Bugenhagen and Melanchthon, the coffin stood beside the pulpit.

By the graveside, Melanchthon did not observe the maxim "Speak no ill of the dead." He stated that Luther had been an instrument of God and emphasized what he had meant for the renewal of the church, but he also stated emphatically that Luther had a difficult character and temperament. After the servicc, they lowered the coffin into the grave in the church. Luther had been in favor of burial outside the city for the sake of tranquility, but such tranquility was not to be: his grave in the church became a pilgrimage site. One advantage, at least, was that Luther continued to draw people into the church.

One of the visitors to Luther's grave was Emperor Charles V, who arrived in 1547, after his armies had occupied Wittenberg. The man who said to him, "Here I stand, I cannot do otherwise," now lay at his feet. Nevertheless, out of respect, the emperor did not touch Luther's grave. The picture of the living emperor standing by the dead Luther was symbolic, because after Luther's death, Rome's position was much better than that of the Reformation. While a struggle ensued among Lutherans as to who should be the true successor to Luther, and reformational theologians continued to be divided, Rome managed to create internal unity through the Council of Trent. The emperor was at the apex of his power, and after his defeat of the Protestant rulers, he managed to reintroduce the mass in many cities and regions.

Käthe

When Luther had sensed that his end had come, he informed Katharina that she did not need to be concerned, because God is able "to provide ten Doctor Martins if the one should die." On February 7, 1546, he wrote her:

> To my dear wife, Katharina Luther, doctor's wife and hog dealer in Wittenberg. My highly esteemed wife, my hands and feet. Do not be concerned about me. I have someone who is able to provide better than you and all the angels put together. He lies in a manger and lies at the breast of the Virgin Mary but also sits at the right hand of God the Almighty Father. Do not be concerned. Amen.[117]

That sounds wonderful, but Luther should have been more concerned about providing for Käthe. After his death there were no ten Martins and not even one new Martin Luther. There was no inheritance, and his will was invalid. Katharina had no money. After Luther had gone to Eisleben, shortly before his death, she had had to borrow money from Melanchthon to buy groceries. Luther had not trusted lawyers, and so he had written his own last testament, which turned out to have no legal weight (see fig. 10.4). The elector wanted to help, and so he declared the document to be legal, but he could not help more because he had little available money due to his various religious wars. The fact that the last testament was declared legal did not help much either. Though Luther's printers had earned a lot of money thanks to him, he could only write in his will,

> I bear witness that there is no ready cash, except for the beakers and valuables listed above in the endowment. Indeed, such a reckoning can be manifest to everyone, since people know how much income I have had from my most gracious lord, and beyond that, I have not received as income one heller or kernel from anyone, except what was a gift, which is to be found cited above under the valuables and which in part is still tied up with the debt. And yet, with this income and with donations, I have built and bought so much, and I ran such a big and burdensome household, that among other things I must acknowledge it as an extraordinary, remarkable blessing that I have been able to manage. The miracle is not that there is not ready money but that there is not a greater debt. I ask this for this reason, that the Devil, since he can come no closer to me, shall no doubt persecute my Käthe in all sorts of ways for this reason alone, that she was, and (God be praised!) still is, the espoused housewife of the man Dr. Martin.[118]

The king of Denmark sent fifty ducats every year, but that was all. From a financial perspective, Katharina could sadly declare that she and her family were beggars—literally. Due to the threat of plague and the emperor's troops, she had to leave Wittenberg. During the trip, the horses pulling her wagon were spooked and threw Katharina from the wagon into a brook. Tired, poor, and afflicted with pneumonia, she arrived in Torgau, the city where she had arrived thirty years earlier

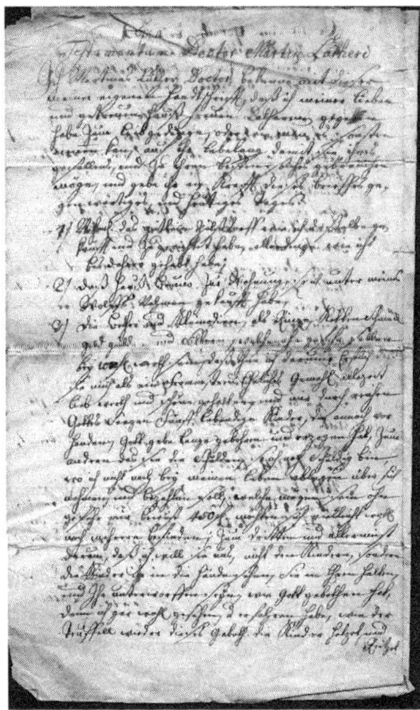

Figure 10.4 Luther's original last testament, dated 1542. Photo used with permission of Gerhard Hund.

as an abducted nun. She died there on December 20, 1552, and was buried in the St. Mary's Church. The only words on her gravestone read, "Blissfully asleep in God."

Simul Iustus et Peccator

Luther needed the grace that he himself had proclaimed. Throughout his life he remained a good example of his view that a Christian remains a sinner all his life and remains justified at the same time. "Through daily remorse and penance," he said, "the old Adam in us must be drowned and together with all sins die . . . and must arise again each day. And then a new man must arise who lives eternally before God in righteousness and purity." But it is not an easy task to drown the old Adam, "for look out: the beast can swim."[119] For many around Luther, his character was a problem. Melanchthon especially suffered much as a middleman between Luther and the people who dared not approach him. Melanchthon therefore often witnessed Luther's fearful bursts of rage when he read or heard something that annoyed him.[120]

Two years after Luther's death, Melanchthon sighed when he said, "I had to bear an almost degrading bondage because Luther was led by his militant temperament and exhibited a cocky self-righteousness, rather than that he would pay attention to his deferential position and the common good."[121]

Luther received much criticism for his abrasive style of writing, his judgments, his unrestrained reactions, and his use of coarse language. But the judgment of Calvin, who also complained about Luther's lack of self-control, was shared by most people: this is just the way he is, and thanks to him we have again received the Word. If everyone were to call him a devil, even then Calvin would have honored him as a unique servant of God.[122] Most colleagues agreed with that assessment. Luther himself was convinced that he himself had not sought the role of reformer, and that is the way he continually presented himself:

> Without being aware of it, God pushed me into working with the gospel. If I had known everything beforehand that I now know from experience, I would not have allowed myself to be pushed. But the wisdom of God is greater than that of people. He simply blinded me as you would put blinders on a horse who must run on a racetrack. Therefore, when I began with this, with great gravity and with genuine feeling, I told him in my little cell that if he wanted to play a game with me, then he should do that for himself, but that he should keep me from letting myself, that is to say, letting my own wisdom, play along. He has powerfully heard this prayer. May he continue to provide his grace.[123]

Luther's researchers have long been busy trying to answer when he ceased being a monk. Was it in December 1520 when he burned the papal bull threatening excommunication, which also declared him to be a fugitive? Was it the ban that caught up to him in early 1521, which formally excommunicated him from the church? Or did he cease being a monk on the day he got married in 1525, because then he also broke his vows of chastity? The answer is found later. He ceased being a monk the day he died, because he was truly a monk his entire life. He was not a monk according to the rules of the church, but he was a monk according to the estimation of Erasmus, who said that the world is a monastery and that we (who are in the world) can live as if we were all monks. The ideal of monkhood can be lived as a head of state, as a mother, as a greengrocer, and also as a married monk. Luther had remained faithful to his vows. All his life he lived a life obedient, chaste, and poor. He had been obedient to God's Word, chaste in his marriage, and poor as a beggar before God, a man without money. "We are beggars." That especially is the language of the monastery. With these his last written words, Luther indicated the essence of being a monk: having nothing of our own to offer but expecting everything from God.

When he entered the monastery, he was asked the question posed to all novices: "What do you seek here?" Luther answered that he was seeking God. That was indeed true. He sought God in Erfurt and found him outside Jerusalem.

Primary Sources and Literature

Primary Sources

Kluckhohn, August, ed. *Deutsche Reichstagsakten: Jüngere Reihe*. Gotha: Friedrich Andreas Perthes, 1893 (in the notes as *RTA*).

Luther, Martin. *D. Martin Luthers Werke, Kritische Gesamtausgabe: Briefwechsel* [Letters]. 18 vols. Weimar: Hermann Böhlau Nachfolger, 1930–1983 (in the notes as WABr).

Luther, Martin. *D. Martin Luthers Werke, Kritische Gesamtausgabe: Deutsche Bibel* [German Bible]. 12 vols. Weimar: Hermann Böhlau Nachfolger, 1906–1961 (in the notes as WADB).

Luther, Martin. *D. Martin Luthers Werke, Kritische Gesamtausgabe: Schriften* [Writings]. 73 vols. Edited by Rudolph Hermann et al. Weimar: Hermann Böhlau Nachfolger, 1883–2009 (in the notes as WA).

Luther, Martin. *D. Martin Luthers Werke, Kritische Gesamtausgabe: Tischreden* [Table Talk]. 6 vols. Weimar: Hermann Böhlau Nachfolger, 1912–1921 (in the notes as WATr).

Melanchthon, Philipp. *Opera Quae Supersunt Omnia*. Edited by Karl Gottlieb Bretschneider and Heinrich Ernst Bindseil. Vols. 1–28 of *Corpus Reformatorum*. Halle: C. A. Schwetschke et Filium, 1834–1860 (in the notes as *CR*).

Scheel, Otto, ed. *Dokumente zu Luthers Entwicklung*. Tübingen: Mohr, 1911 (in the notes as Scheel).

Virck, Hans, ed. *Politische Korrespondenz der Stadt Strassburg*. Vol. 1, *1517–1530*. Strassburg: Karl J. Trübner, 1882 (in the notes as *Pol. Kor.*).

Walch, Johann Georg. *Dr. Martin Luthers sämtliche Schriften*. Vols. 1–23 in 25. Jena: Johann Georg Walch, 1740–1753 (in the notes as Walch).

Literary Sources

Boehmer, Heinrich. *Der junge Luther*. Leipzig: Koehler & Amelang, 1939.

Brecht, Martin. *Martin Luther*. 3 vols. Stuttgart: Calwer, 1981–1987.

Brieger, Theodor. *Die vervollständigten Aleander-Depeschen, nebst Untersuchungen über den Wormser Reichstag*. Gotha: Friedrich Andreas Perthes, 1884.

Fabisch, Peter, and Erwin Iserloh, eds. *Dokumente zur Causa Lutheri (1517–1521)*. 2 vols. Münster: Aschendorff, 1988–1991.

Förstemann, C. E. "Der Studenten-Auflauf zu Wittenberg im J. 1520." *Neue Mittheilungen aus dem Gebiet historisch-antiquarischer Forschungen* 8 (1848): 51–71.

Küchenmeister, Friedrich. *Dr. Martin Luther's Krankengeschichte*. Leipzig: O. Wigand, 1881.

Leppin, Volker. *Martin Luther*. Darmstadt: Primus Verlag, 2010.

Oberman, Heiko A. *Luther: Mensch zwischen Gott und Teufel*. Berlin: Siedler, 1981.

Roper, Lyndal. *Martin Luther: Renegade and Prophet*. London: Penguin, 2016.

Schiess, Traugott, ed. *Briefwechsel der Brüder Ambrosius und Thomas Blaurer: 1509–1548*. 3 vols. Freiburg: Friedrich Ernst Fehsenfeld, 1908–1912.

Schilling, Heinz. *Martin Luther: Rebell in einer Zeit des Umbruchs*. München: C. H. Beck, 2012.

Notes

Introduction

1. *Pol. Kor.* 1.2:512–14.
2. *Joannis Calvini Opera Quae Supersunt Omnia*, ed. Guilielmus Baum, Eduardus Cunitz, and Eduardus Reuss (Brunswick and Berlin: Schwetschke, 1863–1900), 11:705.

Chapter 1: Child (1483–1500)

1. WATr 4: no. 4007.
2. On Mansfeld and mining, see Lyndal Roper, *Martin Luther: Renegade and Prophet* (London: Penguin, 2016), 17–34.
3. WATr 3: no. 2982b.
4. WATr 2: no. 1429.
5. WA 1:44–52, which quotes from *Aesop's Fables*.
6. WATr 4: no. 4192.
7. Luther to Georg Spalatin, January 14, 1520, in WABr 1:610–11.
8. *A True Admonition to All Christians* (1522), in WA 8:637.
9. Martin Brecht, *Martin Luther* (Stuttgart: Calwer, 1981–1987), 2:99.
10. WATr 5: no. 6250.
11. WATr 3: no. 2888a.
12. WATr 3: no. 3839.
13. WATr 3: no. 3566a.
14. *Lectures on Titus and Philemon* (1527), in WA 25:460.
15. Luther to his father, Hans Luther, February 15, 1530, in WABr 5:238–41.
16. WATr 1: no. 933; WATr 2: no. 1388.
17. Luther to Philipp Melanchthon, June 5, 1530, in WABr 5:351.
18. Luther to Konrad Cordatus, May 23, 1531, in WABr 6:103.
19. *CR* 6:156.
20. *Letter of Comfort* (1524), in WA 15:46.
21. WATr 5: no. 5571; WATr 3: no. 3566b.
22. See Volker Leppin, *Martin Luther* (Darmstadt: Primus Verlag, 2010), 34–36.
23. Luther to Klaus Storm, June 15, 1522, in WABr 2:563.
24. *Answer to Duke George* (1533), in WA 38:105.
25. Scheel, *Dokumente*, 1: no. 102.
26. Leppin, *Martin Luther*, 23.
27. *Sermon That Kids Have to Go to School* (1530), in WA 30.2:576.

28. *Lectures on Paul's Epistle to the Galatians* (1531), in WA 40.1:298.
29. WATr 1: no. 137.
30. *Sermon on Psalm 110* (1535), in WA 41:197–98.
31. WATr 3: no. 3526a.

Chapter 2: Student (1501–1505)

1. Scheel, *Documente*, 1: no. 536.
2. WATr 1: no. 119.
3. WATr 5: no. 5346.
4. WATr 3: no. 3767.
5. WATr 3: no. 3593; WATr 5: no. 5346.
6. *Lectures on the Psalms* (1532), in WA 40.2:282.
7. Heinz Schilling, *Martin Luther: Rebell in einer Zeit des Umbruchs* (München: C. H. Beck, 2012), 74.
8. Scheel, *Documente*, 1: no. 536.
9. WATr 1: no. 461.
10. *On Monastic Vows* (1521), in WA 8:573.
11. *On Monastic Vows* (1521), in WA 8:573–74.
12. WATr 4: no. 4707.
13. Volker Leppin, *Martin Luther* (Darmstadt: Primus Verlag, 2010), 30–32.
14. Crotus Rubianus to Luther, October 16, 1519, in WABr 1:543.
15. *On Monastic Vows* (1521), in WA 8:573–74.
16. WATr 1: no. 461.
17. *On Monastic Vows* (1521), in WA 8:574.
18. Val. Bavarus, *Rapsodiae ex ore D. M. Luther* (1549), BII:552, in Scheel, *Documente*, 1: nos. 184–85.
19. *Lectures on Genesis* (1515), in WA 44:782.
20. WATr 4: no. 4414.
21. *Sermons on the Gospel of St. Matthew* (1537–1540), in WA 47:575.
22. *Sermons on the Gospel of St. John* (1538), in WA 45:698.
23. *Sermon on Luke 2:10* (1545), in WA 49:636.
24. *Lectures on the Psalms* (1532), in WA 40.2:282.
25. WATr 1: no. 11.
26. WATr 4: no. 4707.
27. Luther refers to the meaning of the Hebrew word *hanna*, namely, "grace."
28. WATr 4: no. 4707.
29. *On Monastic Vows* (1521), in WA 8:573.
30. *Sermon on Matthew 24:24* (1537–1540), in WA 47:590.
31. WATr 4: no. 303.
32. WATr 5: no. 5374.
33. WATr 4: no. 4414.
34. *Sermons on the Gospel of St. John* (1538), in WA 45:482.
35. *Sermons on the Gospel of St. John* (1538), in WA 45:482.
36. WATr 1: no. 261.
37. WATr 1: no. 518.
38. WATr 2: no. 2283.
39. WATr 5: no. 5346.

Chapter 3: Monk (1505–1511)

1. WATr 1: no. 495.
2. WATr 5: no. 5428.
3. WATr 4: no. 4919.
4. WATr 5: no. 6077.
5. WATr 4: nos. 4414, 5034; WATr 5: no. 6430.
6. WATr 3: no. 2917.
7. *Church Postil* (1544), in WA 21:254.
8. *Sermon on Romans 8:12* (1544), in WA 49:529.
9. *Answer to Duke George* (1533), in WA 38:142.
10. WATr 1: no. 121.
11. *Sermon on the Sacrament of Penance* (1524), in WA 15:489.
12. WATr 5: no. 6017.
13. WATr 6: no. 6669.
14. WATr 1: no. 116.
15. WATr 3: no. 3767.
16. WATr 2: no. 2512; WATr 4: no. 5030.
17. *Sermon on John 5:44* (1529), in WA 29:583.
18. Luther to Johann Braun, September 5, 1501, in WABr 1:17.
19. *Sermons on the Gospel of St. John* (1537), in WA 45.2:295.
20. *Sermons* (1536), in WA 41:582.
21. WATr 2: no. 1558.
22. *Sermons* (1535), in WA 41:681.
23. *Lectures on Genesis* (1535–1545), in WA 43:378.
24. *Sermons on the Gospel of St. John* (1537), in WA 45.2:482.
25. WATr 2: no. 1558.
26. WATr 5: nos. 5375c, 6039.
27. Luther to Elector Johann Frederick, March 27, 1545, in WABr 11:67.
28. *Sermon Prepared for His Friend Provost George Mascow in Litzka* (1512), in WA 1:17.
29. WATr 2: no. 2255a.
30. WATr 5: nos. 5371, 6422.
31. WATr 1: no. 94.
32. *Sermons on the Gospel of St. Matthew* (1537–1540), in WA 47:392.
33. WATr 5: no. 6059.
34. WATr 3: no. 3428.
35. *Sermons on the Gospel of St. John* (1545), in WA 51:89.
36. *Expositions on the Psalms* (1529–1532), in WA 31:226; *Sermon on Indulgence and Grace* (1518), in WA 1:390.
37. *Expositions on the Psalms* (1529–1531), in WA 31:226; *Sermon on Indulgence and Grace* (1518), in WA 1:390.
38. WATr 6: no. 6777.
39. *Against the Papacy at Rome* (1545), in WA 54:220.

Chapter 4: Exegete (1511–1517)

1. " . . . in termino civilitatis . . . ," WATr 2: no. 2800b.
2. WATr 2: no. 2800b.
3. WATr 5: no. 5342a.

4. WADB 7:2; *On David's Last Words* (1545), in WA 54:220.
5. Volker Leppin, *Martin Luther* (Darmstadt: Primus Verlag, 2010), 71.
6. *Lectures on the Psalms* (1519–1521), in WA 5:537.
7. *Sermons on Genesis* (1527), in WA 24:12.
8. *Lectures on the Psalms* (1513–1515), in WA 55.2:12–14.
9. *Lectures on the Psalms* (1513–1516), in WA 3:255, 261.
10. *Lectures on the Psalms* (1513–1515), in WA 55.2:170.
11. *Lectures on the Psalms* (1513–1516), in WA 3:191.
12. *Sermons* (1522), in WA 10.3:10.
13. Luther to Georg Spalatin, December 31, 1516, in WABr 1:82.
14. *Disputation on Indulgences* (1518), in WA 1:627.
15. Luther to Johann Lang, October 1516, in WABr 1:65–66.
16. Luther to Johann Lang, February 8, 1517, in WABr 1:88.
17. *Disputation against Scholastic Theology* (1517), in WA 1:226.
18. Luther to Johann Lang, May 18, 1517, in WABr 1:99.
19. *Preface to the Latin Works* (1545), in WA 54:185–86.
20. *Preface to the Latin Works* (1545), in WA 54:185.
21. *Preface to the Latin Works* (1545), in WA 54:185.
22. *Preface to the Latin Works* (1545), in WA 54:186.
23. *Lectures on Paul's Epistle to the Galatians* (1531), in WA 40.1:207.
24. WATr 2: no. 2540.
25. WATr 5: no. 5532.
26. WATr 2: no. 2318a.
27. Luther to Jerome Weller, July 1530, in WABr 5:519; Luther to Duke Albrecht of Mansfeld, February 23, 1542, in WABr 9:627.
28. WATr 2: no. 1490; WATr 1: no. 1017; WATr 2: no. 2654.
29. WATr 2: no. 2654a.
30. WATr 2: no. 1820.
31. *Disputation on Indulgences* (1518), in WA 1:557.
32. WATr 1: no. 526.
33. Luther to Elector Johann Frederick, March 27, 1545, in WABr 11:67.
34. Luther to Johann Lang, October 29, 1516, in WABr 1:73.
35. Luther to Georg Spalatin, October 19, 1516, in WABr 1:70.
36. Luther to Georg Spenlein, April 8, 1516, in WABr 1:35.
37. *Preface to the German Writings* (1518), in WA 1:378.
38. *Disputation against Scholastic Theology* (1517), in WA 1:228.

Chapter 5: Theologian (1517–1519)

1. Peter Fabisch and Erwin Iserloh, eds., *Dokumente zur Causa Lutheri (1517–1521)* (Münster: Aschendorff, 1988–1991), 1:264.
2. WATr 5: no. 6431.
3. Luther to Albrecht von Mainz, October 31, 1517, in WABr 1:111.
4. *Against Hanswurst* (1541), in WA 51:538.
5. Luther to Albrecht von Mainz, October 31, 1517, in WABr 1:111.
6. *Lectures on the Psalms* (1513–1516), in WA 3:416.
7. *Sermon on Matthew 11:22* (1517), in WA 1:141.
8. Erwin Iserloh, *Luther zwischen Reform und Reformation: Der Thesenanschlag fand nicht statt* (Münster: Aschendorff, 1966).

9. Volker Leppin, *Martin Luther* (Darmstadt: Primus Verlag, 2010), 124.
10. *Disputation on Indulgences* (1518), in WA 1:528; *Address of Martin Luther to Cajetan and the Pope* (1518), in WA 2:29.
11. WATr 5: nos. 5346, 5349.
12. WATr 1: no. 1206. See also WATr 3: no. 3846; WATr 4: no. 5126.
13. Luther to Johann Lang, August 30, 1516, in WABr 1:52.
14. WATr 1: no. 4919.
15. Luther to Georg Spalatin, February 15, 1518, in WABr 1:146.
16. Luther to Christoph Scheurl, March 5, 1518, in WABr 1:152.
17. Luther to Johann Lang, October 5, 1516, in WABr 1:62.
18. Heinz Schilling, *Martin Luther: Rebell in einer Zeit des Umbruchs* (München: C. H. Beck, 2012), 170.
19. Luther to Christoph Scheurl, March 5, 1518, in WABr 1:152.
20. WATr 4: no. 4763.
21. Luther to Johann Lang, March 21, 1518, in WABr 1:154–55.
22. Luther to Johann Lang, March 21, 1518, in WABr 1:155.
23. Luther to Johann von Staupitz, March 31, 1518, in WABr 1:160.
24. Fabisch and Iserloh, *Dokumente*, 2:21.
25. WATr 5: no. 5343.
26. *Heidelberg Disputation* (1518), in WA 1:362.
27. Luther to Georg Spalatin, May 18, 1518, in WABr 1:174.
28. Luther to Johann von Staupitz, March 31, 1518, in WABr 1:160.
29. Luther to Georg Spalatin, May 18, 1518, in WABr 1:173.
30. Luther to Georg Spalatin, May 18, 1518, in WABr 1:173.
31. Luther to Georg Spalatin, May 18, 1518, in WABr 1:173.
32. *Preface to the Latin Works* (1545), in WA 54:186.
33. *Lectures on Genesis* (1535–1545), in WA 42:356.
34. WATr 1: no. 491.
35. WATr 4: no. 5123.
36. WATr 2: no. 2668c.
37. Luther to Georg Spalatin, December 21, 1518, in WABr 1:282; see also Luther to Georg Spalatin, shortly after December 21, 1518, in WABr 1:284–97.
38. Luther to Carlstadt, Amsdorf, Melanchthon, Beckmann, et al., October 4, 1518, in WABr 12:14.
39. WATr 5: no. 5349.
40. WATr 2: no. 2337.
41. Luther to Georg Spalatin, October 31, 1518, in WABr 1:225.
42. Luther to Elector Frederick the Wise, November 21, 1518, in WABr 1:236–46.
43. Luther to Georg Spalatin, November 25, 1518, in WABr 1:253.
44. Luther to Georg Spalatin, December 2, 1518, in WABr 1:260–61.
45. Luther to Georg Spalatin, December 2, 1518, in WABr 1:261.
46. Luther to Georg Spalatin, December 9, 1518, in WABr 1:263.
47. Luther to Johann von Staupitz, February 20, 1519, in WABr 1:344.
48. Luther to Johann von Staupitz, October 3, 1519, in WABr 1:513.
49. *The Fourteen Consolations* (1520), in WA 6:104–34.
50. Luther to Gerardus Listrius, July 28, 1520, in WABr 2:149.
51. Luther to Johann Lang, December 18, 1519, in WABr 1:597.

52. *Commentary on Paul's Epistle to the Galatians* (1519), in WA 2:595.
53. Luther to Johann von Staupitz, October 3, 1519, in WABr 1:514.
54. *CR* 11:613.
55. Preface to the German translation of Philipp Melanchthon's *Commentary on Colossians* (1529), in WA 30.2:68–69.
56. Luther to Justus Jonas, August 17, 1529, in WABr 5:132; Luther to Justus Jonas, beginning of September 1529, in WABr 5:143.
57. Preface to the German translation of Philipp Melanchthon's *Commentary on Colossians* (1529), in WA 30.2:68–69.
58. Luther to Wilibald Pirtheimer, February 20, 1519, in WABr 1:348.
59. Luther to Georg Spalatin, February 24, 1519, in WABr 1:351–54.
60. Luther to Georg Spalatin, March 13, 1519, in WABr 1:359.
61. Luther to Georg Spalatin, July 20, 1519, in WABr 1:423.
62. Walch 15:1200.
63. *Sermon Held in Leipzig* (1519), in WA 2:246.
64. Luther to Georg Spalatin, July 20, 1519, in WABr 1:424.
65. Luther to Georg Spalatin, February 16, 1520, in WABr 2:42.
66. Luther to Georg Spalatin, February 16, 1520, in WABr 2:42.
67. Luther to Johann von Staupitz, October 3, 1519, in WABr 1:514.
68. Luther to Georg Spalatin, March 13, 1519, in WABr 1:360.
69. *Against Hanswurst* (1541), in WA 51:546.
70. *Sermon on Genesis 15:1* (1520), in WA 9:459.
71. *Concerning the Papacy in Rome* (1520), in WA 6:285–324.
72. *Luther's Preface to the Work of Prierias, Epitoma Responsis ad Martinum Luther* (1520), in WA 6:347.
73. Luther to Johann von Staupitz, October 3, 1519, in WABr 1:514.
74. Jacobus Praepositus, prior in Antwerp, and Hendrik of Zutphen, prior in Dordrecht, had studied in Wittenberg.
75. The name is derived from the Latin phrase *sub utraque specie*, which means "under two elements" and alludes to receiving both the bread and the wine in the Eucharist.
76. Luther to Johann von Staupitz, October 3, 1519, in WABr 1:513–14.

Chapter 6: Architect (1520–1521)

1. Luther to Georg Spalatin, February 8, 1520, in WABr 2:36.
2. Luther to Georg Spalatin, February 8, 1520, in WABr 2:36.
3. The bishop of Meissen had forbidden the distribution of one of Luther's sermons in which he advocated the use of the so-called chalice for the laity.
4. Luther to Duke George, January 25, 1532, in WABr 2:251.
5. Luther to Georg Spalatin, July 17, 1520, in WABr 2:144–45.
6. C. E. Förstemann, "Der Studenten-Auflauf zu Wittenberg im J. 1520," *Neue Mittheilungen aus dem Gebiet historisch-antiquarischer Forschungen* 8 (1848): 62.
7. *Sermon on Holy Baptism* (1519), in WA 2:727–37.
8. *Against Eck* (1519), in WA 2:646.
9. *Short Instruction on Indulgences* (1519), in WA 2:59–65.
10. *Sermon on Penance* (1522), in WA 10.3:62.
11. Luther to Georg Spalatin, March 25, 1520, in WABr 2:75.

12. *Lectures on Genesis* (1535–1545), in WA 42:566.
13. Luther to Georg Spalatin, July 9, 1520, in WABr 2:134–35.
14. Luther to Georg Spalatin, July 9, 1520, in WABr 2:134–35.
15. Luther to Georg Spalatin, July 9, 1520, in WABr 2:134–35.
16. Luther to Konrad Sam, October 1, 1520, in WABr 2:189.
17. Luther to Georg Spalatin, October 11, 1519, in WABr 2:341.
18. Luther to Georg Spalatin, October 11, 1519, in WABr 2:341.
19. Luther to Georg Spalatin, August 23, 1520, in WABr 2:169–70.
20. Luther to Georg Spalatin, October 11, 1520, in WABr 2:195.
21. Letter to Elector Frederick the Wise, January 25, 1521, in WABr 2:254.
22. Luther to Georg Spalatin, October 3, 1520, in WABr 2:191.
23. Luther to Georg Spalatin, October 12, 1520, in WABr 2:197.
24. *Disputation against Indulgences* (1518), in WA 1:525.
25. *On Christian Liberty* (1521), in WA 7:44.
26. *Against the Bull of the Antichrist* (1520), in WA 6:597–612, 614–29.
27. *Against the Bull of the Antichrist* (1520), in WA 6:612.
28. *To the Christian Nobility of the German Nation* (1520), in WA 6:404–69.
29. Luther to Georg Spalatin, June 7, 1520, in WABr 2:120.
30. *On the Babylonian Captivity of the Church* (1520), in WA 6:497–573.
31. *To the Christian Nobility of the German Nation* (1520), in WA 6:408.
32. *To the Christian Nobility of the German Nation* (1520), in WA 6:564.
33. *On the Freedom of a Christian* (1520), in WA 7:20–38.
34. Luther to Johann Lang, August 18, 1520, in WABr 2:167.
35. *Open Letter to Pope Leo X* (1520), in WA 7:9.
36. *On the Freedom of a Christian* (1520), in WA 7:21.
37. Luther to Georg Spalatin, November 29, 1520, in WABr 2:220–21.
38. Cited by Heinz Schilling, *Martin Luther: Rebell in einer Zeit des Umbruchs* (München: C. H. Beck, 2012), 233.
39. Luther to Johann von Staupitz, January 14, 1521, in WABr 2:245.
40. *Why the Books of the Pope and His Disciples Were Burned by Dr. Martin Luther* (1520), in WA 7:161–82.
41. *Why the Books* (1520), in WA 7:162.
42. Luther to Johann von Staupitz, January 14, 1521, in WABr 2:245.
43. Luther to Georg Spalatin, December 10, 1520, in WABr 2:234.
44. Luther to Georg Spalatin, December 29, 1520, in WABr 2:242.
45. *RTA* 2:628.
46. Luther to Georg Spalatin, July 15, 1521, in WABr 2:365.
47. WATr 3: no. 3357a.
48. Luther to Albrecht of Mainz, December 1, 1521, in WABr 2:407–8.
49. Luther to Georg Spalatin, March 19, 1521, in WABr 2:289.
50. Luther to Johann von Staupitz, February 9, 1521, in WABr 2:262.
51. Luther to Elector Frederick the Wise, 1521, in WABr 2:354.
52. Luther to Georg Spalatin, February 17, 1521, in WABr 2:396; WATr 3: no. 3357a.
53. WATr 5: no. 5503.
54. *RTA* 2:574.
55. Martin Brecht, *Martin Luther* (Stuttgart: Calwer, 1981–1987), 1:433.

56. *Luther at the Diet of Worms* (1521), in WA 7:838.
57. *RTA* 2:580.
58. *RTA* 2:88.
59. Luther to Georg Spalatin, January 16, 1521, in WABr 2:249.
60. Luther to Georg Spalatin, January 16, 1521, in WABr 2:249.
61. *RTA* 2:82.
62. Luther to Lucas Cranach, April 28, 1521, in WABr 2:306–10.
63. *RTA* 2:82.
64. Text in Volker Leppin, *Martin Luther* (Darmstadt: Primus Verlag, 2010), 180–81.
65. Luther to Lucas Cranach, April 28, 1521, in WABr 2:305.
66. Luther to Georg Spalatin, May 14, 1521, in WABr 2:337–38; WATr 5: no. 5353.
67. Theodor Brieger, *Die vervollständigten Aleander-Depeschen, nebst Untersuchungen über den Wormser Reichstag* (Gotha: Friedrich Andreas Perthes, 1884), 208–11.
68. Letters during his stay at the Wartburg, in WABr 2:330–453.
69. Luther to Archbishop Albrecht of Mainz, December 1, 1521, in WABr 2:408.
70. Luther to Philipp Melanchthon, January 13, 1522, in WABr 2:427.
71. Luther to Georg Spalatin, August 15, 1521, in WABr 2:380–81.
72. Luther to Nicholas von Amsdorf, May 12, 1521, in WABr 2:334.
73. Luther to Philipp Melanchthon, May 12, 1521, in WABr 2:333.
74. Luther to Georg Spalatin, June 10, 1521, in WABr 2:354.
75. Luther to Georg Spalatin, May 15, 1521, in WABr 2:337.
76. *The German Mass and Order of Divine Service* (1526), in WA 19:95.
77. *This Is My Body* (1527), in WA 23:279.
78. Luther to Georg Spalatin, June 10, 1521, in WABr 2:355.
79. Luther to Georg Spalatin, November 11, 1521, in WABr 2:402.
80. Luther to Archbishop Albrecht of Mainz, December 21, 1521, in WABr 2:421.
81. Luther to Philipp Melanchthon, May 26, 1521, in WABr 2:348. Luther used the word "Karsthans," which was a ridiculing or derisive term for farmers.
82. Luther to Philipp Melanchthon, May 26, 1521, in WABr 2:458.
83. Luther to Georg Spalatin, August 6, 1521, in WABr 2:377–78.
84. *Christmas Postil* (1522), in WA 10.1.1:707–8.
85. *On Monastic Vows* (1521), in WA 8:473–669.
86. *On Monastic Vows* (1521), in WA 8:575.

Chapter 7: Reformer (1521–1525)

1. Luther to Philipp Melanchthon, August 1, 1521, in WABr 2:370–71.
2. *Form of the Mass* (1523), in WA 12:208.
3. Luther to Georg Spalatin, December 5, 1521, in WABr 2:410.
4. *A Faithful Exhortation to All Christians to Guard against Turmoil and Anger* (1522), in WA 8:676–87.
5. *A Faithful Exhortation to All Christians* (1522), in WA 8:684–85.
6. Luther to Philipp Melanchthon, January 13, 1522, in WABr 2:426.
7. Luther to Elector Frederick the Wise, March 12, 1522, in WABr 2:470.
8. Luther to Adam Kraft, July 28, 1522, in WABr 2:582.
9. *Sermon on Images* (1522), in WA 10.3:35.

10. *Against the Heavenly Prophets* (1525), in WA 18:70.
11. Luther to Nicholas Hausmann, March 17, 1522, in WABr 2:474.
12. *Three Sermons on the Gospel of Matthew* (1522–1523), in WA 12:470.
13. *Church Postil* (1522), in WA 10.1:728.
14. *Church Postil* (1522), in WA 10.2:60.
15. Luther to Georg Spalatin, March 30, 1522, in WABr 2:490.
16. WADB 7:384.
17. Luther to Georg Spalatin, November 3, 1522, in WABr 2:614.
18. Luther to Wenzeslaus Linck, June 14, 1528, in WABr 4:484.
19. WATr 1: no. 1040.
20. WATr 2: nos. 1317, 2381.
21. WATr 3: no. 3692, and similar remarks in WATr 4: nos. 4690, 5181, 5186.
22. Luther to Wenzeslaus Linck, January 15, 1531, in WABr 6:17.
23. *Assertion of All the Articles of M. Luther* (1520), in WA 7:97.
24. *Open Letter on Translating* (1530), in WA 30.2:627–46.
25. *Open Letter on Translating* (1530), in WA 30.2:636.
26. *Annotations to the Bible*, in WA 48:1–279.
27. *Concerning the Secular Authority* (1523), in WA 11:246–80.
28. *The Right and Power of a Christian Assembly* (1523), in WA 11:408–16.
29. Luther to Georg Spalatin, July 26, 1522, in WABr 2:580.
30. Luther to Wenzeslaus Linck, December 19, 1522, in WABr 2:632; Luther to Georg Spalatin, May 11, 1534, in WABr 3:292.
31. Quoted in Heinz Schilling, *Martin Luther: Rebell in einer Zeit des Umbruchs* (München: C. H. Beck, 2012), 293.
32. Luther to Paul Speratus, June 13, 1522, in WABr 2:559–60.
33. Luther to Johann von Staupitz, June 27, 1522, in WABr 2:567.
34. *Sermon* (1523), in WA 12:74.
35. "All Dear Brothers in Christ, So in Holland, Brabant, and Flanders," in WA 12:77–79.
36. *Spiritual Songs*, in WA 35:91–97, 441–51.
37. Free English translation.
38. Luther to Lambert Thorn, January 19, 1524, in WABr 3:237–39.
39. Luther to Johann von Staupitz, June 27, 1522, in WABr 2:567.
40. *On the King of England*, in WA 23:17–37.
41. *Against Henry VIII*, in WA 10.2:262.
42. Luther to Philip of Hesse, January 7, 1527, in WABr 4:157.
43. *Christian Writing to W. Reissenbusch* (1525), in WA 18:277.
44. Luther to Martin Bucer, April/May 1524, in WABr 12:60.
45. *Christian Writing to W. Reissenbusch* (1525), in WA 18:277.
46. Luther to Wenzeslaus Linck, April 8, 1523, in WABr 3:53.
47. *Why Young Women Can Leave Monasteries* (1523), in WA 11:394.
48. *Why Young Women Can Leave Monasteries* (1523), in WA 11:400.
49. Luther to Georg Spalatin, April 10, 1523, in WABr 3:55.
50. Luther to Georg Spalatin, April 10, 1523, in WABr 3:55.
51. Luther to Hieronymus [Jerome] Baumgärtner, October 12, 1524, in WABr 3:358.

52. Luther to Hieronymus [Jerome] Baumgärtner, October 12, 1524, in WABr 3:358.
53. Luther to Georg Spalatin, November 30, 1524, in WABr 3:394.
54. Luther to Nicholas von Amsdorf, January 2, 1526, in WABr 4:3; Luther to Matthäus Alber, January 4, 1526, in WABr 4:7–9; Luther to Nicholas von Amsdorf, May 12, 1525, in WABr 3:455.
55. *Letter against the Peasants* (1525), in WA 18:399.
56. Luther to Johann Rühell, May 4/5, 1525, in WABr 3:481.
57. Luther to Johann Rühell, June 15, 1525, in WABr 3:531.
58. Luther to Nicholas von Amsdorf, June 21, 1525, in WABr 3:541.
59. WATr 3: no. 3178.
60. Luther to Georg Spalatin, December 6, 1525, in WABr 3:635.
61. Luther to Georg Spalatin, July 16, 1525, in WABr 3:533.
62. Luther to Michael Stifel, September 29, 1525, in WABr 3:584.
63. WATr 4: no. 5117.
64. Luther to Nicholas von Amsdorf, June 21, 1525, in WABr 3:541.
65. WATr 3: no. 2890a.
66. WATr 1: no. 55.
67. Luther to Justus Jonas, October 28, 1535, in WABr 7:317.
68. WATr 4: no. 5117.
69. Luther's Testament, January 6, 1542, in WABr 9:571–87.
70. Luther to Käthe, October 10, 1531, in WABr 6:203.
71. Luther to Philipp Melanchthon, August 2, 1527, in WABr 4:226–27.
72. WATr 2: no. 1563.
73. WATr 1: no. 84.
74. *Incentive to Peace* (1525), in WA 18:311.
75. *Against the Murderous, Thieving Hordes of Peasants* (1525), in WA 18:357–61.
76. *Against the Murderous, Thieving Hordes of Peasants* (1525), in WA 18:361.
77. Luther to Johann Rihel, May 23, 1525, in WABr 3:508.
78. *Against the Murderous, Thieving Hordes of Peasants* (1525), in WA 18:361.
79. *Against the Murderous, Thieving Hordes of Peasants* (1525), in WA 18:360.
80. WATr 1: no. 446.
81. Luther to Nicholas von Amsdorf, May 30, 1525, in WABr 3:517–18.
82. Luther to Johann Lang, March 1, 1517, in WABr 1:90.
83. Luther to Georg Spalatin, January 18, 1518, in WABr 1:133.
84. Luther to Erasmus, March 28, 1519, in WABr 1:361.
85. Luther to Georg Spalatin, April 1, 1518, in WABr 1:163.
86. Luther to Johannes Oecolampadius, June 20, 1523, in WABr 3:96–97.
87. *Sermon* (September 18, 1524), in WA 15:713–16.
88. Luther to Georg Spalatin, November 1, 1524, in WABr 3:368.
89. WATr 2: no. 2086.
90. Luther to Georg Spalatin, November 1, 1524, in WABr 3:368.
91. *On the Bondage of the Will* (1525), in WA 18:786–87.
92. Luther to Wolfgang Capito, July 9, 1537, in WABr 8:99.
93. WATr 2: no. 2420.
94. Luther to Nicholas von Amsdorf, March 11, 1534, in WABr 7:27–40.

95. WATr 4: no. 4028.
96. *Fasting Postil* (1525), in WA 17.2:49.
97. *Little Book on Praying* (1522), in WA 10.2:375–501.
98. *Little Book on Baptism* (1526), in WA 19:539–42.
99. *On the Order of the Congregational Worship Service* (1523), in WA 12:35–37.
100. *On the German Mass* (1526), in WA 19:72–113.
101. Luther to Georg Spalatin, August 3, 1523, in WABr 3:220.
102. *The German Mass and Order of the Divine Service* (1526), in WA 19:48–50.
103. *Spiritual Songs*, in WA 35:419–22.
104. *Spiritual Songs*, in WA 35:474.
105. *Spiritual Songs*, in WA 35:474.
106. *On Music* (1530), in WA 30.2:695.
107. *Preface to the Symphoniae Iucundae* (1536–1539), in WA 50:364–74.
108. *To the Councilmen of All Cities in Germany* (1524), in WA 15:30.
109. *To the Councilmen of All Cities in Germany* (1524), in WA 15:32.
110. Kaspar Glatz to Luther, January 18, 1525, in WABr 3:424.

Chapter 8: Father (1525–1530)

1. Luther to Nicholas Hausmann, June 13, 1526, in WABr 4:88.
2. WATr 2: no. 2590b.
3. Luther to Georg Spalatin, June 17, 1526, in WABr 4:89.
4. Luther to Georg Spalatin, End of June 1526, in WABr 4:97.
5. Luther to his son Hans, June 19, 1530, in WABr 5:378.
6. Luther to Markus Crodel, August 26, 1542, in WABr 10:134.
7. Luther to Georg Spalatin, August 19, 1527, in WABr 4:232.
8. Luther to Nicholas von Amsdorf, November 1, 1527, in WABr 4:275.
9. Luther to Nicholas von Amsdorf, November 4, 1527, in WABr 4:276.
10. Luther to Nicholas Hausmann, December 14, 1527, in WABr 4:299.
11. Luther to Nicholas Hausmann, August 5, 1528, in WABr 4:511.
12. WATr 1: no. 1004; see also WATr 2: nos. 2447, 2578, 3141.
13. WATr 1: no. 437.
14. *Exposition of the Lord's Prayer* (1519), in WA 2:112.
15. *Lectures on the Psalms* (1513–1516), in WA 3:35, 112.
16. *Sermons on Exodus* (1526), in WA 16:490.
17. *Sermon on Marital Status* (1519), in WA 2:170.
18. WATr 3: no. 3566a.
19. WATr 4: nos. 4367, 4364.
20. Veit Dietrich to Käthe Luther, June 19, 1530, in WABr 5:379.
21. WATr 2: no. 2754b.
22. Luther to Joachim von Anhalt, June 23, 1534, in WABr 7:77.
23. Luther to Markus Crodel, September 16, 1542, in WABr 10:147.
24. WATr 5: no. 5494.
25. WATr 5: no. 5490c.
26. Luther to Justus Jonas, September 23, 1542, in WABr 10:149–50.
27. WATr 2: no. 2034.
28. Buying Contract between Luther and Nicholas Hessner, April 19, 1532, in WABr 9:578.

29. WATr 4: no. 4786.
30. WATr 4: no. 4786.
31. Luther to Johann Briessmann, June 20, 1529, in WABr 5:125.
32. Luther to Nicholas von Amsdorf, October 21, 1545, in WABr 11:200.
33. WATr 1: no. 869; WATr 3: no. 2849.
34. Luther to Georg Spalatin, October 4, 1522, in WABr 2:605.
35. WATr 2: no. 1722.
36. Friedrich Küchenmeister, *Dr. Martin Luther's Krankengeschichte* (Leipzig: O. Wigand, 1881), 113.
37. Cited in Heinz Schilling, *Martin Luther: Rebell in einer Zeit des Umbruchs* (München: C. H. Beck, 2012), 339.
38. Luther to Michael Kramer, August 18, 1525, in WABr 3:557.
39. Luther to Philipp Rosenecker, November 11, 1529, in WABr 5:177–79.
40. Luther to Elector Johann Frederick, January 17, 1526, in WABr 4:17.
41. Luther and Johannes Bugenhagen to Stephan Roth, April 12, 1528, in WABr 4:442.
42. Luther and Melanchthon to Elector Johann Frederick, May 1/2, 1528, in WABr 4:447.
43. *On Marital Issues* (1530–1532), in WA 33.3:198–248.
44. Preface to Philipp Melanchthon's *Instruction for Church Inspectors* (1528), in WA 26:195–201.
45. *Exposition on the Prophet Zechariah* (1527), in WA 23:485–86.
46. *Lectures on 1 Timothy* (1528), in WA 26:530–31.
47. *Luther to Wolfgang Capito*, July 9, 1537, in WABr 8:99.
48. WATr 1: nos. 81, 122.
49. *Sermons on the Catechism* (1528), in WA 30.1:129.
50. *Lectures on Deuteronomy* (1525), in WA 14:499.
51. *Whether Soldiers Can Be Saved* (1526), in WA 19:623–62.
52. *Concerning the War against the Turks* (1529), in WA 30.2:107–43.
53. Luther to Philipp Melanchthon, April 24, 1530, in WABr 5:285–86.
54. *Form of the Mass* (1523), in WA 12:208.
55. Martin Brecht, *Martin Luther* (Stuttgart: Calwer, 1981–1987), 2:292–94.
56. *This Is My Body* (1527), in WA 23:38–320.
57. For an extensive report and the references, see Brecht, *Martin Luther*, 2:315–25.
58. Luther to Käthe, October 4, 1529, in WABr 5:154.
59. Luther to Johann Agricola, October 12, 1529, in WABr 5:160.
60. Luther to Justus Menius, second half of March 1531, in WABr 6:61.
61. Luther to Georg Spalatin, April 24, 1530, in WABr 5:291.
62. Luther to Peter Weller, June 19, 1530, in WABr 5:376.
63. Luther to Justus Jonas, June 7, 1536, in WABr 7:429.
64. Luther to Philipp Melanchthon, May 19, 1530, in WABr 5:322–23.
65. Luther to Philipp Melanchthon, May 19, 1530, in WABr 5:322–23.
66. Luther to Wenzeslaus Linck, May 8, 1530, in WABr 5:309.
67. *Expositions on the Psalms* (1529–1532), in WA 31.1:34–182.
68. Luther to Eobanus Hessus, August 20, 1530, in WABr 5:549.
69. Luther to his father, Hans Luther, February 15, 1530, in WABr 5:241.
70. Veit Dietrich to Käthe Luther, June 19, 1530, in WABr 5:379.

71. *Exhortation to the Clerics Who Have Come Together at the Diet of Augsburg* (1530), in WA 30.2:236–356.
72. Luther to Philipp Melanchthon, July 3, 1530, in WABr 5:435.
73. Luther to Elector Johann Frederick, May 15, 1530, in WABr 5:319.
74. Luther to Philipp Melanchthon, June 30, 1530, in WABr 5:399.
75. Luther to Philipp Melanchthon, June 30, 1530, in WABr 5:399.
76. Luther to Johann Brenz, June 30, 1530, in WABr 5:420.
77. *Lecture on 1 Timothy* (1528), in WA 26:86.
78. Luther to Philipp Melanchthon, July 27, 1530, in WABr 5:504.
79. Luther to Johann Agricola, July 27, 1530, in WABr 5:506.
80. Luther to Justus Jonas, June 29, 1530, in WABr 5:408.
81. *Lecture on Paul's Epistle to the Galatians* (1531), in WA 40.2:46.
82. Luther to Georg Spalatin, August 26, 1530, in WABr 5:575.
83. Luther to Justus Jonas, September 20, 1530, in WABr 5:629.
84. Schilling, *Martin Luther*, 473.
85. *Warning to His Beloved Germans* (1531), in WA 30.3:276–320.
86. *Concerning the Secular Authority* (1523), in WA 11:277.
87. *Warning to His Beloved Germans* (1531), in WA 30.3:320.

Chapter 9: Professor (1530–1537)

1. WATr 1: no. 157; WATr 2: nos. 1342, 2437.
2. WATr 2: no. 1463.
3. WATr 2: no. 1404.
4. *Lectures on Paul's Epistle to the Galatians* (1531), in WA 40.1 and 40.2:1–184.
5. WATr 2: no. 1963.
6. WATr 1: no. 146.
7. *Lectures on Paul's Epistle to the Galatians* (1531), in WA 40.1:327–28.
8. Luther to Lazarus Spengler, July 8, 1530, in WABr 5:445.
9. Traugott Schiess, ed., *Briefwechsel der Brüder Ambrosius und Thomas Blaurer: 1509–1548* (Freiburg: Friedrich Ernst Fehsenfeld, 1908–1912), 1:30.
10. Quoted in Heinrich Boehmer, *Der junge Luther* (Leipzig: Koehler & Amelang, 1939), 366.
11. Elector Johann Frederick to Luther, August 30, 1539, in WABr 8:545; Wittenberg University to Elector Johann Frederick, March 20, 1541, in WABr 9:338.
12. *Sermon on Philippians 4:4* (1535), in WA 41:471–72; *Sermon on Luke 2:22* (1539), in WA 47:665–66.
13. *Luther's Exhortation to the Students in Wittenberg* (1542), in WA 49:278–79.
14. *Supplements*, in WA 60:6–15.
15. WATr 5: no. 6404.
16. WATr 5: no. 6404.
17. *Sermon on Galatians 5:16ff.* (1544), in WA 49:588–89.
18. *Formula of the Mass* (1526), in WA 19:75.
19. WATr 1: no. 496.
20. Luther to Dorothea Jörger, April 8, 1535, in WABr 7:172.
21. *Sermons on the Gospel of St. John* (1530–1532), in WA 33:472.
22. *Sermon on 1 Corinthians 4:1ff.* (1535), in WA 41:471; WATr 3: no. 3482.
23. WATr 3: no. 3453; *Sermon* (1534), in WA 37:530–33.
24. *Concerning Baptism—to Two Ministers* (1528), in WA 26:144–74.

25. *Warning to My Beloved Germans* (1531), in WA 30.3:252–320.
26. *Warning to My Beloved Germans* (1531), in WA 30.3:317.
27. WATr 2: nos. 1738, 1741.
28. Luther to the Evangelicals in Leipzig, October 4, 1532, in WABr 6:370–72.
29. Luther to Nicholas Hausmann, January 2, 1533, in WABr 6:411; Luther to Nicholas Hausman, January 14, 1533, in WABr 6:417.
30. Luther to the Evangelicals in Leipzig, April 11, 1533, in WABr 6:450.
31. *Vindication against the Charge of Rebellion* (1533), in WA 38:108.
32. *Expositions on the Psalms* (1529–1532), in WA 31.1:430.
33. WATr 2: no. 2726b.
34. WATr 4: no. 4381; *Sermon* (February 1539), in WA 47:669–70; WATr 5: no. 5216.
35. WATr 4: no. 4013; *Sermon on Circumcision* (1545), in WA 49:556–58.
36. Luther to Georgius Buchholzen, December 4, 1539, in WABr 8:625.
37. Luther to Georgius Buchholzen, December 4, 1539, in WABr 8:625.
38. WATr 1: no. 949.
39. Luther to Jonas von Stockhausen, November 27, 1532, in WABr 6:387.
40. Luther to Elector Johann Frederick, July 9, 1535, in WABr 7:206–8.
41. WATr 5: no. 5519; Luther to Andreas Osiander, September 19, 1532, in WABr 6:364.
42. Luther to Elector Johann Frederick, October 22, 1533, in WABr 6:545.
43. *A Simple Way to Pray, for a Good Friend* (1535), in WA 38:358–73.
44. WATr 3: no. 3481.
45. *Disputations against the Antinomians* (1537–1540), in WA 39.1:342–47.
46. *Contra the Antinomians* (1539), in WA 50:468–77.
47. *That the Government Must Punish the Anabaptists* (1536), in WA 50:6–15.
48. WATr 5: no. 6384.
49. Luther to Justus Jonas, October 28, 1535, in WABr 7:317; Luther to Justus Jonas, November 10, 1535, in WABr 7:322.
50. Quoted in Martin Brecht, *Martin Luther* (Stuttgart: Calwer, 1981–1987), 3:176.
51. *The Smalkald Articles* (1537–1538), in WA 50:199.
52. *Lectures on the Psalms* (1532–1533), in WA 40.3:352; *Disputations* (1537), in WA 39.1:205.
53. WATr 3: no. 3510; WATr 5: no. 6079.
54. *About Councils and Churches* (1539), in WA 50:488–563.
55. *About Councils and Churches* (1539), in WA 50:641.
56. *Lectures on the Psalms* (1513–1516), in WA 3:424.
57. *Sermon on Ascension Day* (1536), in WA 41:591–600.

Chapter 10: Prophet (1537–1546)

1. *Warning to His Beloved Germans* (1531), in WA 30.3:290.
2. *Assertion of All the Articles of M. Luther* (1520), in WA 7:135.
3. *Warning to His Beloved Germans* (1531), in WA 30.3:279.
4. WATr 2: no. 1796.
5. *Sermon on 2 Peter 1* (1523), in WA 14:26.
6. *On Private Mass* (1533), in WA 38:239.
7. *Church Postil* (1522), in WA 10.1.1:13.

8. Quoted in Adalbert Horawitz and Karl Hartfelder, eds., *Briefwechsel des Beatus Rhenanus* (Leipzig: B. G. Teubner, 1886), 303.
9. *Lectures on Genesis* (1535–1545), in WA 43:513.
10. *Short Letter of Comfort* (1540), in WA 51:454–57.
11. WATr 3: nos. 3573, 3579; WATr 4: no. 4719.
12. *Sermon on the Gospel of St. Matthew* (1545), in WA 51:15–16.
13. *Preface to Postil by Johann Spangenberg* (1543), in WA 53:213–18.
14. *Sermon* (1528), in WA 27:409–11.
15. *Sermon on Ephesians 1* (1525), in WA 17.1:428.
16. *Sermon on Luke 24:13* (1529), in WA 29:83.
17. *Sermon on John 8:16–19* (1529), in WA 29:615–16.
18. *Sermon on Isaiah 9:5* (1531), in WA 34.2:515–16.
19. Luther to Elector Johann Frederick, June 9, 1545, in WABr 11:116–20.
20. Luther to Gabriel Zwilling, April 17, 1539, in WABr 8:405.
21. WATr 3: no. 2922b.
22. Luther to Dorothea Jörger, April 8, 1535, in WABr 7:172; Luther to Jacob Praepositus, August 23, 1535, in WABr 7:239; Luther to Philipp Melanchthon, August 29, 1535, in WABr 7:245.
23. Luther to Philipp Melanchthon, May 12, 1532, in WABr 6:309.
24. Luther to Elector Johann Frederick, May 12, 1532, in WABr 6:309.
25. WATr 1: no. 139.
26. *Sermon against Drunkenness* (1539), in WA 47:760–61.
27. *Sermon against Drunkenness* (1539), in WA 47:761.
28. WATr 1: no. 144; Luther to his wife, February 27, 1532, in WABr 6:270; *Lectures on Paul's Epistle to the Galatians* (1531), in WA 40.2:115–16.
29. Luther to Käthe, February 27, 1537, in WABr 8:51.
30. Luther to Georg Spalatin, July 26, 1522, in WABr 2:580; *Against the Clergy* (1522), in WA 10.2:93.
31. WATr 3: no. 3476.
32. WATr 5: no. 6303.
33. WATr 4: no. 4309.
34. Luther to Cruciger, May 1, 1541, in WABr 9:390.
35. Luther to Jacob Praepositus, March 26, 1542, in WABr 10:23; see also the letter of Elector Johann Frederick to Luther, January 18, 1529, in WABr 5:7–9.
36. Luther to Johann Magenbuch, May 15, 1544, in WABr 10:575.
37. Luther to Elector Johann of Anhalt, August 27, 1544, in WABr 10:642.
38. *A Fake Writing of Lies about Martin Luther's Death* (1545), in WA 54:188–94.
39. Luther to Anton Lauterbach, October 19, 1545, in WABr 11:199; Luther to Jacob Praepositus, January 17, 1546, in WABr 11:263.
40. WATr 4: no. 5063.
41. Luther to Philipp Melanchthon, June 18, 1540, in WABr 9:144–46; WATr 4: no. 5100.
42. WATr 5: nos. 5407, 5565.
43. Luther to Käthe, July 2, 1540, in WABr 9:168.
44. Luther to Elector Johann Frederick, June 10, 1540, in WABr 9:134.
45. WATr 4: nos. 5046, 5096.

46. *That Jesus Christ Was Born a Jew* (1523), in WA 11:314–36.
47. Luther to Bernhard, latter half of June 1523, in WABr 3:102.
48. Luther to Heinrich Gnesius, July 9, 1530, in WABr 5:451; Luther to Nicholas von Amsdorf, before February 9, 1533, in WABr 6:427; WATr 2: no. 2634.
49. Luther to Josel von Rosheim, June 11, 1537, in WABr 8:89.
50. *Against the Sabbatarians* (1538), in WA 50:309–37.
51. *Concerning the Jews and Their Lies* (1543), in WA 53:412–552.
52. *Church Postil* (1522), in WA 10.1:569.
53. WATr 4: no. 4542.
54. WATr 4: no. 4639; WATr 5: nos. 5221, 5403.
55. WATr 3: no. 3818.
56. WATr 5: no. 6238.
57. WATr 4: no. 4638.
58. WATr 4: nos. 3969, 3979.
59. Luther to Wenzeslaus Linck, January 1, 1527, in WABr 4:147–48.
60. Luther to Justus Jonas, April 9, 1527, in WABr 8:209.
61. WATr 6: no. 7035.
62. WATr 3: no. 2849b.
63. WATr 1: no. 567.
64. WATr 1: no. 115.
65. Luther to Duke Albrecht of Prussia, May 2, 1545, in WABr 11:83.
66. *An Admonition to All Pastors* (1539), in WA 50:478–87; Luther to Duke Albrecht of Prussia, October 13, 1539, in WABr 8:566–67.
67. *Preface to Theodor Bibliander's Translation of the Qur'an* (1543), in WA 53:561–67.
68. WATr 5: no. 5536.
69. Luther and Johannes Bugenhagen to Elector Johann Frederick, May 10/11, 1541, in WABr 9:407.
70. *Luther's Commentary on the Edict of Karl V* (1531), in WA 30.3:387.
71. Luther to Jacob Praepositus, March 26, 1542, in WABr 10:23.
72. Luther to Nicholas von Amsdorf, August 18, 1543, in WABr 10:370.
73. WATr 5: no. 5506.
74. WATr 6: no. 6893.
75. *Lectures on the Psalms* (1513–1515), in WA 55.2:384.
76. Luther to Matthäus Ratzeberger, March 25, 1545, in WABr 11:59; Luther to Nicholas von Amsdorf, April 14, 1545, in WABr 11:71.
77. *Image of the Papacy* (1545), in WA 54:348–73.
78. Luther to Wenzeslaus Linck, June 20, 1543, in WABr 10:335.
79. *Preface to Prophetiae veteris testament de Christo by Urbanus Rhegius* (1542), in WA 53:397–401.
80. *Sermon on 1 John 3:13ff.* (1545), in WA 49:789.
81. *Answer to the Goat in Leipzig* (1521), in WA 7:631.
82. Luther to Elector Joachim II, December 4/5, 1539, in WABr 8:620–26.
83. *Contra the 32 Articles of the Theological Sharpshooters in Leuven* (1545), in WA 54:425–30.
84. Luther to Jacob Praepositus, January 17, 1546, in WABr 11:264.
85. Luther to Elector Georg von Anhalt, January 29, 1546, in WABr 11:273.

86. Luther to Nicholas von Amsdorf, June 3, 1545, in WABr 11:115.
87. *Against the Papacy at Rome* (1545), in WA 54:206–99.
88. *Against the Papacy at Rome* (1545), in WA 54:218.
89. Luther to Nicholas von Amsdorf, July 9, 1545, in WABr 11:132.
90. Luther to Nicholas von Amsdorf, July 9, 1545, in WABr 11:132.
91. Luther to Jacob Praepositus, April 17, 1544, in WABr 10:554.
92. Luther to Jacob Praepositus, April 17, 1544, in WABr 10:554.
93. *Sermon on Preparing to Die* (1519), in WA 2:685–97.
94. WATr 4: nos. 4787, 4709.
95. Luther to Justus Jonas, December 26, 1542, in WABr 10:226–28.
96. Luther to Matthias Knutzsen and his wife Magdalena, October 21, 1531, in WABr 6:212; Luther to Thomas Tinck, April 22, 1532, in WABr 6:300–302.
97. Luther to Wenzeslaus Linck, June 5, 1530, in WABr 5:344.
98. Luther to Katharina Metzler, July 3, 1539, in WABr 8:485.
99. Luther to Matthias Knutzsen and his wife Magdalena, October 21, 1531, in WABr 6:212; Luther to Thomas Tinck, April 22, 1532, in WABr 6:300–302.
100. Luther to Barbara Lisskirchen, April 30, 1531, in WABr 12:134–36.
101. Luther to Jerome Weller, June 19, 1530, in WABr 5:374–75; Luther to Jerome Weller, July 1530, in WABr 5:518–20; Luther to Jerome Weller, August 15, 1530, in WABr 5:546–47.
102. Luther to Käthe, July 28, 1545, in WABr 11:149.
103. Luther to Käthe, July 28, 1545, in WABr 11:148–52.
104. Luther to Elector Johann Frederick, August 5, 1545, in WABr 11:161.
105. Luther to Jacob Praepositus, January 17, 1546, in WABr 11:264.
106. Luther to Käthe, February 6, 1546, in WABr 11:284.
107. Luther to Käthe, January 25, 1546, in WABr 11:268–70; Philipp Melanchthon to Luther, January 31, 1546, in WABr 11:274.
108. Luther to Philipp Melanchthon, February 3, 1546, in WABr 11:278.
109. Luther to Käthe, February 1, 1546, in WABr 11:276.
110. *Four Sermons Held in Eisleben* (1546), in WA 51:194.
111. WATr 6: no. 6975.
112. Luther to Käthe, February 7, 1546, in WABr 11:286.
113. Luther to Käthe, February 14, 1546, in WABr 11:300.
114. WATr 5: no. 5677.
115. *Annotations to the Bible*, in WA 48:241; Notation, February 16, 1546, in WABr 12:363.
116. The account is found in Joachim Bauer, *Martin Luther: Seine letzte Reise* (Rudolstadt: Gerhard Seichter, 1996), 54–111.
117. Luther to Käthe, February 7, 1546, in WABr 11:286–92.
118. For the text of the testament, see Tibor Fabiny, *Martin Luthers letzter Wille: Das Testament des Reformators und Seine Geschichte* (Bielefeld: Luther-Verlag, 1983).
119. *Small Catechism* (1529), in WA 30.1:257.
120. *CR* 5:292.
121. *CR* 6:880.
122. Herman J. Selderhuis, ed., *The Calvin Handbook* (Grand Rapids, MI: Eerdmans, 2009), 57–63.
123. WATr 1: no. 1206.

General Index

Page numbers in bold italic refer to illustrations.

Scripture Index